PERSONS AND VALUES

Persons and Values

SELECTED PAPERS

Volume II

J. L. MACKIE

EDITED BY
JOAN MACKIE
AND
PENELOPE MACKIE

CLARENDON PRESS · OXFORD
1985

Oxford University Press, Walton Street, Oxford OX2 6DP

London New York Toronto
Delhi Bombay Calcutta Madras Karachi
Kuala Lumpur Singapore Hong Kong Tokyo
Nairobi Dar es Salaam Cape Town
Melbourne Auckland
and associated companies in
Beirut Berlin Ibadan Mexico City Nicosia

Oxford is a trade mark of Oxford University Press

Published in the United States
by Oxford University Press, New York

British Library Cataloguing in Publication Data
Mackie, J. L.
Persons and values.——(Selected papers; v. 2)
1. Philosophy
I. Title II. Mackie, Joan
III. Mackie, Penelope IV. Series
192 B1647.M12
ISBN 0-19-824678-1

Library of Congress Cataloging in Publication Data
Mackie, J. L. (John Leslie)
Persons and values.
Includes index.
1. Ethics——Addresses, essays, lectures.
2. Self——Addresses, essays, lectures.
I. Mackie, Joan. II. Mackie, Penelope. III. Title.
BJ1012.M327 1985 170 84-23100
ISBN 0-19-824678-1 (v. 2)

Printed in Great Britain by
Butler & Tanner Ltd, Frome and London

PREFACE

THIS is the second of two volumes of selected papers by J. L. Mackie, who died in December 1981 at the age of sixty-four. Like its companion volume, *Logic and Knowledge*, it is based on a selection made by Mackie himself a few months before his death. Of the nineteen papers published here, seven have not appeared in print before. The present volume is not a complete collection of John Mackie's papers on ethical subjects. A full bibliography of his published writings, including those on moral, political, and legal philosophy, will be found in *Morality and Objectivity*, the memorial volume edited by Ted Honderich (Routledge and Kegan Paul, 1985).

Chapters I-X and Chapter XII of the present collection were chosen by Mackie for a volume of his papers on 'moral philosophy and related topics', for which he suggested the title 'Persons and Values'. Chapters XVIII and XIX consist of material that he planned to rework as a single paper for inclusion in the volume. Although the greater part of Mackie's work on moral philosophy was done in the later years of his life, which saw the appearance of his *Ethics*, *Inventing Right and Wrong* (1977), his *Hume's Moral Theory* (1980), and the publication of numerous articles, he wrote and published work in this field throughout his career. As is evident from his choice of papers and their ordering, Mackie's selection was designed to represent his contributions to a wide range of ethical topics over many years. He contemplated adding a postscript to the collection, giving his retrospective comments on the papers, but his illness and death interrupted the project, and the postscript was not written.

Personal identity and responsibility are the subjects of the first four chapters: the 1980 paper 'The Transcendental "I"' and 'The Grounds of Responsibility', published in 1977, are accompanied by 'Multiple Personality' and 'Responsibility and Language', two papers written over twenty years earlier, the first of which has not appeared in print before. Chapter V, a paper first published in 1969, examines subjective and objective elements in aesthetic judgements, giving an account of aesthetic evaluation that complements Mackie's subjectivist theory of moral value.

In Chapter VII, first published in 1973, while not endorsing any form of utilitarian theory, Mackie defends act-utilitarianism against certain arguments purporting to show that it is self-defeating. Utilitarian theory is also discussed in Chapter VI, 'Sidgwick's Pessimism' (1976), where the chief topic is the relation between egoism and moral principles, a theme that appears, in various forms, in many of Mackie's writings on moral philosophy.

'The Third Theory of Law' (1977), a well-known critique of Ronald Dworkin's legal theory, is printed here as Chapter X, while 'Can There Be a Right-Based Moral Theory?' (1978), with its advocacy of a central place for rights in moral philosophy, appears as Chapter VIII. Chapter IX, 'The Law of the Jungle: Moral Alternatives and Principles of Evolution', originally published in 1978, discusses the relevance of sociobiology to ethics, a theme continued in Chapter XII, 'Co-operation, Competition, and Moral Philosophy', which examines the contributions of biological and cultural evolution to the development of morality, and their implications for ethical theory. In the final papers in his selection, 'Parfit's Population Paradox' and 'The Combination of Partially-Ordered Preferences' (Chapters XVIII and XIX), both written in 1980 and printed here for the first time, Mackie addresses himself to a group of puzzles concerning the combination of moral principles.

In preparing the volume for publication we have added to Mackie's own selection the papers printed as Chapters XI and XIII–XVII, four of which have not been published before. All dating from the period 1979–80, they show Mackie at work on themes characteristic of his moral philosophy. Chapter XI, 'Bootstraps Enterprises', which appears in print for the first time, is a contribution to a debate with Ronald Dworkin on the issue of objectivity in ethics and legal theory. Ethical objectivity is also one of the chief topics of Chapter XV, in which Mackie argues that retributive elements in attitudes to punishment, and in moral attitudes in general, support a subjectivist conception of ethics; the paper might be regarded as a companion piece to Chapter XII. Mackie's advocacy of a right-based moral theory (in opposition to utilitarianism, in particular) is carried further in Chapters XIV and XVI: in Chapter XIV ('Rights, Utility, and Universalization') on the basis of a critique of R. M. Hare's version of utilitarianism, and in Chapter XVI (which has not appeared in print before) by means of an examination of the problem of external costs. Chapter XIII, 'The Three Stages of Universalization', also published here for the first time, criticizes attempts to base utilitarianism on the thesis of universalizability, adding to the discussion presented in Chapter 4 of *Ethics, Inventing Right and Wrong*. 'Norms and Dilemmas', another paper not previously printed, is a short critical examination of Derek Parfit's suggestion that rational benevolence can provide a solution to various 'prisoners' dilemmas' involving public goods and harms.

At the time of his death Mackie's papers included further unpublished material on moral and political philosophy that he intended to use for a book on theories of justice and rights. We hope to publish this material, for which we could not find space in this collection, in a separate volume in due course.

Oxford   P. M.
February 1985

ACKNOWLEDGEMENTS

WE are very grateful to all the copyright holders and editors concerned for permission to reprint in this volume those papers that were originally published elsewhere. These include three of the most recent papers, all published only after the death of the author and in collections for which they were specially written: in respect of these we express our thanks to *Acta Philosophica Fennica* for permission to reprint 'Morality and the Retributive Emotions' from *Edward Westermarck: Essays on His Life and Works*, edited by Timothy Stroup (Helsinki, 1982); to the University of Minnesota Press for permission to reprint 'Rights, Utility, and Universalization' from *Utility and Rights*, edited by R. G. Frey (Minneapolis, 1984); to Van Nostrand Reinhold for permission to reprint 'Co-operation, Competition, and Moral Philosophy' from *Cooperation and Competition in Humans and Animals*, edited by A. M. Colman (Wokingham, 1982). We also express our thanks to *The Australasian Journal of Philosophy* for permission to reprint 'Responsibility and Language'; to Peter A. French, Theodore Uehling Jr., and Howard K. Wettstein, editors of *Midwest Studies in Philosophy*, Vol. III, 1978 (*Studies in Ethical Theory*), and the University of Minnesota Press for permission to reprint 'Can There Be a Right-Based Moral Theory?'; to *The Philosophical Quarterly* and Basil Blackwell for permission to reprint 'Sidgwick's Pessimism' and 'The Disutility of Act-Utilitarianism'; to Princeton University Press for permission to reprint 'The Third Theory of Law' from *Philosophy and Public Affairs*, Vol. 7, No. 1, © 1977 by Princeton University Press; to the Royal Institute of Philosophy and Cambridge University Press for permission to reprint from *Philosophy* 'The Law of the Jungle: Moral Alternatives and Principles of Evolution'.

CONTENTS

I

MULTIPLE PERSONALITY

ALL of us here, I expect, are fairly familiar with the sort of case that is described as being one of multiple personality, or split personality—familiar, that is to say, with descriptions of these cases, for the cases themselves are rather rare. The classic description is that of Sally Beauchamp in Morton Prince's *The Dissociation of a Personality* (1905), and there have also been literary treatments, for example in Stevenson's *Dr Jekyll and Mr Hyde*.

What is characteristic of these cases is that a human individual, what we would normally take to be a single person, has a different character and different modes of behaviour at different times, and also that there are systematic breaks in his memories. There may be two or more personalities, and if we call these P_1, P_2, etc., then when the individual is exhibiting personality P_1, he may remember his experiences at the other times when he was exhibiting P_1, but perhaps none of the experiences that he had when he was exhibiting P_2, and so on; but these memory breaks may not be symmetrical: P_1 may remember P_2, and yet P_2 not remember P_1, and so on.

Although this type of case is well-known to all of us, it is apparently not yet familiar to the general public. At any rate, when a film, entitled *The Three Faces of Eve*, portraying a case of triple personality, and based on what purported to be a scientific case-history, was shown recently it created quite an impression, and the filmgoers, at least in Dunedin, went away shaking their heads and saying, 'It makes you think, doesn't it?' though it was not clear exactly what thoughts it had provoked.

One would be inclined to say, then, that such a film might have an educational value, as it introduced the public to phenomena of which it was previously ignorant, but in talking about the film to a psychiatrist, a Freudian, I found that he was very critical of both the film itself and the book on which it was based, and contemptuous of all the reviewers who had praised either of them. I tried

Previously unpublished. On the typescript is a note in Mackie's hand: 'Read to a New Zealand philosophy conference in 1957 or 1958'. The typescript, preserved from that time, bears no additions or alterations.

to discover the grounds of his hostility, and as far as I could make
out, they were as follows.

He was not denying that such phenomena occur, but he was
condemning the interpretation and the explanation of them given
in the book and the film, and he was also doubting whether the
actual case recorded in *The Three Faces of Eve* was a genuine
multiple personality case at all. In the first place, then, he was
saying that in this particular case the woman who appeared to take
on three different personalities was merely *acting*. When someone
wondered how the woman in the film could be so different at
different times, the psychiatrist retorted, 'How do you think the
actress did it?' He thought that the psychiatrists who wrote the
book were either extremely gullible or themselves fraudulent, that
in one way or another they were very ready to be deceived and to
pass the deception on to the public. All this, of course, is merely a
comment on this one case-history, but it has the general implication
that we should be very wary of accepting as genuine what is
claimed to be a case of split personality. But what about the few
genuine cases that do occur? My psychiatrist was saying that we
should not describe even a genuine case, even one in which there
is no acting, no fraud, as one where there are a number of different
persons at different times in command of the same body.

His first reason was that this way of putting it presupposed an
extreme dualism of mind and body, it suggested that there were
persons, souls, psychic entities separable from and independent of
bodies, which could simply move in and take over, in turn, a
particular bodily apparatus of brain and nerves, or of which any
number could inhabit the same body, on the principle that spirit
does not occupy space, whereas he was himself convinced that
psychic phenomena can occur only in connection with physiologi-
cal processes, and have no separable or independent existence.

His second reason was that this 'three persons' story was a
pseudo-explanation, that it purported to explain the phenomena
but did not. This should, I think, be stated as an alternative to the
first objection: the three-persons story might imply that there are
souls that are independent of any bodily apparatus, and is then
open to the first objection, but alternatively it might be merely a
summary of the phenomena themselves; to say that there are these
three persons successively present might be merely to say that the
individual acts in three systematically different manners at different

times, and has correspondingly systematic memories and failures of memory, and then this story is open to this second objection, that as a proposed explanation it is empty or circular.

My psychiatrist's third objection to this three-persons story, which could, I think, be combined with either the first or the second, was that this story puts an end to explanation. You ask, 'Why does this woman act in these three different ways, and have these odd breaks in memory?' You receive the answer, 'Because she is three different people at these different times', and then no further explanation of how the three persons came to be there is either required or permitted. The multiplicity of persons is taken as an ultimate fact. As against this, the psychiatrist would want to say that the different personalities can and should be seen and understood as developing out of a single psychic history, in accordance with psychological structures and laws that are universal, that are found to operate in normal people, and in those that are abnormal in other ways, as well as in cases of split personality. He would also say that the different personalities have relations to one another quite different from those which any three bodily distinct persons have to one another, even over and above those relations that are forced on them by having to share the same body. In general there will be some memories shared by any two personalities, and even if the individual in each state does not remember at all what he does in any of the other states, yet there are caused transitions from one state to another: something experienced in one state helps to bring about the appearance of one of the other personalities.

A fourth objection would be that the story about the different persons is, sometimes at least, part of the malady itself; it is one of the things that is wrong with the patient that he sees himself at other times as another person, and this is just an extreme way of rejecting what is really a part of himself; so that if a psychologist adopted literally the three-persons story he would be incorporating into his theory the *content* of his subject's delusion.

Now I have some sympathy with all of these objections, but I think we can accept the substance of all of them without either giving up the three-persons story or robbing it of all value, admitting all the time, of course, that we must take care to distinguish genuine multiple personality cases from simulated ones.

As for the first objection, I should agree in rejecting any extreme dualism of mind and body, any notion of a soul or self that can enter or leave, control or inhabit a body, but I find the view that *one* soul is thus permanently attached to each body just as philosophically objectionable as the view that two or three or more souls can inhabit the same body, either simultaneously or in turn. This is not a special reason for rejecting a plurality of persons in the one body, it is a reason for rejecting the view that the supposed kind of relation holds at all between the body and the person. And in fact this metaphysical view about an independent soul or self is used far more frequently to assert that in all cases there is an absolute and permanent identity of the person to whom each spatio-temporally continuous human body belongs than to assert that the same body can be possessed by a multiplicity of persons. In any case, statements about multiple personality can be worked out without implying any such dualism. Granted that there cannot be a disembodied soul, a soul or person or personality is still not just a collection of bodily parts, but consists of bodily parts organized and functioning in a particular way. And if the same parts, or mainly the same parts, are differently organized and function differently, they can be said to make up different souls or persons or personalities, at any rate in the sense in which much the same electrical components, differently connected, could make up two different wireless sets, or even two different pieces of equipment, one a wireless set and one an amplifier.

As for the second objection, I should say that the talk about more than one person or personality *could* be used merely to sum up the observed or observable differences in behaviour and breaks in memory; if it is so used, it will not *explain* such behaviour, and if it is then offered as an explanation it will be circular, but if it is used merely as a summary description it is harmless. But alternatively this talk about multiple personality could be used as an explanatory hypothesis, as saying something about psychic structure and organization—it would be epistemologically comparable with such other psychological hypotheses as those about unconscious mental processes, about the *ego* and the *id*, and so on. Developed in this way, it could be a real explanation, not an empty one: it could have a meaning that was not a mere summary of the observations nor yet a metaphysical doctrine about a plurality of immaterial souls.

In either case, whether the talk about multiple personality was a summary of observations or an explanatory hypothesis, we could meet the third objection by agreeing that whatever the status of multiple personality statements may be, they need not and should not be taken as final, as putting a stop to any search for further explanations. The divisions of personality are caused, have an historical development, and presumably are not completely *sui generis* but are capable of being understood as the working out in particular circumstances of more general psychological laws. In particular, there must be some gradations, some sequence of intermediate conditions by which individuals can pass from what we call a normal state into one of split personality, and the different personalities must still have causal relations with one another.

As for the fourth objection, the fact that the patient himself, in some cases, sees himself as divided into different persons is not necessarily evidence against the truth of this description: the patient in talking in this way *may* be deluding himself and others, but he may be describing quite correctly a situation of which he has a peculiarly intimate knowledge. Wanting to reject a part of himself, he may so far succeed as to destroy his unity as a person.

If we take the appropriate precautions, then, it seems to be at least permissible to say that the cases in question are cases of multiple personality. But should we speak, in these cases, of a plurality of *personalities* or of a plurality of *persons*? So far I have not made any distinction between these, but it is now time to draw one.

'Personality' I take to be a term belonging to psychological theory. It could be used in a simply descriptive way, and then to say that Bill Smith has one personality on Monday and a different one on Tuesday is merely to say that he behaves differently on the two days. Or it could be used dispositionally, and then to say that Bill Smith has a different personality on Tuesday is to say that he has a radically different set of dispositions, that not only what he does but what he would do if such-and-such happened is quite different from what he did and would have done on Monday. Or, again, the word 'personality' could be used to refer to a supposed psychic structure or organization, the postulated ground of the disposition to which the word in its previous sense referred, and then to say that Bill Smith has different personalities on Monday and on Tuesday is to offer a psychological hypothesis about a change in psychic organization which would explain the differences in behaviour and in disposition. But whichever of these three senses the word 'personality' has, it seems that to speak about more than one *personality* is much more guarded and cautious than to say that there are different persons, that this same body which we recognize as Bill Smith's is not that of the same person on Monday and on Tuesday. If we speak in these cases of a plurality of persons, we seem to be saying something much more sweeping and much more dangerous. My next task, then, will be to see just what more we would be saying if we spoke about a change of person as contrasted with a change of personality, and then to enquire whether we are ever justified in saying this much more.

It may help to answer this question if we digress for a time onto the well-worn topic of personal identity, and reconsider what is or can be meant when we say about some normal individual that he is the same person as the individual who was called by the same name yesterday or twenty years ago. And in considering this, we should begin by reflecting on what is meant by the identity of a material object.

I take it that we have the notion of 'the same thing', of an identical material object persisting through time, because occurrences of this sort are common in our experience: at t_1 at a certain place, there is an object of a certain sort; a little later, at t_2 in the same place or not far away, there is an object of much the same sort; and at any time between t_1 and t_2 there is an object of the same sort in the same region, in such a way that the succession of objects forms a continuous spatio-temporal track along which some features persist without change and others change continuously. That is to say, it is the combination of spatio-temporal and qualitative continuity that gives us the notion of an identical persisting material object. Also, I take it that when we say that this is the same object as the one we observed earlier, it is this spatio-temporal and qualitative continuity that we are asserting, we are saying that there is a continuous track between the two observed things. Of course we do not always, or even in the majority of cases, observe this continuity: it is not our usual evidence, our normal ground for saying that this is the same thing as that. In most cases sufficiently close resemblance, together with the fact that the differences were predictable or are explainable, and the possibility of a spatio-temporal continuity, is enough to justify us in saying, 'This is the same thing'. But although the latter are our usual grounds for asserting identity they do not include all or even the major part of what 'identity' means, of what we are asserting. It is the two continuities that make the difference between 'the same thing' and 'a similar thing' or even 'an exactly similar thing'. No doubt if the world were different, or were discovered to be different, we might use the word 'same' in another way. If it were frequently found that a certain thing disappeared, passed out of existence, and then shortly after a very similar thing appeared, came into existence, in the same region, in such a manner that there were close causal connections between the features of the first and the second thing, then we might change the meaning of 'same' so that we could say that the second thing was the same as the first, that is, we might make identity cover both continuous and a special sort of interrupted existence. Or again, if with the advance of physical science we discovered that all or most of the things to which we have been ascribing a continuous existence have in fact an intermittent existence, with imperceptibly brief gaps, such as we know to be possessed by a figure on a cinema screen, we might similarly change the meaning of the word 'same' so as to be able to apply it in the same cases as we now apply it, despite the change in what we believe about those cases. But at present the identity of a material object means spatio-temporal and qualitative continuity. We are not asserting, or at any rate we do not need to assert and could have no good reason for asserting, over and above these continuities, any absolute identity of a substance to which the qualities belong.

When we come to the identity of a person, however, it is much less plausible to say that what we are asserting is the combination of spatio-temporal with qualitative continuity. With a material object, it is difficult to see what there could be, other than continuity or perhaps the quasi-continuity just mentioned, to make the difference between 'same' and 'similar', but with persons there are clearly other factors that could make this difference. *Prima facie*, the point of an assertion of personal identity lies in an alleged unity of interest and responsibility. That is, I today take a special sort of interest in what is going to happen to John Mackie tomorrow, and John Mackie tomorrow will feel a special sort of responsibility for what I do today, will experience pride or shame or guilt, whichever is appropriate. I say 'a special sort', because I can take an interest in the fortunes of others, but not the precise sort of interest that I take in my own fortunes; I can love my neighbour, and I can even love him as much as or more than myself, but I cannot literally love my neighbour *as* myself. Similarly I can feel a kind of responsibility for what others do: a New Zealander with a taste for cricket may feel pride or shame about the performance of the New Zealand team in the first Test, I may feel a direct responsibility for what my children or my students do, over and above the indirect responsibility that I have in so far as I have helped to cause them to do it; but neither of these is quite like the responsibility that I feel for my own past as well as present actions.

It might be objected that although unity of interest and responsibility is something implied by personal identity, it is not the primary meaning of personal identity; my identity, it may be said, is a thing of which I have a direct awareness, and which is presupposed in talk about any other sort of identity, where we take for granted the persisting identical perceiving subject that can make and compare observations strung out in a sequence in time. This, it might be said, is the key to the failure of Hume's attempt to explain away personal identity in a manner analogous to that in which he explained away necessary connection: the absolute identity of the self cannot be just an idea constructed out of a certain sequence of impressions, because there would have to be an absolutely identical self to have all the impressions and to do the constructing.

Now admittedly there is what we can call a direct awareness of one's own identity through short periods: I am aware of myself as continuing from one half-minute to the next. Moreover, in all our talk about sameness we rely heavily on the principle that identity is transitive, and by repeated application of this principle to my direct awarenesses I can build up a picture of my own identity over a considerable period, perhaps a whole day. But this sort of awareness of identity is interrupted by deep sleep or an anaesthetic, and it is not in this way that I know myself, when I wake up, as the same person who went to sleep. It is, of course, by memory that I know this, but memory of a special sort. It is not just that I remember that certain events occurred, but rather that I remember actions and experiences as seen from the inside, it is not just that I remember that John Mackie did such-and-such, but rather that I remember doing it, I have a memory which closely resembles an experience of a present action of my own. It is as if in the present

I were performing these actions. Of course this private memory basis of personal identity is strongly reinforced by the fact that other people ascribe to me the actions that yesterday's I did.

It seems to me that it is out of experiences of all these kinds that we build up the notion of an identical person, and I do not think that if I were to develop this account I should be faced with the necessity with which, it is alleged, Hume is faced, of having to assume the existence of that absolutely identical metaphysical self which he tried to explain away. Indeed, not only do I have no more success than Hume did when I look into myself and try to catch this strange entity, but besides I cannot think what use it would be if I caught it. It seems to me that the present self with which I wish to assert the identity of past and future selves is my empirical self, with all its thoughts, feelings, purposes, and individual character, not a mere substratum to which these in some quite mysterious sense 'belong'.

But if we reject this notion of an absolutely identical metaphysical self, we must ask what else we could be asserting when we assert personal identity. It is not merely the identity of the person's body as a material object, though this is commonly taken for granted and perhaps included in the ordinary concept of personal identity. Nor is it, I think, the collection of experiences by means of which we are aware of our own identity; when we say 'the same person' we are not merely saying that there is such a collection of experiences, for if we were saying just this, there would be no doubt at all that in the abnormal cases where the chain of experiences fails, where someone loses his memory, he is no longer the same person, though it is still the same human body as before. So I return to the suggestion that what is being asserted in personal identity is this special unity of responsibility and interest, that the future Bill Smith matters to the present Bill Smith, and that the present Bill Smith is responsible for what the past Bill Smith did.

This account of personal identity has the merit of preserving a connection with the earlier history of the word 'person'. The 'persona' is originally the mask through which a classical actor spoke, and so the character that he represented, and then by an easy analogy, the legal entity represented by anyone who appeared in a court of law. The notion of a person as something represented, and in particular as a legal entity, a subject of rights and duties, is central in the history of the meaning of the word, and my account of the identity of a person as a unity of responsibility and interest makes the present meaning continuous with these earlier ones.

After this rather long digression, let us go back and apply this account of personal identity to the cases of multiple personality, and see whether we are there justified in speaking not merely of more than one personality but of more than one person. We should have to say, in accordance with this account, that Sally is the same person as Miss Beauchamp if and only if what happens to Sally matters, in that special way, to Miss Beauchamp, and if Miss Beauchamp is responsible for what Sally does, and vice versa. But this has an unfortunate consequence. We may originally have hoped that we could find some way of settling the question about the identity or difference of persons on the basis of which we could decide questions of moral responsibility; we may have hoped to be able to say either 'Sally and Miss Beauchamp are different persons, *and therefore* Miss Beauchamp is not responsible for Sally's actions' or else 'Sally and Miss Beauchamp are the same person, *and therefore* Miss Beauchamp is responsible for Sally's actions'. But we cannot now do this. We cannot first decide whether they are the same person or not and then use this decision in order to settle problems of moral responsibility, for we can only determine whether they are or are not the same person by first deciding the questions about moral responsibility. But then, how *are* we to decide the questions about moral responsibility?

The other part of my meaning for personal identity, namely a special sort of interest, may be easier to check. We may, by enquiry or experience, find out whether Miss Beauchamp cares about what happens to Sally or not, and vice versa. But in checking this, we should observe two precautions. First, we must be on the lookout for deception, we must guard against the possibility that Sally may *say* that she doesn't care what happens to Miss Beauchamp when she really does care. Secondly, it is obvious that if the personalities alternate in appearance the fact that they share the same body will imply that each of them can't help caring about some things that could happen to the other; for example, if Miss Beauchamp breaks her leg then Sally will have a broken leg next time she appears. But for Sally to care about this would *not* be for her to care about what happens to Miss Beauchamp as Miss Beauchamp, so in making this check we should see whether each personality cares about things whose effects fall exclusively on the other personality: for example, does Sally care if Miss Beauchamp suffers embarrassment?

Now suppose that we can settle the question whether there is unity of interest, can we use the answer to this to settle in turn the question about responsibility? We can if we take a certain view of the nature of responsibility. If to be responsible for an action is simply to be a fit recipient of reward or punishment for that action, and if rewards and punishments should be given simply as inducements and deterrents, then it clearly follows that there is responsibility if and only if there is unity of interest. If and only if Sally cares what happens to Miss Beauchamp will it be possible, by guaranteeing to reward or punish Miss Beauchamp, to induce Sally to behave well or to deter her from behaving badly. On such a utilitarian theory of responsibility, which regards punishment simply as deterrence, unity of responsibility coincides with unity of interest, and therefore if we can answer the question about unity of interest we can give the same answer to the question about responsibility, and thus we shall be able to apply the whole of our test for personal identity, and decide definitely whether we have here two persons or one.

A different conclusion would follow if, while still saying that to be responsible for a wrong action is just to be a fit recipient of punishment for it, we regarded the function of punishment as being not deterrence but reformation. The answer to the question whether Miss Beauchamp should be punished for Sally's wrong actions depends on (a) whether Miss Beauchamp needs to be reformed in this particular respect and (b) whether Sally can be reformed by anything that happens to Miss Beauchamp. In view of the great difference between the two personalities, the fact that they display different characters, different sorts of feeling and response, it is most unlikely that either question (a) or question (b) could be answered in the affirmative. In so far as responsibility is related to reformation, then, two distinct personalities cannot have unity of responsibility.

If we turn to a retributive theory of rewards and punishments, and say that there is such a thing as a *desert*, which cannot be further analysed in terms of deterrence or inducement or reformation or anything else, then we are called upon to answer the question 'Does Miss Beauchamp deserve reward or punishment for Sally's good or bad actions?' and to answer it without any further guidance. The retributive principle that right actions deserve reward and that wrong actions deserve punishment clearly means that if a certain person has done a right action then that person deserves reward, and so on; but this would help us only if we could *first* decide whether Miss Beauchamp was the same person as Sally or not, and we cannot do this. Even if we were to revive the doctrine of a metaphysical self it would not help us, because since this notion is metaphysical in the bad sense its application is purely arbitrary: if selves are non-empirical entities to which empirical actions, experiences, etc. belong, then we can as easily postulate two selves, or twenty selves, as one, whether there is a change of personality or not. As soon as we raise the question whether the metaphysical self to which a certain body belongs is the same at all times or not, it becomes unanswerable: we regard the metaphysical self as explaining personal identity only so long as we do not even consider the possibility of many selves for one body. On the retributive view, then, we are faced with the blunt question, 'Does Miss Beauchamp deserve reward or punishment for what Sally does?' and we are called upon to answer it without any further guidance; but then, it seems to me, we cannot answer it at all. Any answer would be purely arbitrary. And this is a reason for rejecting the retributive view.

It might be objected that my account could lead to paradoxical results. If we hold that responsibility is a matter of both deterrence and reformation, then it seems that we may have to say that Sally and Miss Beauchamp are the same person for one purpose and different persons for another purpose: we shall have to give up any sharp distinction between the identity and the difference of persons. Again, it is possible that Sally might care about what happened to Miss Beauchamp, but not vice versa, and so, on the deterrent view, Miss Beauchamp would be responsible for Sally's actions, but not vice versa. Would we then have to say that Miss Beauchamp is the same person as Sally but that Sally is not the same person as Miss Beauchamp? Are we to deny that identity is symmetrical? But these, I suggest, are similar to other puzzles that have been propounded about identity—for example, if people were to divide in the way that amoebae do, so that person A split (physically) into two persons A_1 and A_2, and each of these satisfied all the ordinary criteria for being the same person as A, would we have to say that A_1 is the same person as A, and that A is the same person as A$_2$, but that A$_1$ and A$_2$ are different persons? Do we have to deny that identity is transitive? It seems to me that all such puzzles should be treated in the same way: each one calls for some decision about what our words are to mean. In ordinary conditions we have criteria for personal identity which, while they do not *logically* guarantee that personal identity should be symmetrical and transitive, do *practically* guarantee this as long as people behave in the normal way. And similarly, as long as people behave normally, an individual who is the same person at different times for one purpose is likewise the same person at different times for any other purpose. But if we encounter abnormal cases, either the imaginary ones of amoeba-like division or the real ones of multiple personality, we may have to decide *either* to stick to our ordinary criteria for personal identity and abandon its definiteness or its symmetry or its transitivity, *or* to preserve the definiteness or the symmetry or the transitivity of personal identity by making the criteria more stringent in some way. But it is an issue that calls for a decision precisely because there is no possible answer to the metaphysical question, 'But is there *really* more than one person here: is Sally *really* Miss Beauchamp or not?'

I began by referring to the Dunedin filmgoers who went away from *The Three Faces of Eve* saying, 'It makes you think', and I shall conclude by trying to indicate what it might have made them think. I suggest that not only do these rare cases of multiple personality pose metaphysical and ethical problems about how to describe and deal with these cases themselves, they also throw some reflected light on personal identity and moral responsibility even in the great mass of normal cases. They compel us to abandon the facile assumption that in some sense that is important, and yet that neither requires nor admits of any further analysis, each named human individual is absolutely the same person from the cradle to the grave and possibly beyond, and that at every time after he becomes an adult he is morally fully responsible for everything he has previously done since he became an adult. They compel us to analyse personal identity, and the most suitable analysis seems to be one which admits of degrees and of irregularities in the identity of a person. And here we must take account of the point made by my Freudian psychiatrist, that cases of multiple personality have a history, that such a condition can grow gradually out of, and perhaps gradually return to, what we ordinarily recognize as a normal state. The different personalities of Miss Beauchamp are like a normal person's different moods pushed to an extreme. The breaks of memory, the diminution of mutual interest or concern between these personalities, are just an extreme case of those divisions of attention which every one of us can observe in himself; conflicts of motives and forgetting that results from repression are perfectly normal psychological phenomena. Since this is so, we should relax a little the absoluteness of the personal identity which we ascribe even to a normal individual. The question, 'Why did you do this?', addressed to Miss Beauchamp about an action of Sally's is pointless and unanswerable, and in a similar way the question, 'Why did you do this?', addressed even to a normal person about one of his past actions may in some circumstances be somewhat blunted, and we may have to accept something less than a direct answer. And even among normal people there are very great differences and fluctuations in the extent to which Bill Smith today has that special sort of interest in what will happen to Bill Smith tomorrow or ten years hence, and if responsibility depends at all on unity of interest it will differ and fluctuate correspondingly. These facts need not make us abandon altogether the notions of moral and legal responsibility, of the appropriateness of rewards and punishments, incentives and deterrents, but they do help to force us to give up any simple retributive theory, and they make us at least hesitate about the justice, as well as the efficacy, of certain rewards and punishments, and especially of long-range or long-term penalties.

II

THE TRANSCENDENTAL 'I'

WHAT theme unites the images of Zeno Vendler mounted on a horse and watching, through Hannibal's eyes, the battle of Cannae, of Peter Strawson blazing a trail through a jungle of phenomena, and of Elizabeth Anscombe floating in a tepid bath? It is of course, the transcendental 'I'.[1]

Vendler's argument is best stated from his own point of view. For reasons that Kripke and others have stressed, Zeno Vendler, this man that I am, could not have been born at any other period, or of parents other than those who actually generated me. Yet I can imagine living at a different period, I can imagine my being Hannibal or Claudius. But the impossible cannot be imagined; so it must be possible that I should be Hannibal or Claudius. But Claudius has one individual essence, and Vendler has another, so Vendler could not be Claudius and cannot be imagined to be Claudius. The 'I' that is the subject of such a transference 'has no content and no essence; it is a mere frame in which any picture fits; it is the bare form of consciousness' (p. 117). 'The transcendental "I" is not a thing ... The transcendental aspect of my being consists in nothing else but in the realization that I, as a subject of experience, am only contingently tied to the senses of this body, ... in one word, it consists in my ability to perform feats of transference' (p. 118).

Anscombe's argument turns upon a contrast between the use of 'I' and what would be the use of a proper name '*A*', which everyone used of himself (a human being, a person with a body), though each person also had another name which others used of him. A hint of the contrast is given by the term 'self-consciousness', which

Reprinted from *Philosophical Subjects: Essays Presented to P.F. Strawson*, edited by Zak van Straaten (Clarendon Press, 1980).

[1] See Zeno Vendler, 'A Note to the Paralogisms', in *Contemporary Aspects of Philosophy*, edited by Gilbert Ryle (Stocksfield, 1977), pp. 111–21; P.F. Strawson, *The Bounds of Sense* (London, 1966), pp. 162–70; and G.E.M. Anscombe, 'The First Person', in *Mind and Language*, edited by Samuel Guttenplan (Oxford, 1975), pp. 45–65.

'is something real . . . which "I"-users have and which would be lacking to "*A*"-users, if their use of "*A*" was an adequate tool for their consciousness of themselves' (p. 51). But the crucial question is whether 'I' is or is not a referring term of some kind or other. If so, it is 'secure against reference-failure. Just thinking "I . . ." guarantees not only the existence but the presence of its referent' (p. 55). The 'conception' through which 'I', if it is a referring term, either a name or a demonstrative, attaches to its object can only be 'the thinking of the I-thought, which secures this guarantee against reference-failure' (p. 55). Though '*A*', in use, would also be guaranteed to have a reference, it would not be guaranteed to have the right reference, since what I take to be part of my own body may not be so. Consequently, '*if* "I" is a referring expression, then Descartes was right about what the referent was' (p. 58). Its referent can be nothing but a (stretch of a) Cartesian Ego. But Descartes's position 'has . . . the intolerable difficulty of requiring an identification of the same referent in different I-thoughts' (p. 58). 'How do I know that "I" is not ten thinkers thinking in unison?' (p. 58).

Anscombe therefore takes the difficulties of the Cartesian position as completing a *reductio ad absurdum* of the suggestion that 'I' is a referring expression of any kind. 'Getting hold of the wrong object *is* excluded, and that makes us think that getting hold of the right object is guaranteed. But the reason is that there is no getting hold of an object at all. With names, or denoting expressions (in Russell's sense) there are two things to grasp: the kind of use, and what to apply them to from time to time. With "I" there is only the use' (p. 59).

Anscombe's negative conclusion, then, is similar to Vendler's. There is nothing to which 'I' refers; 'I am E.A.' (or 'Z.V.') is not an identity proposition. But their positive accounts diverge. Whereas Vendler stresses feats of transference, Anscombe at least centres the use of 'I' in such thoughts as 'I am sitting', 'examples of reflective consciousness of states, actions, motions, etc. . . . of this body. These I-thoughts . . . are unmediated conceptions (knowledge or belief, true or false) of states, motions, etc. of this object here' (p. 62). She sets aside such typically Cartesian thoughts as 'I am thinking about thinking', 'I hope, fear, love, etc.', and even 'I have a headache' and 'I see a variety of colours'. It is a corollary of her view that 'No problem of the continuity or reidentification of "the I" can arise' (p. 62); it is merely that the same human

being has different I-thoughts at different times. A 'lapse of self-
consciousness' is just a lack of 'unmediated agent-or-patient conceptions of actions, happenings, and states'. But these conceptions,
she maintains, 'do not involve the connection of what is understood
by a predicate with a distinctly conceived subject'. The notion of
such a subject is just a '(deeply rooted) grammatical illusion'
(p. 65).

Strawson, too, speaks of an illusion, though not a grammatical
one. He argues that Kant exposed and, less completely, explained
'a natural and powerful illusion' by which 'we mistake the necessary unity of consciousness for ... an awareness of a unitary subject' (p. 163). Reconstructing and completing Kant's account, he
says that while 'a certain character of connectedness and unity' in
a temporally extended series of experiences, yielding 'experience of
a unified objective world', 'makes room for the idea of *one* subjective or experiential route through the world', and so provides 'as
it were, the basic ground for the possibility of an empirical use for
the concept of the subject of such an autobiography, the concept
of the self', this is not in itself enough. It is also vital that 'our
ordinary concept of personal identity does carry with it empirically
applicable criteria for the numerical identity through time of a
subject of experiences (a man or human being) . . . which involve
an essential reference to the human body'. This 'supplies an absolutely firm basis for a genuinely object-referring use of names and
personal pronouns, in sentences in which states of consciousness,
inner experiences, are ascribed to the objects referred to by the
name or pronouns' (pp. 163-4). But 'the fact that lies at the root of
the Cartesian illusion' is that 'When a man (a subject of experience)
ascribes a current or directly remembered state of consciousness to
himself, no use whatever of any criteria of personal identity is
required to justify his use of the pronoun "I" to refer to the subject
of that experience' (pp. 164-5). Yet Strawson insists that when 'I'
is thus used in 'criterionless self-ascription', it does not 'lose its role
of referring to a subject'. He suggests that it can still refer to a
subject because either it issues from the mouth of an empirically
identifiable person or, if used in soliloquy, it is used by a person
who would acknowledge the applicability of ordinary empirical criteria to the question of his own identity with someone who performed some earlier action. '"I" can be used without criteria of
subject-identity and yet refer to a subject because, even in such a

use, the links with those criteria are not in practice severed'
(p. 165).

Strawson, then, is partly in agreement but partly in disagreement
with Anscombe and Vendler. Like them he holds that 'a purely
inner and yet subject-referring use for "I"' is an illusion. Consequently 'If we try to abstract this use, to shake off the connection
with ordinary criteria of personal identity ... what we really do is
simply to deprive our use of "I" of any referential force whatever.
It will simply express, as Kant would say, "consciousness in
general"' (p. 166). But what Strawson here says that we may try to
do, Anscombe and Vendler think we have done. They say that the
central use of 'I' is this non-referring one, whereas Strawson says
that the ordinary use remains referential, because the links with
empirical criteria of identity are not in practice severed. (Also,
unlike Anscombe, Strawson does not shy away from the characteristically Cartesian thoughts: for him it is especially states of consciousness, inner experiences, that are self-ascribed immediately
and without criteria.)

We have, then, two issues. Are Strawson, Anscombe, and
Vendler all in the right in their general support of a Kantian against
a Cartesian view? And, where they differ, is Strawson right against
the others in saying that 'I' remains a referring term?

On this second question, the view of Anscombe and Vendler is
paradoxical. Surely ordinary speakers commonly at least intend to
use 'I' as a referring term. On first learning the jargon they would
say confidently that it is one. If this is a grammatical illusion, it is
one nearly all of us share. Also, as Anscombe admits, the rule for
the truth of propositions with 'I' as subject is

If X makes assertions with 'I' as subject, then those assertions will
be true if and only if the predicates thus used assertively are true
of X.

—for example, 'I am sitting' said by E.A. will be true if and only
if E.A.—that human being—is then sitting. It is hard to see how
'I', so used, can be failing to refer to X (or E.A.) if that is how it
helps to determine the truth or falsity of the assertion. Again,
Anscombe admits that children sometimes use their own names
instead of 'I', and that this could conceivably be the standard
practice. But, she says, what is semantically a name in other
people's mouths will not be so in one's own: 'it will not signify like

a name' in one's own utterances (p. 64). This is what consistency requires her to say; but it underlines the paradox.

However, Anscombe and Vendler have arguments to support their initially surprising claims. Anscombe's main argument is that no reference other than the Cartesian one (to which there are, she believes, decisive objections) could be guaranteed against the two kinds of reference-failure, the lack of a referent and the risk of a wrong reference, the risk that what I take to be I might not be I. This is how 'I' differs from '*A*', the hypothetical second name that every human being uses of himself. But what does this show? Surely only that the *sense* of 'I' differs from that of '*A*'. If 'I' has a reference, then the way in which it gets its reference differs from the way in which '*A*' gets its; but 'I' might still have a reference, and might even happen always to have the same reference as '*A*'. But how could there be a sense which guaranteed 'I' against both kinds of reference-failure?

As Locke saw, the basic fact, which also gives a clue to the answer to this question, is the occurrence (in each of us), both at the same time and in temporal succession, of co-conscious experiences, of both the Cartesian and the Anscombian varieties—awareness of feelings, bodily positions, intentional movements, and so on. These, as they occur, joining on to a pre-existing co-conscious system (from which components are also constantly dropping off) are ascribed to a single supposed subject. Why, or even how, we do this is for the moment irrelevant, though I shall revert to it later; it may well be a sophisticated, learned, performance; but it is enough that it occurs. Built on this occurrence is a linguistic rule for the use of 'I': each item that enters this co-conscious system is I-ascribed, that is, it is appropriately reported by such sentences as 'I am writing', 'I have a headache', 'I wonder whether ...' Thus it is linguistically, and therefore trivially, guaranteed that whatever I take as 'I' *in this way* is I; but the reality on which this linguistic procedure is based is just the serial co-consciousness of experiences and thoughts. But if 'I' is then used with the intention of referring, must it either refer to a Cartesian Ego or, if there is no such thing, and yet it is intended to refer to such, *always* involve a failure of reference? No, because there is something which in all normal cases really will be writing, or having a headache, or wondering, and so on: the human being who uses such sentences assertively either in conversation or in soliloquy. And even in abnormal cases, where the asserted predicate is not true of this human being—I have a delusion that I am writing—it is still about this human being that I am mistaken. So in fact, though not by the above-mentioned linguistic rule alone, reference to this human being will be secured. However, this is not the only linguistic rule for the use of 'I'. Another is that if someone says to X 'You are ...', X can agree by saying 'Yes, I am ...' or disagree by saying 'No, I'm not ...' That is, 'I' is located partly as a counterpart to 'you' (and to 'he' and 'she' in certain uses). And this tends to fix its reference as being to the human being who uses it. (But of course this works both ways: the meanings of 'you' and 'he' and 'she' are also affected by the fact that they are counterparts of 'I'.) 'I', therefore, is governed by at least two meaning rules: one which makes it refer to whatever it is whose self-consciousness it expresses, which is at best factually and contingently this human being, and one which binds it directly, linguistically, as Anscombe's 'A' is bound, to the human being who uses it. The over-determination of meaning by such initially divergent rules might conceivably cause trouble; but since the rules contingently converge in the end, it does not.

I want to say that when the first rule is implemented—the one linked with self-consciousness—we have a guarantee against the second kind of reference-failure: there is no danger that what I thus take to be I might not be I. And only then. The second rule, like that for 'A', secures us only against the first kind of reference-failure: it ensures that there is a referent somewhere around. But it might be objected that even the first rule does not achieve this. The reference of the 'I' that expresses self-consciousness to this human being could conceivably fail, and it can be deliberately abandoned. It would fail if I were to become disembodied, which is conceivable though it may well be physically impossible, and it is abandoned when, with Vendler, we engage in feats of transference. And in these marginal cases the over-determination of meaning by the two rules does cause trouble: in employing one rule we have to ignore the other.

This brings us to Vendler's argument, which seems straightforward and, given its assumptions, conclusive. It is necessary that Z.V. is not Claudius. But I can imagine my being Claudius, so it is not necessary that I am not Claudius. From this it does not, indeed, follow that I am not Z.V. But it does follow that I am not necessarily Z.V., and hence that 'I am Z.V.' cannot be a true identity statement if both 'I' and 'Z.V.' are rigid designators. 'I' cannot be used as a rigid designator, as a name or a definite description used referentially, both in 'I am Z.V.' and in 'I might have been Claudius'.

Once it is thus set out explicitly, we can see that the argument does not show that 'I' is never used to refer to a thing (or person or human being), but only that there are some uses in which it does not rigidly designate a human being, and hence that if it does then rigidly designate anything, this will have to be a Cartesian Ego. It follows that if there is another use in which it does rigidly designate the human being who uses it, 'I' must be ambiguous. But this is only to put in other words what was suggested above, that 'I' is governed by two meaning rules which initially diverge, though they converge again in ordinary circumstances. Vendler's examples of transference stress that there are special kinds of thinking in which the divergence is unresolved. I as a subject of consciousness, or perhaps as a mere pseudo-subject in a series of co-conscious experiences, might have been Claudius, though I, this human being, could not.

But should we speak here of a subject or of a pseudo-subject? Vendler is wrong to say that the 'I' which is the subject of transference is 'the bare form of consciousness', though he is right to say that it is a frame in which any picture fits. When I imagine being at Cannae, it is *my* being at Cannae that I imagine, not that of a bare form of consciousness. (After all, a good many thousand 'forms of consciousness' were there, but this is not the central part of what I imagine.) Yet it is not, in general, that I imagine there being experiences linked by co-consciousness to my actual ones: I do not have to think of myself, at Cannae, remembering the twentieth century. I ascribe the imagined experiences to a subject. I need not imagine them as linked by co-consciousness to the present series, and *a fortiori* I do not merely do this. (Nor is it merely that I am joining them to this series just by imagining them: for that would be true of anything I imagined, and so cannot explain the distinctive element of my imagining *my* being there.) But still we have the nagging question, is it to a real subject or to a pseudo-subject that I ascribe them? As we noted, there is a real subject of my actual experiences—these imaginings among them—namely this human being. So when I imagine whatever is the subject of my actual experiences as being at Cannae, it is to this human being that I in effect ascribe the imagined experiences; but not directly, not explicitly, and that is how I avoid the contradiction of supposing this human being to have lived at a different time. The two premisses of Vendler's main argument—'Z.V. could not have lived at a different period' and 'I could have lived at a different period'—both call for fuller interpretation. As I have argued elsewhere about such Kripkean modal theses, the first really means only that we have a way of thinking and speaking about the same individual with respect to counterfactual possibilities that precludes this. We think of the same individual, even in counterfactual possibilities, as being whatever persistent thing of that kind has the same origin.[2] Possibilities for this individual (human or non-human) are possible divergences from its actual history. But the second premiss brings out another way in which I can think, with respect to counterfactual possibilities, of this special individual, myself. I hold on to myself merely as the subject, whatever it may be, of these present experiences. The counterfactually imagined experiences are made its simply by direct fiat. I do not construct an apparently objective course of events and then have to identify myself with some item already in it: rather I tell a story about myself as centre.

It may be objected that if the subject of these present experiences happens to be this human being, then it could not have been at Cannae. This is true in/the sense that (unless we allow travelling backwards in time) there is no objectively describable possibility which we would count as this human being's being at Cannae. But that does not conflict with the fact that in constructing a subjective, egocentric, story I can think of 'I' simply as the subject, whatever it may be, of these present experiences and not include any features of any individual essence which would prevent me from coherently imagining this subject's being at Cannae.

In this, as with many similar puzzles, some vagueness or equivocation about the scope of a definite description is a source of trouble, and care about such scope is the formal treatment required for clarity. Since the subject of my present experiences is in fact this human being, we can say truly, giving the description large scope, 'As for the subject of my present experiences, it is not possible that it should have been at Cannae', but also, giving it small

---

[2] Cf. my *'De* What *Re* is *De Re* Modality?'*, in *The Journal of Philosophy*, Vol. 71 (1974), pp. 551-61, and my *Problems from Locke* (Oxford, 1976), pp. 152-9.

scope, 'It is coherently imaginable that the subject of my present experiences should have been at Cannae'. And 'I' may well have one sense, though perhaps not its only one, in which it is equivalent to this definite description.

The conceivability of disembodiment is no more of a problem. I can conceive that the subject, whatever it may be, of my present experiences is not and has not a body; yet if that subject is in fact this human being, which would cease to exist if this body ceased to function, there is no objectively describable possible state of affairs which would count as this subject's being disembodied.

We can cope, then, both with Anscombe's argument and with Vendler's. They fail to disprove what indeed seems to be the case, that 'I' not only is regularly a referring term, but also regularly refers to the human being who uses it. But this reference is secured by two different rules which constitute different senses for 'I'. One rule links it, like Anscombe's '*A*', directly to this human being. The other rule links it directly only to the subject, whatever it may be, of these experiences, and therefore only indirectly and contingently to this human being. In feats of transference and in the conceiving of one's own disembodiment the latter sense only is employed: the former would yield a contradiction and is in practice ignored.

On one central issue, then, I am agreeing with Strawson against Anscombe and Vendler. But I doubt whether Strawson would accept this talk of two senses for 'I'. He insists that even in the uses which correspond to what I have just called the latter sense the links with empirical criteria of personal identity are vital. '"I" can be used without criteria of subject-identity and yet refer to a subject. It can do so because—perhaps—it issues publicly from the mouth of a man who is recognizable and identifiable as the person he is by the application of empirical criteria of personal identity; or, even if used in soliloquy, is used by a person who would acknowledge the applicability of those criteria in settling questions as to whether he, the very man who now ascribes to himself this experience, was or was not the person who, say, performed such-and-such an action in the past' (p. 165). But this seems wrong. There have been philosophers, from Joseph Butler to Richard Swinburne, who have denied that anything empirical constitutes decisive criteria for personal identity, and I think that about the analysis of our present ordinary concept of personal identity they are right.[3] If so, not only they but also those whom they correctly report do not 'acknowledge the applicability of those criteria'. Nor is it only by issuing publicly from the mouth of an identifiable man that 'I' refers to a subject. Anscombe remarks that our imagination makes something of the idea of mediums and possession, arguing that the following communication is conceivable (and presumably also understandable): 'Try to believe this: when I say "I", that does not mean this human being who is making the noise. I am someone else who has borrowed this human being to speak through him' (p. 60). Such considerations as these show that the use of 'I' to refer to a subject is not contemporaneously parasitic upon any links with empirical criteria of the identity of a human being. (But the example is also a difficulty for Anscombe herself. To explain how our imagination makes something of this idea, she compares the notion of possession with that of an interpreter who quotes his principal's words, including 'I', in direct speech. But this is different: the principal is normally another human being who is being *quoted*, but if there were a case of possession, it would be some other 'spirit' speaking directly, then if not there.)

Strawson also says: 'It is not easy to become intensely aware of the immediate character, of the purely inner basis, of such self-ascription while both retaining the sense of ascription to a subject and forgetting that immediate reports of experience have this character of ascriptions to a subject only because of the links I have mentioned with ordinary criteria of personal identity' (p. 166). What he speaks of forgetting is what I would deny. Since, as he says, such self-ascription is immediate and has a purely inner basis—what I have called being joined on to a series of co-conscious experiences—what *present* role can the alleged links with ordinary criteria play? Strawson does not explain this, and it is hard to see how they can be playing any role, in view of ways in which they can be broken or dispensed with, for example in thought about mediums and possession or in a Butler-Swinburne-everyday concept of the absolute identity of a person.

On the other hand, taking up a theme that was set aside earlier, we can allow that these empirical criteria are historically important: they will have contributed to the development of the concept of a unitary subject to which experiences (etc.) are ascribed. In what he calls 'the coup de grâce to Cartesianism', Strawson, following Kant,

---

[3] See *Problems from Locke*, pp. 192–5.

argues that Descartes's rational psychology is powerless to defend its conclusions against alternative but equally empty theories. Perhaps there are a thousand souls simultaneously thinking the thoughts that one man's utterance expresses. 'How could the—or each—soul persuade itself of its uniqueness?' (p.168). Anscombe echoes this: 'How do I know that "I" is not ten thinkers thinking in unison? Or perhaps not quite succeeding. That might account for the confusion of thought which I sometimes feel' (p.53). But these intendedly rhetorical questions themselves hint at an answer.

The approximation to harmony that my thoughts display is some evidence, though not conclusive evidence, of a single thinker, of a source whose parts, if it has parts, are closely interconnected. As jam sessions go, my mental performances are fairly successful. If there were a thousand, or even ten, souls thinking in near unison, this would call for some explanation of how it was achieved. Nevertheless, it is obvious that historically the notion of a single subject of experiences is borrowed from that of a single human being: in particular, it is other people's view of me as one person that has consolidated my unitary view of myself. Again, it is no accident that what I have called the two senses of 'I' converge. They grew up together: they developed in virtue of their convergence in the ordinary central uses. Each of us learned to use 'I' to refer to the subject, whatever it may be, of his co-conscious experiences because he was having those experiences in circumstances in which the corresponding predicates were true, and many of them observably true, of this human being. So when Strawson says that 'immediate reports of experience have this character of ascriptions to a subject only because of the links ... with ordinary criteria of personal identity', we can accept this if 'because' has a causal, historical, sense; what I deny is that we should accept it if 'because' stands for a contemporaneous linguistic constraint.

We finally return, then, to the other major issue, that between Kant and Descartes. Am I now rejecting what Strawson takes as Kant's insight and opening the way for the acceptance of a Cartesian Ego after all? Not quite. I am conceding to Descartes that whatever sophistication and learning may lie behind our present competence, we do now have a way of ascribing experiences, states, and actions to a supposed single subject, independently of any criteria for its unity and identity through time and without any contemporaneous reliance on the equation of this subject with a body or a human being, and we can therefore coherently engage in feats of transference or speculations about disembodiment which would conflict with such an equation. My essence is thinking and nothing but thinking in the sense that thinking alone is contemporaneously involved in this ascription. But I agree with Kant and Strawson and Anscombe and Vendler, against Descartes, that such a method of ascription does not suffice to introduce a thing to which these items belong and whose existence involves thinking alone, which is ontologically distinct from the body and of which we know, just in virtue of this method of ascription, that this thing can continue to exist whether there is a body or not. Descartes's mistake was to suppose that something whose style of introduction into our thought and speech involved nothing but thinking was thereby shown to be such that its existence involved nothing but thinking. The truth of the matter is that 'I' in one sense—as we may call it, the transcendental 'I'—genuinely refers to something which is introduced in the style of a Cartesian Ego, and yet what makes this a successful reference to an actual persisting thing is the fact that there is a human being, a body alive and functioning, which is not only the user of this 'I' but also the subject of the thoughts by way of which it refers.

There is, however, a further question: is the ordinary concept of *I* itself Cartesian? That is, is *I* not merely introduced in the style of a Cartesian Ego but also conceived as having an individuality independent of anything physical? Two considerations point in this direction.

First, can I still perform feats of transference once I know that I am in fact a human being, for whose existence and persistence the existence and persistence of this body—or at the very least this central nervous system—are needed? I should have to put this knowledge aside. I cannot include it within my transference imaginings without making them internally incoherent. But it will not be easy to put this knowledge aside if I am thinking of *I* just as the subject, whatever it may be, of these experiences, and thereby leaving the door wide open for its identification with this human being. It will be easier to do so if I have a positively Cartesian concept of myself and firmly deny my ontological dependence on my body.

Secondly, can I perform feats of transference with regard to you? If so, how? We ordinarily recognize, of course, that every *he* is an *I* to himself, but this recognition enables me only to understand that *you* can imagine your being at Cannae; it does not give *me* a way of imagining your being at Cannae. Yet I seem able to do this (for example, to imagine your being at Cannae with me). This would be a further difficulty not only for Anscombe and Vendler but also for Strawson, since I cannot regard it as possible that you, that particular human being, should have been at Cannae. I already believe that you have experiences, act intentionally, and so on, and I know something of what these experiences and actions are. So I can think of you, in one sense, as the subject, whatever it may be, of those experiences and actions, and I just might be able to ignore the fact that it was by way of my identification of you as that human being that I came by such knowledge as I have of your thoughts and actions, and so coherently imagine that that same subject, whatever it may be, existed at an earlier period. But again it will be much easier to think of something identical with you as existing at an earlier period if I have some category available, so that I can think of you, at Cannae, as the same so-and-so as you are now, and the appropriate category will be that of a Cartesian Ego, something which exists simply as a subject of thoughts and actions and which has, and can be thought of even in fantastically counterfactual imaginings as having, an absolute identity sustained neither by bodily continuity nor by chains of co-consciousness.

I am inclined to think, then, in view of our readiness to engage not only in first person but also in second and third person transferences, that our present ordinary concept of *I* (and of *you* and *he* and *she*) is partly Cartesian, and that in whittling down the meaning of the transcendental 'I' to 'the subject, *whatever it may be* ...' and thereby allowing it to have a genuine reference to this human being, I am proposing a conceptual reform. A mere analysis of this part of our concept would equate 'I' rather with 'the subject, which exists in and by being a subject ...', and therefore would compel us to say that though this is intendedly a referring term, it always fails of reference. For the arguments which suggest that our ordinary concept is (partly) that of a Cartesian Ego have no tendency to show that there really are any such things.

III

RESPONSIBILITY AND LANGUAGE[1]

In this article I propose to examine two contributions to the theory of responsibility that have been made by philosophers of the 'linguistic' school: Professor Hart's Aristotelian Society paper on 'The Ascription of Responsibility and Rights', which has been reprinted in *Logic and Language, First Series* (pp. 145-166), and Professor Ryle's remarks in *Dilemmas* (pp. 4-5). My main intention is to use this examination to develop some positive suggestions of my own, but I shall also be criticizing the accounts given by Hart and Ryle, and I believe that this criticism will provide detailed illustrations of certain general weaknesses in the linguistic method of philosophizing.

Before we come to criticism, however, let us consider a concrete example of the assigning of responsibility. In Sydney some time ago a motor cyclist was exceeding the speed limit; a traffic policeman, also on a motor cycle, chased him, and soon they were both travelling, according to the reports, at 70 m.p.h. Then an unobservant citizen stepped off a bus into the policeman's path; in the crash that resulted the other man was killed at once; the policeman died next day.

There was some disagreement as to who was responsible for this accident. The police announced that when they caught the original speedster they would charge him with causing the two deaths. The general public was inclined at first to hold the policeman responsible for the other man's death, but tended to change its mind a little when he died himself. So far as I know, no one said that the man who stepped off the bus was to blame for his own death and the policeman's, but this is a view that could conceivably be held. In addition to these three simple answers to the question 'Who was responsible?' there are several less obvious or more complex ones— for example, that no one was responsible, that some unmentioned

Reprinted from the *Australasian Journal of Philosophy*, Vol. 33, No. 3 (December 1955). References are to *Logic and Language, First Series*, edited by A. Flew (Oxford, 1951) and G. Ryle, *Dilemmas* (Cambridge, 1954).

[1] Based on the presidential address given to the Annual Congress of the Australasian Association of Psychology and Philosophy in August 1954.

person or persons were responsible, that the responsibility was shared, or that perhaps even apart from such sharing someone was not fully but only partly responsible, and so on. But for simplicity I shall consider only the three straightforward answers.

The answer we choose will depend on what we take to be the normal, proper, or expected course of events: the person that we hold responsible is the one who steps outside this expected pattern. Thus if we assume, as apparently the police did, that it is normal and proper for traffic police to pursue, relentlessly and with all the means in their power, those who break the speed limit, and that it is normal and proper for people to step off buses without taking precautions against motor cycles passing at 70 m.p.h., but that it is not normal and proper for cyclists (other than police in pursuit of a criminal) to break the speed limit then we shall hold the cyclist responsible. The behaviour of the policeman and the bus traveller belonged, on this view, to the normal pattern, but that of the cyclist was an intrusion into it.

On the other hand, the general public is inclined to take a less legalistic view, and not to identify what is normal and proper with strict conformity to the law and the police regulations. It might hold, therefore, that the cyclist's conduct, though illegal, was yet normal and expected, including his increase in speed when chased, whereas it was not normal, not 'reasonable', for the policeman to go to such lengths to catch a speedster. Making these assumptions, the general public would conclude that the policeman was responsible for the accident.

We can even imagine how we might come to hold the bus traveller responsible. If, perhaps under the influence of an excessive reading of crime stories, we come to regard both law-breaking and the all-out pursuit of law-breakers as two parts of a normal social activity, as together constituting something like a game, but a very important game, with which the rest of society should not interfere, then we might regard the man who stepped off the bus as the intruder into this field of normal activity, and so as being responsible for the accident.

That is to say, to hold someone responsible for some occurrence is to take his action as the cause of that occurrence, and Professor Anderson has shown[2] that the cause of an event is its necessary

---

[2] See 'The Problem of Causality', this *Journal*, Vol. 16, No. 2 (August 1938).

and sufficient preceding condition *within some field*. In seeking the cause of an event we are assuming some field and looking for the differentia which marks off within that field the cases where the event occurs from those where it does not. This differentia is not itself part of the field, but an intrusion into it. It follows that the answer to the question 'What is the cause of this event?' will vary according to the field with implicit reference to which the question is asked.

But in determining responsibility we do not choose the causal field quite arbitrarily; our choice is determined by our moral expectations, our views about what is normal and proper. The person responsible is the one whose action is the cause in relation to this morally determined field. Thus if (in relation to *some* field) a man's action is the cause of some bad result, but this is not the morally normal field, that is to say, if the bad result would not have followed his action if the normal pattern of expectations had been fulfilled, we do not hold him responsible. This is why we do not hold a man responsible for results which he could not 'reasonably' have anticipated, but we do hold him responsible for results which, we say, he should have anticipated, whether he actually did or not.

This means that determining whether a person is responsible for something, whether it is part of his 'action' in a moral sense, is not a thing that can be done in advance of moral judgement. We cannot first decide what each person did and then proceed to pass a series of moral judgements; for to decide what each person 'did', in the sense of 'was responsible for', presupposes a system of moral judgements. This leads to a curious inversion of the utilitarian account of moral judgement. According to utilitarianism, you determine whether one act is right or wrong by looking at its results; but we have found that you cannot determine what events are to count as *its* results without first deciding whether it is right or wrong.

This paradox may be illustrated by another recent case. A Mr Cazneaux had made a will leaving property to his wife, and a Miss Hamilton had witnessed it. After Mr Cazneaux's death, his wife sought proof of the will, but Miss Hamilton refused to say that the signature was hers, because she regarded as unjust the rule which allows a solicitor or a doctor a fee of one guinea for attesting a will, while other people who attest wills get nothing. The judge, no doubt in agreement with public opinion, said that Miss Hamilton was doing wrong, because she was preventing Mrs Cazneaux from getting the money to which she was entitled. But Miss Hamilton said that it was not *she* who was preventing Mrs Cazneaux from getting her money, but rather the unjust rule against which she was protesting. And clearly the judge was arguing in a circle. In holding Miss Hamilton responsible for the delay, he was assuming that her action was wrong, and that the rule, whether perfectly just or not, was good enough to go on with. But the reason he gave for the wrongness of her action was that it was causing this delay.

The account I have suggested would, if it is correct, explain what is happening when we hold someone responsible, and it shows that responsibility, in this sense, is relative to a prior system of moral views. But, someone may object, when is a person *really* responsible; for instance, how can we tell which of the three men was really to blame for the death of the passenger on the bus? I shall comment later on this question.

Let us now turn to Professor Hart's account of responsibility. He says that sentences about human actions, like 'he did it', are often not descriptive but ascriptive, that they ascribe responsibility, and that this is rather like ascribing rights. Also, action and responsibility are defeasible concepts, and in this respect resemble many legal concepts, such as contract. Contract is a defeasible concept, Hart says, because no genuine set of necessary and sufficient conditions for a contract can be given: some positive conditions are needed for the existence of a contract, but these are not sufficient; there are various contingencies which can *defeat* the claim that there is a contract, there are various defences against such a claim, e.g. that the supposed contract resulted from misrepresentation or duress or was for an immoral purpose. Similarly, human action or responsibility is a defeasible concept because the claim 'he did it' can be challenged and defeated by a great variety of defences, e.g. that it was accidental or by mistake or under compulsion or great provocation. It is, Hart thinks, a great mistake to take the distinction between a bodily movement and a human action—the sort of thing for which we are responsible—to be that in the latter case there occurs along with or before the physical movement a mental event called 'willing' or 'having an intention'. An 'intention' is not a mental event for whose absence the various defences are alternative pieces of evidence; in fact it is nothing positive at all; the word 'intention' is merely a comprehensive way of referring to the absence of one or more of the defences.

Let us examine the logic of this account. First, is there really no set of necessary and sufficient conditions for such things as contract and action? From what Hart himself says, it would appear that there is such a set. There are certain positive features—let us call them A and B—which are necessary and, in the absence of any defence, sufficient for a contract. There are various defences which would defeat the claim that there is a contract—let us call them K, L, M, N. Then if this is the complete range of defences, the complex term $AB\bar{K}\bar{L}\bar{M}\bar{N}$ is the necessary and sufficient condition of a contract. Hart admits this in a footnote (p. 152), but suggests that this is a vacuous way of providing a necessary and sufficient condition. But if he admits this, what is he denying?

For one thing, he is denying that there is any *short* list of *positive* features which constitute a definition of contract; he is arguing that the non-availability of the various defences can't be reduced to or taken as evidence for the presence of a single positive feature, that $\bar{K}\bar{L}\bar{M}\bar{N}$ is not equivalent to any simple term C. But even if this is true it would not indicate that contract—or any similar defeasible concept—is non-descriptive, that there is any need to introduce a special ascriptive way of using language.

I think, however, that the footnote was added in a weak moment; the rest of the text indicates that this is not Hart's real view, that in at least two ways this account is to be modified.

First, when a judge says that there is a contract, he is not giving even a complex description of the situation, he is not asserting $AB\bar{K}\bar{L}\bar{M}\bar{N}$, but he is giving a decision on the basis of the facts described by counsel, who may not even have mentioned some of the defences: I think this means that the judge is assigning certain rights and duties, he is ordering the parties to perform the actions to which the contract binds them. Similarly when we ascribe responsibility we are making a decision, not describing the facts but judging in the light of them, and such a judgement is not to be considered true or false, but rather correct in certain circumstances but requiring modification in other circumstances, e.g. if some new defence is raised. Thus what Hart should have admitted is merely that the complex term $AB\bar{K}\bar{L}\bar{M}\bar{N}$ gives not a necessary and sufficient condition of a contract, but a sufficient condition of a situation in which it is correct for a judge to decide that there is a contract—

not a necessary condition, since it may be correct for the judge to give this decision in such a situation as AB$\bar{\text{K}}$, where the other defences, L,M,N have not even been mentioned.

However, what needs to be brought out here is that the word 'contract' hesitates between meanings of different sorts: to say 'there is a contract' is sometimes to make the purely descriptive statement that a situation of the kind AB$\bar{\text{K}}$$\bar{\text{L}}$$\bar{\text{M}}$$\bar{\text{N}}$ has occurred, but sometimes, especially when a judge says it, 'there is a contract' is an instruction to the parties, and others, to act in certain ways. After the judge has given his decision, the sentence 'there is a contract' may also have a further descriptive meaning, namely that there is a legally recognized contract, and it is worth noting that if the judge in giving his decision uses 'there is a contract' with *this* meaning, he is at once stating something and making his statement true: his words in their prescriptive sense *are* the legal recognition which his words in this second descriptive sense assert to have been given. 'The ascriptive use of language' seems to be a name for an unanalysed mixture of meanings, whereas the mixture can be analysed into these various descriptive and prescriptive meanings.

Secondly, Hart sometimes suggests that AB$\bar{\text{K}}$$\bar{\text{L}}$$\bar{\text{M}}$$\bar{\text{N}}$ would not be a definition of contract because the set of defences can never be complete, that the correct list of defences would be of the form K,L,M,N, *etcetera*. New circumstances can arise to which the existing law does not clearly apply; it does not determine the judge's decision and so the judge has to make a decision in another sense, he has to decide whether some new defence should be admitted as a ground for deciding that there is not a contract. This would mean, I think, that the concept of contract has what Waismann calls 'open texture'. Now it is a fact quite well known and generally recognized in legal theory that there are cases where judges pretend to be applying an existing law and are in fact making new law. In view of this, if we want to use legal terms like 'contract' to refer both to the existing law and to the law that judges may make in the immediate future, we must admit that these terms have open texture.

Hart does not make it clear whether he thinks that 'responsibility' and 'human action' are like 'contract' in this respect, that a new defence might be suggested against an imputation of responsibility, and that we should just have to decide whether to accept this sort of defence or not. But let us suppose that this is his view.

Hart would then be saying that in two different ways the meaning of 'action' goes beyond any set of necessary and sufficient conditions of the form $A B \bar{K} \bar{L} \bar{M} \bar{N}$, that there are two different levels at which an element of decision enters. On the one hand in ascribing responsibility we are not describing the facts but assigning blame (i.e. in part expressing a certain emotion) in the light of our possibly incomplete knowledge of those facts, and on the other hand there is some indeterminacy in the set of criteria that we take to justify blame or to excuse persons from blame: *we* may have to decide whether to admit some new type of excuse.

But if the condition for, say, contract is of the form '$A B \bar{K} \bar{L} \bar{M} \bar{N}$ *etcetera*', what is the precise force of the 'etcetera'? Is it like the 'etcetera' in '2, 4, 8, 16 etcetera'? Does the validity of every new defence follow in a rigid way from that of the already recognized ones? Obviously if it were, the 'openness' of the concept would be illusory, all the defences could be summed up under some principle, as this series can be summed up under the formula 2^n. Or does this 'etcetera' mean that new defences may be added in a completely arbitrary way? If so, the addition of a new defence simply changes the meaning of the legal term 'contract', and it seems strange to say that it is part of the meaning of a term that its meaning may be changed. Yet what other possibility is there? I think what is meant must be that the range of already recognized defences sets some limits to what the judge may do, but within these limits he makes an arbitrary choice. He is free legally, in fact, though not in legal fiction, to change the law by stretching precedents in one way or another, but he can only stretch a precedent, not create an absolutely new one, and he cannot stretch it too far. The 'etcetera' then means that the meaning of 'contract' may be changed in the immediate future, but only a little bit at a time.

I believe that this detailed elucidation of Hart's view points to a general criticism not only of Hart, but of the linguistic method. In Hart's treatment a number of different issues are bundled together. He speaks as if it were a single feature of the ascriptive use of language, as opposed to the descriptive use, that an ascriptive concept cannot be defined in terms of a set of necessary and sufficient conditions—he must mean, though he does not say it, a necessary and sufficient set of conditions, or a set of conditions which are severally necessary and jointly sufficient. If my analysis is correct, Hart is really asserting that there are three features which mark these concepts off from ordinary descriptive ones: (i) the conditions are not few and positive, but include many negative ones, (ii) the set of conditions does not determine the meaning of such a concept, but only indicates the situations in which it is correct for someone to do a bit of ascribing, and not all the conditions are necessary to make this correct, (iii) the set of conditions is never complete, so that these concepts have open texture: their meaning is partly indeterminate and is open to supplementation.

Now this whole discussion is concerned with the use of language, that is, with the very sort of topic with which linguistic philosophy claims to deal competently. Yet, although Hart's article is more lucid and more definite than many specimens of linguistic philosophy, it does not bring out these three features clearly. What particularly needs to be brought out is this. With regard to the second of these three features, legal terms and terms like 'responsible' contain a prescriptive element, which must be distinguished from their descriptive element, and also if we say that in certain circumstances it is *correct* for a judge to give such-and-such a decision, we are ourselves making or quoting a further, higher level, prescription: we are prescribing when the judge is to prescribe. And with regard to the third of these features, legal terms, and the phrase 'the law' itself, are used loosely to cover the law as it is, the law as it will be made, and the rules that permit the remaking of the law, and this loose usage tends to conceal the difference between these distinct types of prescription, to suggest that there is throughout a single stable system of law. Hart's failure to make these points sharply enough illustrates the fact that talking in detail about the ways in which we use expressions may not bring out clearly the general points that are being made even on this topic. Especially, the issues are obscured by Hart's invention of a special ascriptive use of language: when we get the issues clear we see that even if Hart is right ascription is not a way of talking irreducibly different from others that are commonly recognized, but includes descriptions, perhaps complex and perhaps partly indeterminate, and also instructions and perhaps the expression of emotions. The tendency to recognize and indeed welcome an indefinite multiplicity of ways of using language, which is a feature of the linguistic movement and which is illustrated here in a mild way, can have the effect of concealing facts even about the use of language.

So far I have been merely finding out what Hart is saying: it is a further question whether what he says is true. First, is he right in insisting upon the irreducible multiplicity and heterogeneity of defences to the claim that there is a contract? It is true that defences of one class that he mentions, 'defences which refer to the general policy of the law in discouraging certain types of contract', are of a different sort from most of the others. The very way in which Hart describes this class indicates that such a defence would show, not that there is no contract in the common-sense meaning of that word, but merely that the law refuses to enforce such a contract. When on these grounds the judge says there is no contract he is negating the prescriptive part of the meaning of this phrase, he is declining to instruct that these provisions should be fulfilled, and he may also be denying, at the same time that he is making false, the statement that there is a legally recognized contract. The defence that the claim is barred by lapse of time comes under the same heading. The other types of defence, those referring to the knowledge or the will of the defendant, or to a change of circumstances, all seem to come under another principle, that the parties did not really agree to do what a literal enforcement of the contract would now involve.

But this is exactly what Hart will not have: he dismisses Sir Frederick Pollock's view that 'true, full and free consent' is a necessary condition of a contract, maintaining that such a doctrine 'is only accurate as a statement of the law if treated as a compendious reference to the defences with which claims in contract may be weakened and met'; such consent is not a positive psychological element. In the same way Hart maintains that 'intention' is not a positive psychological element in responsible human action, but only a compendious reference to the absence of various defences. But how does he establish this? In the case of contract, merely by referring to the procedures of the courts: but of course this does not prove or even probabilify his conclusion. It is, as Hart has to admit, still possible to maintain that the various defences are merely evidence of the absence of free consent. Hart thinks that to maintain this would be a piece of unreasonable obstinacy, but he has really nothing to say against it, and introspectively it is clear that there is such a thing as consenting. The only effective case that could be made out against the occurrence, or the relevance in law, of this psychological element would be one based on behaviourist or pragmatist or logical positivist assumptions; such

assumptions would lead to the conclusion that since the presence
of consent is practically verified in court by the non-availability of
the various defences—or, what comes to the same thing, by the
impossibility of pointing to behaviour of a kind that would indicate
non-consent—the meaning of the word 'consent' must be just the
absence of these defences. Hart explicitly repudiates behaviourism
(p. 165) and tacitly rejects the principle of verification (p. 154), but
of his two reasons for doing the latter, the one depends upon his
lack of precision about necessary and sufficient conditions and the
other is that his defeasible concepts involve decisions, and are not
purely descriptive. So far as the *descriptive* part of the meaning of
these concepts is concerned, Hart *is* identifying the meaning with
the method of verification.

This brings me to my second general criticism of linguistic philosophy: one main theme running through it is still a sort of
crypto-logical-positivism. No one, these days, is game to assert the
principle of verification, but many people argue as if it held good.
And Hart is one of these. His real but unstated argument against
Pollock is that consent is verified simply by the non-availability or
failure of the various defences, and so it must mean nothing more
than their absence.

Even in the procedure of the courts, however, there may be
something to support Pollock against Hart, not so much in ordinary practice in the lower courts, but rather in the way in which
the higher courts deal with new and difficult problems. In ordinary
practice, lawyers may treat 'consent' as the mere absence of the
various defences; but on the rare occasions when a higher court
has to make a new decision, surely the judges do sometimes consider, as a real question, whether the new defence is or is not
evidence of the absence of consent. In other words, *sometimes* the
'etcetera' in the list of criteria for a defeasible concept *is* like that
in '2, 4, 8, 16 etcetera'. The judge takes some of the already recognized criteria to indicate a principle, and considers whether this
principle would justify the proposed new defence as well.

It seems, then, that Hart greatly exaggerates the heterogeneity of
the defences against the claim that there is a contract. They boil
down to two main types, those concerned with the policies of the
legal system and those concerned with the occurrence of a genuine
agreement on the matter in dispute. And we can see why there
should be these two types of defence once we realize the dual nature

of the statement 'there is a contract', that on the one hand it asserts that there is an agreement and on the other hand it gives the support of the legal system to actions in accordance with this agreement. In view of this, it is natural that a defence is either a denial that there is an agreement or a reference to some feature that would make the legal system withhold its support.

But one further point may be made before we leave this topic: there is a problem concealed in the notion of *free* consent. There is always some inducement to enter into a contract, some influence bearing upon each party, and the decision of each to enter into the contract arises from some mental state. When we call an act of consent free we are not saying that it is uncaused or uninfluenced, but merely that it was free from *undue* influence, and that the mental state from which it arose was not an abnormal one. But what the law recognizes as undue influence or an abnormal mental state will depend upon the general policies of the legal system, the moral views it represents. So that although I have distinguished 'genuine agreement' and legal policy' as two principles covering, between them, the whole range of defences, these two are not quite independent: what counts as genuine agreement depends in part on the policy of the legal system. This is, I believe, a sound point, but it was made not by Hart, but, a long time ago, by Hobbes.[3]

Can the defences against the claim that a person is responsible be boiled down in a similar way? At first sight it would seem that they can. First we have a set of defences which assert in one way or another that the agent did not intend his action, e.g. that Smith hit someone accidentally, inadvertently, or by mistake for someone else. Secondly we have a set of defences which diminish the degree of disapproval that we commonly feel; we blame Smith less for the attack if it was in self-defence, under provocation, or if he was forced so to act by a threat from some other person, and we do not blame him at all if we find that he was mad. The ascribing of responsibility has these two aspects, the assertion that the agent intended this action and a disapproval of this sort of action, and naturally enough any defence against the imputation of responsibility is either a denial that the action was intended or an account of circumstances which would put the action into a class of which we disapprove less or not at all.

And again the first part of this view is exactly what Hart is

[3] See *Leviathan*, Chapter 20.

arguing against. He says that there is no such common psychological element as intention, for whose absence the various defences are so many distinct modes of bringing evidence. But can he seriously maintain that accident, inadvertence, and mistake are just a collection of defences, quite arbitrarily thrown together, a mere heap of items with no common principle? Surely, despite what Hart says, intending, like consent, is an introspectively recognizable state of mind. It is true that it is only by stretching the notion of intention beyond any definite psychological meaning that we can say that *all* of the defensible actions are unintended. But the sting is taken out of this argument when we admit that only *some* of the defences come under this heading, e.g. that the occurrence of provocation does not make the act any less intentional.

Nevertheless this account will not quite do. An act is intended in the strict psychological sense if the agent envisages the result and aims at it. Perhaps with a bit of stretching this psychological sense can include the case where the agent aims at one result but accepts, puts up with, another result which he sees to be a necessary concomitant of the first: if in order to save yourself in a shipwreck you push someone else off a raft that is too small to support you both, you may be said to intend that he should be drowned, though you do not *aim* at this. But you cannot in any strict psychological sense be said to intend a result which you do not envisage at all. Yet there are plenty of cases where someone is held responsible for an unenvisaged result, where it is said that he should have foreseen it and provided against it. There is such a thing as culpable negligence, whereas if showing that an act was literally unintended were a complete defence against the charge of responsibility, there would be no such thing. Also, this account in terms of intention does not explain the case where someone is held responsible for harm that results, without his intention, from some other wrong or criminal act. If while standing on a crowded railway platform you snatch a woman's handbag and cause her to fall under a train, you are more likely to be held responsible for her death than if you had caused her to fall by stooping to retrieve a parcel of your own.

But the difficulties may perhaps be cleared up if we make use of the account of responsibility that was suggested by the example of the cyclist and the policeman. To hold a person responsible for some harm that is done is to take him to be the cause of it, in relation to a causal field that is chosen in the light of one's own moral views about what is proper or expected. *Now* it is easy to see how culpable negligence occurs. The negligent act is regarded as culpable because it is outside the system of expected actions, it is the cause relatively to this field. It is to be expected that rifles which, without inspection, you imagine to be unloaded will sometimes be loaded: expecting this, we cannot also happily accept the practice of pointing an uninspected rifle at someone and playfully pressing the trigger. So if a man does this, and the other man is killed, we hold the man who pressed the trigger responsible—that is, we take his action to be the intrusion into the peaceful, to be expected, course of events. Similarly we hold the bag-snatcher responsible for the woman's death because, or if, we look on bag-snatching as something beyond the pale, as outside the proper system of activities. On the other hand, the man who stoops to pick up his own parcel is less likely to be held responsible, because picking up one's own parcel is more likely to be accepted as a normal procedure, though there may be some doubt about its propriety on a very crowded platform.

This treatment may also explain why intention in the literal psychological sense is so important. As we have seen, it is not that the absence of intention is a defence; it is rather that the presence of intention establishes a *prima facie* case for the prosecution. If you intend someone's death and bring it about, this in itself puts you beyond the pale, sets your act outside the field of morally acceptable activities, and therefore it will be taken, in relation to this field, as the cause of the death. The correctness of this analysis seems to be confirmed by exceptional cases where a person may aim at an end that is held to be evil, and bring it about, and yet not be held responsible. In some societies the seduction of virgins is regarded as a bad thing, and yet it is accepted as normal and proper for young men to try to seduce virgins. In such a society, if a girl is seduced, *she* is blamed and not the young man; it was her business, it is said, to preserve her virginity. The man is not blamed, for his endeavours are taken to be normal and proper, i.e. to be part of the causal field: the intrusion into this field was the girl's carelessness. Where absence of intention *is* a defence (e.g. where harm is done accidentally or inadvertently), what is important is not the *mere* absence of intention but the fact that what one did was perfectly normal.

The same treatment might explain the other defences, those in terms of provocation, self-defence, compulsion, and madness. Each of these defences inclines us to accept the action as part of the normal scheme. We expect people to react violently when provoked, we approve of self-defence and in general of the choice of the lesser evil, which is called compulsion, and we do not make moral demands upon people who are mad. But this works only if these are taken as defences, not as pleas in mitigation, as negating responsibility, not as lessening it. It must be admitted that the notion of a lower degree of responsibility is a confused one: it suggests that the action in question is a completely wrong one, but that the agent didn't quite commit it, doesn't fully own it. It suggests that what the agent did can be more or less a cause, and contrarily less or more a part of the causal field, but no clear meaning can be given to such notions. What must be meant is that there is full responsibility but for a less wrong act. That is to say, to see what is happening here we must take account of the emotional side of the notion of responsibility, which was mentioned above. Where there is said to be reduced responsibility, the act in question is being taken as the cause, as wholly outside the field of moral expectation, but is of a sort less strongly disapproved than others. It is the emotion of disapproval which admits of degrees.

I suggest, then, that the whole variety of defences against the claim that something is a human action, that the agent is responsible, may be explained by these two principles, that to hold a person responsible is to take him as the cause of the bad result within a field that is determined by one's moral views, and that the degree of guilt assigned depends upon the strength of one's disapproval. This is not to say that all the defences are homogeneous, that they all point to the absence of a single factor called intention; but it is to say that the situation is less haphazard than Hart's account would suggest.

If any systematic account of responsibility, such as this, is correct, there is, then, a further weakness in Hart's treatment, which again exemplifies a widespread weakness in linguistic philosophy. Hart has stopped short of an adequate account of what it is to ascribe responsibility precisely because he is reluctant to go beyond the analysis of language. He leaves responsibility as an irreducibly defeasible concept, whose use is governed by a large set of heterogeneous criteria, whereas these could have been related to two connected principles. And I think he stopped short because such an explanation goes beyond language to the facts: it could not be discovered by investigating 'the use of language' if this is conceived as a study of equivalences and differences between sentences, of the fitting of words into sentence-frames, and suchlike philological questions. But such an explanation can be reached by investigating the use of language, if this means finding out what we use language for, discovering, among other things, what situations are referred to by various expressions.

This connects with another general difficulty for the linguistic movement which has been emphasized, for example, by Mr Passmore. Is linguisticism philology or metaphysics? Is the linguistic philosopher talking just about language, or is he talking in a roundabout way about the facts? If it is the latter, there may be some justification for this roundabout approach in that other philosophers may have been misled by language, and special attention to language may be needed if we are to avoid being misled. But still attention to language can be only a part of the philosopher's activity, and indeed he will be able to clear up linguistic puzzles only by studying the facts directly as well. And if he is talking about the facts, he cannot establish the answer to his main questions by a study of language alone. If he tries to get answers to philosophical questions from language alone, he is merely using, in a concealed way, the Aristotelian appeal to common sense. Especially in morals and in scientific method linguisticism can lead to a sort of conformism or conventionalism. Such-and-such are the criteria commonly used to distinguish right from wrong, therefore these are *the* criteria of right and wrong. Induction is a valid procedure in science, because it is the way in which scientists proceed. These are what are recognized as good reasons in ethics or in science: what further justification of them could you seek or get? And so on.

But the linguistic philosopher need not get stuck in what has been called 'vicious linguisticism'; he can work through language to the facts. But then he needs something more than linguistic evidence to support his view of what the language is attempting to describe: he must observe how things really are. Now Hart is failing to do this; in so far as he is asserting something objective, he is using the evidence of linguistic procedures as if it showed conclusively what the facts are like. For example, because we use the word 'intention' defeasibly, intention must be a purely defeasible concept, there cannot be a positive psychological state or process called intending. But this argument is parallel to and no more valid than the argument which linguists commonly ascribe to their opponents, that since there is a word 'intention' there must be a thing to which it refers. Neither way of arguing from language is at all conclusive: what we must do is look at mental processes, especially our own, and see whether there is one such process to which the word 'intending' refers. I think that we do find such a process, but that the word 'intention' is often stretched beyond the cases in which this process actually occurs.

I now want to turn briefly to some of Professor Ryle's remarks, in his recent book, *Dilemmas*, about the problem of responsibility and determinism, the problem whether, if all human actions are caused, people can ever be to blame for what they do. Throughout this book Ryle proposes to solve philosophical puzzles by showing that they arise from litigations between what are really two or more different lines of thought; we think there is a contradiction because we take two theories to be rival solutions to the same question, and we can remove the difficulty by showing that they are solutions to two different questions. So the responsibility–determinism dilemma can be resolved when we see that 'The proposition that people tend to behave as they have been trained to behave is [an] answer to the question, "What differences are made to a person by the scoldings and coaxings he has received [etc.]" ... But the proposition that some behaviour is reprehensible is a generalization of the answers to questions of the pattern "Was he wrong to act as he did, or did he do it under duress or in an epileptic seizure?"' (p. 5).

This approach enables Ryle to solve some dilemmas correctly, but I think that it can very readily be misused. My criticism of it links with what I was saying about the conformist tendency in linguisticism. This tendency appears, for example, in the endeavour to find a proper place for all ordinary respectable activities, to ensure, for example, that religion and science should have each its own sphere and that they should not encroach upon each other. In at least some cases I believe that the spheres are not separable: the different questions do bear upon each other, and there is a real conflict between the answers that people are conventionally inclined to give to them.

For example Ryle says (pp. 69-70) that people used to be worried by the conflict between the supposedly scientific account of human nature offered by the economists, that 'Man was a creature actuated only by considerations of gain and loss' and the account offered by ordinary experience, and he says that the problem is solved, the two accounts reconciled, once we realize that the economists are really talking about men only in so far as they concern themselves in marketing matters. But this will not do, for many of the affairs in which men act generously, hospitably, or in devotion to some branch of learning are *also* economic affairs. If it were necessary for economic theory that men should always seek to maximize profits in so far as they engage in marketing matters, then economic theory would really conflict with ordinary experience. The two spheres cannot be separated: the answers to the different questions do conflict. And I believe that as a matter of history this conflict has been resolved not by any demarcation of spheres but by the economists' having stopped talking about the Economic Man, by the intrusion, we might say, of common sense into economic theory.

Nor can the determinism-responsibility dilemma be resolved by merely pointing to the difference between a causal question and a moral question—a solution strangely reminiscent of Kant's attempt, in Section III of the *Fundamental Principles*, to solve the antinomy of freedom and necessity by suggesting that we occupy different points of view when we think of ourselves as free and as determined. Blaming someone for an action may or may not be compatible with recognizing it as caused; it will depend what blaming is; in particular it will depend on whether blaming involves a reference to an uncaused cause.

Now if holding someone responsible is, as I have said, taking his act to be the cause in relation to a field determined by our moral views, then there is indeed no conflict between responsibility and determinism: what is thus taken as the cause may quite well be an effect in some other field. But using my account of responsibility we can easily see how the appearance of a conflict arises. For one thing, in thus assigning responsibility, in selecting this act as the cause, we are precluded from treating it as an effect in *this* field. If this act were itself an effect in relation to this field, we should assign responsibility to *its* cause. This transferring of responsibility backwards from effect to cause is a logical consequence of the nature of responsibility as I have described it, and only a slight confusion is therefore needed to give rise to the view that responsibility can be assigned only to a cause which is itself completely uncaused.

But another way of looking at the problem is this. As I said much earlier, my account of responsibility is a relative one, it does not answer the question, 'But who is really, absolutely, responsible?' But if you persist in asking this question you are looking for some act which will be a cause, not merely in relation to the field that is determined by some actual set of moral views, but in relation to any field whatsoever. And this would have to be an uncaused cause. In other words, absolute responsibility would require indeterminism.

An adequate treatment of the determinism–responsibility dilemma, then, would require a distinction between two senses of 'responsible', the relative and the absolute. Relative responsibility, with which I have been dealing in most of this article, is compatible with determinism, but absolute responsibility is not. Now it is true that Ryle only touches on this problem, and does not pretend to deal thoroughly with it, but even so the little he says is misleading. It suggests that there is a sphere in which moral thought can have free play, unhampered by considerations of causality. But a great deal of moral thought has involved a belief in absolute responsibility, in objective blameworthiness, so that Ryle's solution could serve to cover up a real problem, and to protect a false moral view from the criticism that can be brought against it from the side of causal theory. I should agree with Ryle, then, that philosophy is often concerned with litigation between spheres of thought, but I should say that it is a mistake to start with the assumption that spheres of thought are separable and do not really conflict. And this is a mistake into which a linguistic philosopher is particularly liable to fall.

IV

THE GROUNDS OF
RESPONSIBILITY

'AN action is voluntary when what the agent does is controlled by
his will; or, when what he wants straightforwardly determines what
he does; or, when his desires issue in action.' It would be natural
to give some such account as these, preserving the etymological
connection between 'voluntary' and will, want, or desire, but also
somehow indicating the double relation between the wanting and
what is done, that the former both brings about the latter and is
fulfilled by it. And we could sketch a related but more complicated
account of intentional action. But Professor Hart (in the lectures
and essays collected in *Punishment and Responsibility*) repeatedly
criticizes accounts of this sort, on two main grounds. He does not
believe that such an analysis can be coherently developed or applied
in an illuminating way. But also, even in so far as it does point
correctly to certain psychological elements, it focuses attention on
the wrong things. What is important as a ground for liability to
legal penalties is not that agents should ' "have in their minds" the
elements of foresight or desire for muscular movement. These
psychological elements are not *in themselves* crucial. ... What is
crucial is that those whom we punish should have had, when they
acted, the normal capacities, physical and mental, for doing what
the law requires ... and a fair opportunity to exercise those capacities'. (*Punishment and Responsibility*, p. 152; all page references in
the sequel are to this volume.) Capacity and opportunity, Professor
Hart holds, are what matter, rather than foresight and the execution of desire as such. He thinks that mistakes about this have
fostered bad arguments against responsibility for negligence and
have delayed the recognition of other ways in which diminished
capacities for self-control should limit responsibility. But I believe
that what I have called the natural account can be defended against
such objections.

Reprinted from *Law, Morality and Society: Essays in Honour of H.L.A. Hart*, edited
by P.M.S. Hacker and J. Raz (Clarendon Press, 1977).

For the sake of clarity, let us introduce a distinction like that commonly drawn between a fact and a concrete event, and enshrine it rather arbitrarily in the words 'act' and 'action'. Acts, like facts and results, will be tied tightly to descriptions, though to gerundival phrases rather than to that-clauses: an act will always be the act of doing or bringing about such-and-such. An action will be the whole concrete performance, which will incorporate or involve as many acts as there are non-equivalent true descriptions of it. Then instead of saying, as we might have said without this distinction, that an action may be intended or intentional under one description but not under another which also applies to it, we can say simply that it is acts and results, not actions, that are intended or intentional, or that fail to be so, and that the same action can involve some acts that are intended and some that are not. We also need Bentham's distinction between what is directly intended, either as an end aimed at or as a means to such an end, and what is obliquely intended either as a second effect of a means or as a further consequence of an end, including as obliquely intended both results which the agent foresees with certainty and ones which he sees as likely to follow what he directly intends. *Mens rea* must relate, like intention, to specific acts or charges: the agent's *mens* can be *rea* with regard to a particular *actus reus*—which is an act, not an action—only if he intended that act either directly or obliquely.

In 'Acts of Will and Responsibility' Professor Hart examines the theory that besides the knowledge of circumstances and foresight of consequences required for *mens rea* there is another, more fundamental, psychological, element required for responsibility, that the 'conduct' (including omissions) must be 'voluntary'; this is more fundamental in that it may still be required for offences of strict liability where *mens rea* or even inadvertent negligence is not. He agrees that there is in non-voluntary conduct some kind of defect, different from and more fundamental than lack of knowledge and foresight, but he finds obscure such phrases as 'acts of will', conduct 'not governed by the will', and the like, which have been used in attempts to describe it. There is, he notes, a theory which would give such phrases an exact meaning, which was expounded clearly, early in the nineteenth century, by Dr Thomas Brown and, following him, by John Austin, remnants of which have come down into the legal textbooks. This theory is that a human action, strictly speaking, is 'merely a muscular contraction'—what are ordinarily called actions are combinations of muscular movements and some of their consequences—and a voluntary action is a muscular contraction caused by a pre-existing desire for that contraction. But, though simple and clear, this account cannot, Professor Hart thinks, 'intelligibly or correctly characterize ... a minimum indispensable connexion between mind and body present in all normal action and generally required for responsibility' (p. 99). He criticizes it on two main grounds, that it cannot account for the voluntariness and involuntariness of omissions, and that in ordinary positive actions desires for muscular contractions do not occur. In its place he puts an account which deals separately with positive interventions and omissions. Involuntary movements are ones which 'were not appropriate, i.e. required for any action (in the ordinary sense of action) which the agent believed himself to be doing' (p. 105). An omission (for example a failure to do some positive action demanded by the law) is involuntary if the agent either is unconscious and therefore unable to perform any positive action or, though conscious, is unable to make the particular movements required for the performance of the action demanded by the law. In the Notes added later, Professor Hart expresses dissatisfaction with this account of involuntary movements, and suggests instead that the defective cases are 'those where the bodily movements occurred though the agent had no reason for moving his body in that way' (pp. 255-6). But this still seems wrong; if a doctor is testing my knee-jerk reaction I may have a reason for kicking up my leg—perhaps I want him to report that I am in sound health—but the movement may still be involuntary. What would make it voluntary is not my having a reason but my moving it for that reason, and this leads us back towards the rejected theory of movements caused by desires. The same is true of another phrase Professor Hart uses, that involuntary movements are 'not subordinated to the agent's conscious plans of action' (p. 105).

Since it is difficult to formulate any stable alternative account, let us look again at the Brown-Austin theory. This had two salient features: the first, that it took something as both the object and the causal product of the same desire; the second, that it identified this something with a muscular contraction. Professor Hart's criticism is fatal to this second feature, but it does not touch the first. (There is, indeed, a well-known argument against the first feature, that a desire is so logically connected with its object that they cannot also

be related as cause and effect. But this 'logical connection argument', it is gradually being realized, is thoroughly fallacious. The
fact that an adequate description of a desire will have to include a
description of its object in no way prevents the desire and its object
from being distinct occurrences, as a causal relation between them
requires.) Let us see, then, if we can salvage this first feature while
abandoning, as we must, the second—that is, find something other
than a muscular contraction to play the double role of object and
causal product of desire.

Suppose that I voluntarily shut a door. When I start to do this,
I desire the result, the door's being shut, though perhaps only as a
means to some further end. From long experience I know that I
can shut the door and I know how to do so; hence when I desire
the door's being shut and have no strong contrary motive I decide
to shut the door; the movements that constitute my shutting of the
door then take place and bring about that result. In such a straightforward case the desire leads causally to a pre-formed decision or
intention to shut the door, this in turn leads causally to the appropriate muscular contractions and bodily movements, and these in
turn to the door's being shut. I am normally aware of my bodily
movements though not of the muscular contractions, but I do not
normally desire or intend either of these. I do not need to. Long
practice and habitually established skills enable me to bring about
many results while thinking only about the result, not about any
of the essential intermediate links in the causal chain.

This example suggests a general account: an action is voluntary
if it incorporates some directly intended act, where a directly intended act is the bringing about of some result by a causal process
which starts with a desire for that result and a decision to bring it
about. The sense in which voluntariness is more fundamental than
mens rea would then be that an action is voluntary if it incorporates
some directly intended act, whereas there is *mens rea* only if the
particular feature which is the *actus reus* is itself either directly or
obliquely intended.

But this is not quite correct. First, the step of pre-formed decision or intention is not essential for voluntariness: an unopposed
desire may lead directly to appropriate movements. I can just do
something without deciding to do it. But, secondly, it is not necessary for voluntary action that any desired result should actually be
realized. I want the door to be shut and in consequence begin the

appropriate series of movements; but the door is jammed, so that I fail to shut it. Though nothing that I desired has come about, those initial movements were voluntary. Though not themselves desired and not the object of any explicit decision, it is enough that they were such as would normally fulfil the desire that brought them about and that they came about because they were so associated with its fulfilment. They were what I had learnt to do in execution of such a desire, having been 'reinforced' in this respect by normal success. An action may be voluntary, then, even though nothing plays the double role of object and causal product of desire—the muscular contractions are not desired, and the result which is desired may not come about. It is enough that the action incorporates some movement which is (in the sense indicated) appropriate for the fulfilment of a desire that causally brings it about.

This resembles Professor Hart's formula that an action is involuntary if the movements that constitute it 'are appropriate to no action which [the agent] believes himself to be doing' (pp. 105-6). But there is the vital difference that in my account what the movements are to be appropriate to is the fulfilment of a desire that causes them, not just something that the agent believes he is doing, and the appropriateness can be explained by a more complex relation to that desire. Voluntariness is constituted by certain causal patterns in which desires play a leading role.

It is easy to check that this account gives the right answers in such cases of non-voluntary conduct as those listed by Professor Hart (pp. 95-6). It resembles what he calls a toned-down version of the Brown–Austin theory, which he admits to be 'broadly acceptable' but dismisses as 'not very informative' (p. 103). But I think that when it is spelled out a little more fully it gives just the information that we need to understand how voluntary positive actions differ from non-voluntary ones.

But it is still exposed to Professor Hart's other criticism, that it does not apply to omissions. Now an omission corresponds to what we have called an act rather than to an action, and even where the *actus reus* is an omission, it may be an aspect of a positive concrete action, and the latter can be voluntary in the way already explained. If I am driving a car in the normal way, while conscious, but go past a red light without noticing it, the *actus reus* is an omission, a mere negation, failing to stop, but all the time I have been doing something positive, maintaining a slight pressure on the accelerator, making small movements of the steering wheel, watching and responding to road conditions other than the unnoticed signal, and all this is (in the sense explained) appropriate to and a causal product of the desire that the car should proceed along the road. My failing to stop is merely a negative feature of a positive voluntary action. Of course, this does not make the omission itself voluntary. On the other hand if the omission is involved in a piece of positive behaviour which is itself non-voluntary, then *a fortiori* the omission will be non-voluntary.

Omissions, like positive acts, can be intended, either directly or obliquely, and will then be voluntary. But they can also be voluntary in a weaker, negative sense, that the failure to perform the omitted act was caused by the lack of any sufficiently strong desire. If the agent had had some sufficiently strong desire whose fulfilment would have involved the omitted act, or to whose fulfilment that act would have been appropriate, then it would have been performed in execution of that desire; so the omission can be causally ascribed to a lack of desire. Omissions which are involuntary in this sense will be so by Professor Hart's criteria too, since they will have to be causally ascribable to something other than either a desire or the lack of a desire, and this will be some lack of capacity or opportunity. But the converse may not hold. An omission could be voluntary in our sense but involuntary in Professor Hart's, since the lack of a desire that would have brought about the required action might itself be regarded, in some cases, as resulting from the lack of a capacity to form such a desire. Positive acts and actions can also be voluntary in this weaker sense: a habitual, semi-automatic, action may be causally ascribable not to any desire which it fulfils or to which it is appropriate, being a learned means to its fulfilment, but merely to the lack of any sufficiently strong desire. My aimless walking along the road is voluntary in that I would stop if I either wanted to stop or wanted to do something else.

The stronger and weaker senses of 'voluntary' are connected by the fact that in each case what is said to be voluntary is causally dependent upon what the agent wants: it is due to his wanting something or to his not wanting something strongly enough, and where it is due to his wanting something it is either a carrying out of what he wants or at least an appropriate step towards this.

This account of voluntariness, especially of the stronger, positive, sort, leads naturally to a further explanation of intending and intentionality. The central case is that of an act which is both directly intended and carried out. This is both the object and the causal product of a desire, but the intending combines with the desire the belief that the intending will lead straightforwardly to the fulfilment of the desire which it includes. There can be a bare intention to do something, where this combination of desire and belief occurs but the causal process stops short before it issues in any action. There can be intentions for the more distant future—I intend now to do something tomorrow—where the desire is for the future achievement and the belief is that this desire will persist until the specified time and will then lead to its own fulfilment. Attempts and doing something with some further intention also fit easily into this account.

The notion of something's being obliquely intended fits best into an admittedly ideal picture of a fully deliberate action. If an agent brings into consideration and weighs thoroughly everything he knows about the nature and circumstances and likely consequences of a proposed action, and performs the action as a result of this deliberation and in fulfilment of the decision in which it culminates, then he has intended a rather complex act which includes all the features of the action known to him. He has accepted its undesired or neutral components for the sake of the desired ones, knowing that he cannot have these without those. Aspects of the action which are not directly intended either as desired ends or as means may still be known parts of this complex intended act: it is in this that their being obliquely intended consists. But this is an ideal case, and as soon as we move from it to actions which are less deliberate, or impulsive, or result from passion, or rage, or terror, this description becomes less apt. An agent may have known that a certain further consequence would result from what he did, and yet through imperfect deliberation not have explicitly included it in the act which he literally intended. One can bring something about knowingly but not intentionally.

I think, then, that a coherent account of voluntariness and intentionality can be developed on fairly traditional lines and in a way that preserves the close connection between voluntariness and will, want, and desire. But does it lead, or allow, us to draw the boundaries of responsibility in the right places? Or is it easier to do this if we work, as Professor Hart recommends, with the notions of capacity and opportunity, asking 'Could he have done otherwise?' or 'Had he any real choice?'

One problem concerns duress and 'necessity'. Actions performed under duress or necessity—where acting otherwise would have led with practical certainty to the death of the agent himself, or of persons close to him, or to some similar disaster—are clearly voluntary in our stronger sense; but we may well feel inclined to excuse them on the ground that the agent had, in the circumstances, no real choice.

But though this is a colloquially natural way of speaking, it would be more accurate to say that he did have a choice but to spell out what that choice was—for example, between doing what some tyrant demanded and having his relatives safe, and defying the tyrant and having them tortured or killed. Though his being confined to just these alternatives was not voluntary, the agent's choosing one of these complex alternatives rather than the other was wholly voluntary and intentional. And to hold him responsible for his intentional act, adequately described, is appropriate and has no undesirable implications. Even if X is in itself morally wrong or dishonourable or illegal, it does not follow that X-rather-than-Y must be so.

Instead of taking duress or necessity as negating responsibility because it deprives the agent of any real choice, we should see each of these as helping to determine the precise act for which he is responsible, as adding justifying or mitigating circumstances to the description of what he intentionally did.

Another problem concerns the actions of the kleptomaniac, the compulsive drinker, the psychopath, and of one who executes a suggestion made under hypnosis. In some important sense each of these has no real choice, cannot do otherwise; yet his actions seem to be voluntary in terms of the proposed account, they carry some desires that he has into effect. But we may hope to identify some ground of responsibility that will make such people not responsible, or perhaps less than normally responsible, for these actions.

However, even if the question 'Could he have done otherwise?' gives the right answer in these cases, it gives it for the wrong reason. It is liable to mix up considerations relevant to the ordinary grounds of responsibility with the metaphysical problem of determinism and free will. If causal determinism holds, there is a sense in which no one could have done otherwise, and we need at least

Persons and Values

to do some work to distinguish the determinist's 'could not have done otherwise' from that which denies the ordinary grounds of responsibility. But, also, if we state the test in this way we may wonder why the compulsive drinker is not responsible for drinking whereas the compulsive mathematician presumably is to be given credit for his achievements, and likewise the compulsive reformer, the compulsive patriot, the compulsive scribbler, and the compulsive mountaineer.

An alternative explanation would qualify the voluntariness of certain actions by reference to one or both of two models, of which one impugns an agent's unity through time and the other his unity at any one time. First, what is a voluntary action of mine at a certain time may express motives which are very poorly representative of my relatively permanent character and personality; the self whose voluntary action it was may be less than normally continuous with my present self. 'I did it, but I wasn't myself at the time.' Secondly, we may follow Freud, or Plato, in comparing the mind of an individual with a society, and in distinguishing different groups of elements and different styles of interaction between them. There may be a central personality or ego within which desires and purposes interact by conscious deliberation that is an analogue of parliamentary debate, but other desires or impulses which arise in the same human being and which may causally determine and purposively control his movements, but which are outside this central personality and do not participate in this debate, but may either be 'censored' and suppressed or get their way by some less rational process. Thus a voluntary action of this human being may fail to be a voluntary action of his central personality.

Extreme variants of these two models work with the notion of an absolute self: my unity and identity are unequivocal, but completely alien spirits may fight with me for control of my limbs and sometimes take complete possession of my body. But the more plausible variants are built on the rejection of this metaphysical theory; they presuppose that such unity and identity as we have at the best of times depend upon connections and interactions and continuities which are themselves matters of degree. However, philosophical considerations could show only the possibility of these models. It must be an empirical question whether they are exemplified in particular cases or types of case. This will not be an easy question. No neat tests will directly decide the answer, and it is all too easy for someone to use one or other of these models as an excuse; but that does not prevent there being a real issue whether, or how far, they are exemplified. These models formulate questions which we should like psychologists to answer.

These models bring out, better than does the question 'Could he have done otherwise?', what is wrong about the actions of the kleptomaniac and the rest. The compulsive drinker at other times, and perhaps even when he is starting to drink, wishes that he did not get drunk, whereas the compulsive mathematician or mountaineer is on the whole happy with his addiction.

But the psychopath (or perhaps one kind of psychopath), the person who is quite lacking in sympathy and shows no capacity for moral feeling or moral reasoning, escapes both these accounts. His actions are, by our criteria, voluntary in relation to his whole permanent personality, whereas Professor Hart would say that they are not voluntary because he lacks the capacity for self-control. However, it is less confusing to say firmly that his actions are voluntary and his acts intentional, but that there may be other reasons for not holding him responsible, that voluntariness and intentionality are necessary but not sufficient conditions for legal responsibility. The reasons for not holding such a psychopath responsible are significantly different from those that cut other agents off from their unintended acts and non-voluntary actions. The psychopath is in some ways like a young child. Of him in particular it is plausible to say that he is not a moral agent; I shall try to show later how this bears upon legal responsibility.

Would our account lead us implausibly to rule out responsibility for negligence? Here we need some distinctions. If the agent foresees as likely certain harmful results of what he is about to do, but none the less deliberately goes ahead, and such results occur, then those results are themselves obliquely intended. If he is only vaguely and generally aware that harm of a certain sort could result from his carelessness, so that he knows that he is being negligent in that respect, it would be more accurate to say that his negligence itself is obliquely intended, but not its results. If we took it as a necessary condition of responsibility for a certain *actus reus* that that act should itself be intended, then this would exclude responsibility for the results of inadvertent negligence, though not for negligence itself. But if we took as our necessary condition for responsibility only voluntariness in the weaker sense, then there could be responsibility for the results of inadvertent negligence. Of these it may be true to say that if the agent had had a sufficiently strong desire that they should not come about he would have taken more care, and it is only where we can say this that it seems reasonable to impose responsibility for the results of negligence. (But I am not saying that voluntariness in the weaker sense, or even in the stronger, is in itself a sufficient condition of responsibility: as I have hinted with respect to psychopaths, there may be other grounds for excuse.)

Judgements about responsibility which are in themselves acceptable, and which indeed pretty well coincide with those which Professor Hart reaches by a different route, can be largely based on and at any rate reconciled with our version of the natural and traditional account of voluntariness and intentionality. But what of the charges that these psychological elements are not *in themselves* crucial, that what matters for liability for punishment is that those whom we punish should have had the normal capacities for doing what the law requires and opportunity to exercise them—in effect, that what matters is not so much what they did or how they did it, but what else they could have done? This charge is the more forceful since we have had to refer to a different principle to explain the non-responsibility of psychopaths, whereas this is already covered by Professor Hart's principles of capacity and opportunity.

Our view of what matters here will naturally depend upon our view of the aim and justification of legal penalties and of the point, in relation to these, of recognizing any excusing conditions. Bentham, having located this aim and justification in deterrence, tried to explain the excusing conditions by arguing that penalties which violated these restrictions would be ineffective in deterrence. But Professor Hart has shown that this argument is fallacious. Though one can be deterred only from voluntary acts (or omissions), one may be more effectively deterred by the annexing of penalties to all acts of a certain sort rather than just to the voluntary ones, since one might hope that one's own voluntary act might escape punishment by the false pretence that it was not voluntary. Alternatively, anyone who took retribution to be the aim and justification of legal penalties would naturally take the psychological elements to be what matters: it is only what an agent voluntarily does that can in itself deserve punishment. But Professor Hart also rejects this approach. He sees both legal penalties and the excusing conditions attached to them as parts of a compromise between the protection of society and the freedom of individuals, as elements in 'a method of social control which maximizes individual freedom within the coercive framework of law' (p. 23).

His argument is, I think, that penalties attached only to infringements of the law where the agent has the capacity and opportunity to comply with the law interfere less with individual freedom just because the agent can avoid them. This interpretation agrees with Professor Hart's use of the analogy between the mental conditions that excuse from criminal responsibility and those that invalidate wills, contracts, marriages, and the like (pp. 44–5). The function of these institutions of the private law is to carry individual preferences into effect, and the invalidating conditions tend to ensure that only genuine preferences, real choices, are thus made effective. Similarly, the excusing conditions maximize, within the coercive criminal law, 'the efficacy of the individual's informed and considered choice in determining the future and also his power to predict that future' (p. 46).

We must concede that individuals would be less free under a criminal law that did not recognize these excusing conditions, and also that there is some important analogy between these and the invalidating conditions in the civil law. But the analogy does not seem to hold in quite the suggested way. It is surely not that while the civil law tries to ensure that people enter into contracts, marriages, and the like only if they really want to, the criminal law tries to ensure that they go to jail only if they really want to. We must allow for the fact that whereas the aim of the civil law is to carry bequest-making choices, contract-making choices, and so on into effect, the aim of the criminal law is not to carry law-breaking choices into effect but to discourage them.

Let us, then, take this as the starting point of our explanation, noting that the criminal law is addressed primarily to rational agents who are presumed in general to have some tendency to respect the law. It seeks to regulate conduct in the first place by attaching an adverse legal characterization to certain types of voluntary and especially intentional acts and omissions, some but not all of which also have adverse moral characterizations. This legal characterization is the primary thing: it is intended to—and to a considerable extent does—control conduct independently of any sanction. Deterrence and penalties for non-compliance are secondary, reinforcing the motive of direct respect for the law. If we ask why, given that there is a social need for the regulation of conduct, we should have a device of this rather than of some other sort, the answer will be that it has many merits, but one of them is that it represents the compromise of which Professor Hart speaks between individual freedom and the protection of society. But this is an answer not to the more special question, why recognize excusing conditions, but to the very basic question, why work with a law that is addressed primarily to rational—and socially rational, not just egoistically rational—agents. Given that this is the nature of the (criminal) law, and that penalties are intended only to back up the immediate discouragement of adverse legal characterization, it follows that penalties will be appropriate only in so far as they are attached to the very items to which those adverse characterizations are first assigned, that is, choices, or voluntary and especially intentional acts and omissions. To be punishable an act must first be legally wrong. Most of the excusing conditions then follow immediately: they are signs of the absence of intentional or at least voluntary acts to which adverse legal characterizations are typically applied. The true analogy between the invalidating mental conditions in civil law and the excusing conditions in criminal law is then this: they both negate the positive psychological feature of action in fulfilment of desires which fairly represent the agent as a coherent person, while it is contract-making (and the like) with this feature to which the civil law seeks to give effect, and harm-doing with this feature which the criminal law seeks to discourage.

The psychopath who is 'not a moral agent' stands outside this system of social control. Adverse legal characterizations do not make sense to him, because he lacks moral responses with which they could be linked. Punishing him may indeed help to deter others, but it cannot have any of the normally intended effects on the psychopath himself.

Of the psychopath, then, it is correct to say that he is not responsible because he lacks the normal capacities for doing what the law requires. But this is a very different reason from that which makes people non-responsible for their non-voluntary actions and, in general, for their unintended acts, and different even from the reasons for which we may excuse the kleptomaniac and others whose actions, though voluntary, are not voluntary actions of their relatively permanent central personality. I think it is confusing to group all these different excusing conditions under the heading of lack of capacity or opportunity, and to take as the decisive test such questions as 'Could he have done otherwise?', 'Had he any real choice?', which misleadingly suggest that if causal determinism—or even some approximation to it—holds the essential requirement for legal responsibility is negated.

If we ask 'Why should we not punish unintended and even non-voluntary harmful acts and omissions, or the voluntary and intended acts of those who are not moral agents?', then Bentham's answer 'Because this would be ineffective as deterrence and would therefore be just useless further harm' is both false and irrelevant. A more relevant answer is retributivist in form, 'Because none of these acts is of the sort that can be legally wrong.' But we can go further and ask about the point of a system which works primarily by the legal characterization of voluntary and intentional acts of socially rational agents, and Professor Hart's stress on a compromise between individual freedom and the protection of society will be part of the answer to this basic question. But if it is here rather than as a direct answer to our previous question that Professor Hart's point is in place, the positive psychological elements of voluntariness and intentionality—an essentially traditional but slightly modified account of which I gave in the first part of this article— are crucial *in themselves*, not simply as signs of capacities and opportunities. The capacities summed up in the phrase 'moral agent' are indeed also crucial. But since these different factors are crucial in different ways, it is more illuminating to distinguish them than to run them together under a single heading; and our account will be less exposed to irrelevant intrusions if we ground responsibility on what a certain sort of agent did and how he did it than on the possibility of his having acted otherwise.

V

AESTHETIC JUDGEMENTS—
A LOGICAL STUDY

I WHAT AESTHETICS IS NOT

What are we doing when we say that one literary work is good and
another bad, or that one poem is great and another insignificant,
or that one painting is beautiful and another ugly, or when we
distinguish a fine musical composition, or a fine musical performance, from a poor one? If two critics disagree about the merit of
some work, can such disagreement be resolved, is there any way of
deciding that one critic's judgement is correct and the other mistaken? Can judgements of value about art be themselves justified
or defended, or are such judgements essentially arbitrary and subjective? Is there, or should there be, a *science* of criticism, or is the
evaluation of literature and art and music a field in which everyone
is free to follow his fancy, and one man's fancy is as good as
another's?

These are rather abstruse second order questions: in asking them,
we are quite literally reflecting, looking back on, the first order
activity of actually making critical judgements. But they are important ones. It is widely believed that literature and art and music
matter, that the appreciation and enjoyment of them play a part,
perhaps a large part, in the kind of life that is most worth living;
it is widely believed that the study of the arts, of literature in
particular, is a large and important part of education. But this
would hardly make sense if there were no real difference between
good works and bad ones.

To examine these value judgements, we must mark them off from
judgements of other kinds which critics also make, and which in
practice are almost inextricably mixed up with judgements of value.
We must mark off the study of artistic merit from other ways in
which the arts can be studied.

For example, there is the history of the various arts: the art

Reprinted from *The Pluralist* (June 1969).

historian as such aims at a purely factual record, telling us that such-and-such works were produced at such-and-such times, and showing how various styles have developed and flourished and fallen into disuse.

Also, there is the psychology of art: we can investigate psychological questions of why artists produce works of art, and of what mental processes contribute to artistic creation. We can enquire whether art is a form of fantasy, or whether, as Freud says, it is a path back from fantasy to reality. And, of course, as well as the psychology of the artist, there is the psychology of artistic appreciation to be considered too.

From psychology we could go on to the sociology of art, to consider the functions of the various arts in society. Of particular interest and importance here is what we might call the historical sociology of art, the study of the different functions that the arts have fulfilled in different historical periods and of how works of art reflect the social tensions and the intellectual problems of their time.

Biographical studies of artists, which may throw light on their aims and intentions, are distinct from but related to all of these.

These are all genuine fields for investigation: but they are all distinct from our present field, that of the evaluation of art. Besides, we can borrow and apply here a principle that has been much discussed in ethics, and I believe thoroughly established there, that whatever conclusions we may reach in these factual investigations, we cannot from such conclusions alone derive any judgements of value. A discovery or an insight, however sound or however penetrating, about the history or the psychology or the sociology of art, or even about the intentions of artists, will not in itself tell us anything about the merit of particular works of art or of artistic styles or movements. Value judgements, about how good or beautiful or great a work is, are distinct from all sorts of factual judgements, and do not follow from these alone. But, as we shall see, this does not mean that all factual judgements are irrelevant to judgements of value: there can be indirect connections between them.

I shall for the present leave aside these factual questions, and also all that body of philosophical aesthetics which has been linked with, or has formed part of, the idealist systems of metaphysics. In these, the whole universe has been treated as being somehow a product or an activity of Mind or Spirit, and Art has naturally been given a place as one particular mode of Spirit, as a particular kind of mental act or activity, identified perhaps with intuition or imagination. I would reject this, primarily because there are general philosophical objections to metaphysics of this sort. It would be gratifying if philosophy could prescribe, *a priori*, the role that art is to play, and could derive from its role prescriptions and rules for all the particular arts: but unfortunately nothing of the sort is possible, and philosophers have to be content with humbler tasks.

There is one particular part of this idealist aesthetics which sometimes survives independently of the rest of the system. This is the doctrine that the real work of art or 'artistic object' is never an ordinary physical thing, but a mental or spiritual entity. On this view works of art are not bought and sold, they are not kept in art galleries, they are not even types of which the tokens are kept in libraries or heard in concert halls: they reside exclusively in minds. The work of art is first an idea in the mind of the artist, and then an idea in the minds of the audience, the spectators, the appreciators who by creating this idea anew are, so to speak, subordinate artists. However, there is no good reason for adopting this view, and there is at least one good reason for rejecting it, namely that it makes the supposed true work of art inaccessible to checks of any sort. If the true work of art is tucked away in somebody's mind, we can never determine what qualities or what merits or faults it may have. This doctrine is in fact a device for mystification, and if we accepted it we should always have to allow comments on the imperfection of what we ordinarily call the work, the public, readily observable, object, to be rebutted on the ground that the real work, in someone's mind, was free from these imperfections. On this view the adverse critic merely condemns himself: in finding fault with a supposed work of art he is merely confessing his own poverty of imagination; he is admitting that he has failed to reconstruct the great work conceived not only by the original artist but also by other, more perceptive, appreciators. I suspect that this all too charitable doctrine sometimes encourages would-be artists to present very inferior wares—the sort of free verse which consists of a few rather obvious remarks spaced out with heavily dramatic pauses, the plays or the paintings which, as it were, stand waiting for significance to be read into them.

2 SUBJECTIVISM AND OBJECTIVISM

We return, then, to the view that works of art are ordinary objects, which are there to be seen or heard or read. What account can we give of judgements of their artistic merit?

One initially plausible view is that such judgements are essentially expressive: in calling a painting beautiful we are simply expressing feelings that it arouses in us. Beauty, on this view, is a fictitious quality, an illusory projection onto the work of art of the pleasure or admiration which belongs properly to the spectator alone. The critic, in evaluating a work, is just responding emotionally to it, and a piece of critical writing is a sort of expressive poem—even if it happens to be in prose—provoked by the original work. This description fits a good deal of evaluative criticism, not only the direct and naïve responses of the child or the layman, but also much that is said by critics of wide experience and developed taste. But our problem is to decide whether this is *all* that is possible.

Slightly varying this pure subjectivist theory, we may note that there are fashions in art and music and literature, much as there are fashions in dress or in hair-styles, though the fashions in the arts change more slowly. That being so, a critical judgement may express not an innocent private response, but rather a sophisticated, learned response: the reputable critic is the one who manages to react in whatever way the top people are reacting at the moment. On this modified view there can be such a thing as the cultivation of taste: but it consists essentially in keeping abreast of the changes of style, in being in touch with the centres of artistic fashion. But again we must ask, is this *all* that is possible? Can an aesthetic judgement not be anything more than an emotional response, whether sophisticated or naïve?

At the other extreme from these simple subjectivist views is the objectivist doctrine that there is an objective aesthetic quality, which is what we call 'beauty'. It is the possession of this quality that marks off the great works of art from the inferior ones. This quality may be hard to discern, but on this theory it is just as real, just as objective, as any ordinary quality: it is there waiting to be seen or to be perceived. But this theory also says that beauty is a quality of a very special sort: to perceive beauty in anything is automatically to admire it, to derive from it a special aesthetic pleasure or enjoyment. Beauty is not *just* a quality: it is a *value* as well.

But this is a very puzzling suggestion, in several respects. Is this alleged quality indefinable and indescribable? How is anyone to start looking for it, and how can anyone know whether he has found it? Is it plausible to suggest that the presence of this one quality accounts for merit in all the extremely diverse arts? What sort of quality could we hope to find at once in a good novel, a good painting, a symphony, a statue, and a block of flats? Besides, there are philosophical difficulties in the notion of a quality which is *necessarily* connected with the relations of being liked and being admired, a quality the perceiving of which is *ipso facto* a species of enjoyment. Surely a quality at once as elusive and as odd as this is just the thing to be explained away in the subjectivist manner, as a projection of our feelings onto the works of art.

3 STANDARDS OF JUDGEMENT

Perhaps the pure subjectivist theory, and the pure objectivist one, have both gone wrong in the same way. Each of them has assumed that an aesthetic judgement is made *in one move*. But again we can usefully borrow an account of value judgements which has been worked out and discussed particularly with regard to ethics, the core of which is that a value judgement involves at least two moves, and that we can begin to see light if we distinguish them.

To explain this, let us consider a very simple analogy. If I say that a certain carving knife is a good carving knife, I am judging it by reference to certain standards or criteria. To be a good carving knife it must be sharp, it must keep its edge and not be easily blunted, it must be well-balanced, and so on. There is a set of features possession of which makes it good. All these good-making features are perfectly objective: it is a question of simple fact whether a given knife is sharp and so on. They are also what are called *natural* features: to mention them is merely to describe the knife, not to commend it. But when I say that this is a good carving knife I am both saying, or hinting, that it has these good-making natural characteristics, and also commending it on that account.

This example, simple though it is, is typical. In making an evaluative judgement we are at once saying or hinting that the object judged has certain natural characteristics, and commending it, or perhaps condemning it, on that account. The good-making characteristics are natural features which we are using as criteria or standards of value: we commend something which satisfies these standards, and condemn something which fails to satisfy them. Evaluative judgement is relative to standards or criteria, and presupposes them. But it is we who take these as standards of value. At the risk of describing as if it were a conscious and deliberate act what is often an unconscious one, we may say that we decide to value highly things which satisfy a set of criteria which we choose for that purpose. There is nothing which is, in its own nature, and apart from our choice of it, a standard of value, in aesthetics or in any other field. There is no characteristic which *requires* that we should admire or enjoy the things that possess it. No doubt there are reasons why we choose particular standards for particular purposes: obviously there are practical considerations underlying our choice of the criteria for a good carving knife. But whatever these reasons may be, there is an ineradicable element of choice in the transformation of any natural feature into a standard of value.

4   THE CHOICE OF STANDARDS

What natural characteristics, then, might be chosen as criteria of aesthetic value? There is a wide range of possible standards and there is no good reason to suppose that we must adopt a single criterion or system of criteria for all the arts. Indeed, it is a question that might be worth looking into just why we group precisely these activities together as arts—for example, why we separate poetry, drama, and the novel from other sorts of writing, other ways of using language, and group them along with sculpture and painting and music. Perhaps this is due to some historical accident, perhaps what these arts have in common is only the negative characteristic that they are not obviously and directly useful, or perhaps there is a significant similarity in the mental processes through which the works of these different arts are produced. But however we answer this question, we have no right to assume that what brings all these activities together is that their best products have features in common, that there is a single set of standards by which they may all be judged. And in fact different criteria seem to be appropriate to the different arts.

(i)   Rhetorical force
A lyric poem, for example, often makes a single point, or a small

number of closely related points; it presents a view or feeling or attitude about some subject. The only relevant question may be whether it makes its point effectively. That is, the criteria by which we judge a lyric poem may be closely related to those by which we judge rhetoric: we can assess such a poem in much the same way that we assess a debating speech. And just as we should be able to judge the quality of a debating speech irrespectively of whether we agree or not with the debater's case, so we should be able to judge the rhetorical quality of a poem irrespectively of whether we sympathize with its sentiments.

When we read Montrose's poem,

> *My dear and only Love, I pray,*
> *This noble World of thee*
> *Be govern'd by no other Sway*
> *But purest Monarchie.*
> *For if confusion have a Part,*
> *Which vertuous Souls abhor,*
> *And hold a Synod in thy Heart.*
> *I'll never love thee more . . .*

we can recognize the force of the case which he puts for constancy in love, whether or not we agree with it, and whether or not we share the political prejudices which he weaves into it. But we can recognize equally the force with which a slightly later poet puts the contrary case:

> *Speak not to me of constancy,*
> *That frivolous pretence,*
> *Of cold age, narrow jealousy,*
> *Disease, and want of sense . . .*

Even this criterion of quasi-rhetorical effectiveness is not, however, a simple one: just as there are different kinds of oratory, so there are different ways in which a poem can be effective, and what is effective with one audience may well be ineffective with another. Usually the force of a poem will depend in part at least on its formal structure: its parts will be relevantly related to one another, there will be some sort of unity that holds them all together. But in this case the form will not be an end in itself, and can hardly be taken on its own as a criterion of aesthetic value: it is rather an instrument, a means to the rhetorical effect.

(ii) Representation

Another possible aesthetic criterion is success in representation. It is obvious that a great deal of art has been at least partly representational. This is true of short stories, novels, and drama; many paintings represent scenes or people, many sculptures represent human or animal figures, and one possible way of judging them is by their degree of success in representation. Of course, this criterion tends to be out of fashion at present, at least for the visual arts. Certainly there is no reason for saying that all art *must* be representational, for taking representation as an exclusive and universally applicable aesthetic standard. But once we have seen that we do not need a single universal and exclusive standard of merit, there is no reason why we should not accept representation as one criterion among others.

Of course, representation would be rather pointless if it merely gave us weakened copies of what we could see better for ourselves in the ordinary world; but in fact representational art can show us things of which we should otherwise be unaware. When people dismiss representation in art, often it is not representation as such, but only particular kinds of representation that they are rejecting. Artists who lost interest in what we may call the photographic representation of the detailed appearance of things were still intensely interested in representing colour or light or movement or vitality.

The drug mescaline is said to open to those who take it 'a paradise of colours'. But the testimony of at least one person who has tried it suggests that what it does is to enable ordinary people to see things with 'the painter's eye', to suspend their attention to their practical concerns, and to attend to colours in their own right (not just as the colours of objects), to colour patterns, spatial patterns, and so on. Now a painter can by selection and emphasis draw our attention to just such visual aspects of reality which we do not normally notice, which we either do not see at all or are only dimly aware of, because they have little bearing on our practical interests. But this is a variety of representation too.

To some extent the different varieties of representation are in competition with one another: one feature can be adequately represented only at the price of not representing some of the others: we cannot expect the artist to represent everything at once. But we can use as a standard of artistic merit the degree of his success in representing one or other feature.

However, this criterion is not equally applicable to all the arts. Architecture is not representational at all, and into music representation can enter only in a very minor way. A lyric poem may describe a scene, but this is hardly ever its main point; a lyric may be said to represent an attitude or a state of feeling, but I think this would usually be an inaccurate way of speaking: more often such a poem does not so much *represent* an attitude or feeling as *express* one. But Shakespeare's sonnet on lust (Sonnet CXXIX) consists essentially of a vigorous, pointed, description of a general state of affairs:

> *Th' expense of Spirit in a waste of shame*
> *Is lust in action; and till action, lust*
> *Is perjured, murderous, bloody, full of blame,*
> *Savage, extreme, rude, cruel, not to trust;*
> *Enjoyed no sooner but despised straight . . .*

The novel and the drama necessarily involve a large element of representation: typically they show us people in certain relations and certain settings, they represent human thoughts, feelings, purposes, and actions. But whereas in painting representation may be largely an end in itself, in literature it is more often a means to something else. The point is not just that something has been successfully represented: the reader usually has a further interest in what is represented, and he may ignore the medium, seeing straight through it to the subject, the human material. And it will then be natural to use some features of that subject as further aesthetic criteria. While the writer's success in representation can be taken as one of our criteria, then, it seems that it should here be only one of a set of criteria, and probably not the leading member of the set.

(iii) Realism

Realism is not the same as representation. If we take representation as a criterion, the question is only whether the work succeeds in presenting something to a given audience. But if we make realism a standard, then we raise the question whether what is presented is *true* of what it claims to portray. A novel set, say, in the United States Senate passes the test of representation if it gives us a vivid picture of personalities, motives, political forces interacting and determining a sequence of events: but it will pass the test of realism only if that picture is not only vivid but also correct, only if it shows us how the Senate actually does operate. We may well apply this sort of test to a portrait: we can ask whether it is a true likeness of the person whose portrait it is supposed to be. Or we may well ask whether a landscape painter has correctly brought out the character of what he is painting, particularly if he is trying to show us scenery of a strange or unfamiliar kind—for example, a painter trying to present to English viewers the landscapes of Central Australia. But in either case we must not equate realism with photographic or anatomical accuracy: since there are different kinds of feature to be represented, there are also different kinds of feature about which we can ask whether they are represented faithfully, whether the picture shows them as they really are.

(iv)   Social Realism

A variant of this is the criterion of *social realism*, which may be applied particularly to literature and has been applied especially by Marxist critics. That is, we judge, say, a novel not only by asking whether it depicts tensions and problems which actually occur, but also by asking whether what it depicts is socially significant, whether it is concerned with what is central and typical in the society of its time, and perhaps also whether it is predictively true, whether it indicates correctly the direction in which society is moving and the manner in which those struggles are going to be resolved. But there are at least two difficulties about this suggestion. First, to use such a criterion at all presupposes that we can pick out what is central or typical, that we can set aside as trivial problems which may be quite real, but are somehow off the centre of the social stage. The use of this criterion in its predictive form, especially, presupposes that we know in advance how society will develop, how its conflicts are going to be resolved. Marxists are prepared to make such presuppositions, but they may well be mistaken, and if they are this criterion simply cannot be applied. Second, there is a danger that in demanding that literature should be true to the movement of society we may be asking it to do what it can do only clumsily, and forbidding it to do what it can do well. Literature excels in presenting individuals in their full individuality, and in showing a course of events that is determined by the interaction of the individuals concerned, not predetermined by some supposed general trend of events, and if it concentrates instead on what is typical or allegedly universal it may become a very ponderous vehicle for conveying an essentially simple message. Admittedly, however, this is only a danger, not a necessary fault; plenty of good novels have been written about social stresses and conflicts, but only by showing these operating in and through genuine human individuals, not stereotypes or merely representative figures.

(v)   The Artist's Intention

It is sometimes suggested that we should take as a criterion of aesthetic value the degree to which a work fulfils the artist's intentions. No doubt we *could* use this as a criterion, wherever we have independent information about what the artist's intentions were. (Of course, where we have this information, our *immediate* criterion is not the fulfilling of intentions as such, but whatever concrete goals the artist set before himself.) But if (as is usually the case) we have no guide to the artist's intentions except the work itself, if we have to infer what the artist intended to produce from what he actually has produced, then this becomes a thoroughly circular and pointless procedure. Seeing the finished work, we must infer that the artist intended to create just such a work as this, and we have no choice but to conclude that this intention has been perfectly fulfilled. If we used this criterion honestly, we should end up by saying that anything that even purports to be a work of art is perfect in its own way. This is not a standard of judgement, but a way of abandoning the very attempt to make discriminations of value. Used honestly and consistently, therefore, this criterion would be self-defeating. We are, however, tempted to use it dishonestly: having picked out, in some other way, the works that we are going to commend, we then apply this criterion exclusively to them, and offer this as an explanation of their merit. But since it is logically guaranteed that any work at all will satisfy this standard, it cannot provide any genuine explanation of the distinctive merit of the works to which it is thus applied.

(vi)   Creativity

It is often suggested that artistic creation is a unique kind of activity, and that true works of art are distinguished from inferior productions by the creative spirit that is embodied in them. I am much more willing to accept the first of these contentions than the second. What is meant by 'artistic creation' or the 'creative spirit' may be psychologically identifiable and distinct from other spirits or activities, but what we can thus psychologically identify as creative may give birth to products that have little or nothing to do with art. I am sure that, psychologically speaking, one can feel and be just as creative as any original artist in merely baking a cake in accordance with the recipe in the cookery book, or in making a table with a do-it-yourself kit. Creativity, in this sense, is a purely mental characteristic of the producer: it does not survive or even leave any image of itself in the work. If we think we can discern creativity in some works, and can use this to discriminate the good works from the bad ones, then I believe we are using this word as a name for something else, something not to be explained in psychological terms. If so, we should make this new meaning explicit, we should try to identify as a feature of the work this new thing that we are calling creativity. And this goes for psychological criticism in general. Suppose we say that one work is inhibited, that another is uninhibited or spontaneous. If these terms are used literally, they apply not to the work but to the producer: we are guessing, rightly or wrongly, at his psychic condition, and whether this condition is healthy or unhealthy, it tells us nothing about the artistic merits of his work. But if we are using these terms to refer to what are genuinely characteristics of the work, then they have still to be given meaning in this new sense. The fact that we understand them as psychological terms is no guarantee that we can understand them when they are applied in a new sense to a quite different kind of subject. Though this may seem paradoxical, artistic creativity makes much better sense as an ethical criterion than as an aesthetic one. Artistic creation may be something that contributes to the goodness of life, just as an uninhibited person may be morally better, as a person, than an inhibited one. But this is neither here nor there when we come to an aesthetic evaluation of the works of art that they produce.

(vii)   Evocation of Emotion

One of the most persistent of critical theories is that artistic merit has something to do with the evoking of feeling, of emotion. No doubt many works of art do evoke feelings, and this might be taken as a criterion of merit. (We should, of course, sharply distinguish this suggestion, that the evocation of feeling is an aesthetic criterion, from the view, mentioned earlier, that critical judgements are themselves simply expressive of an emotional response.) However, this suggestion does not stand up very well to closer examination. We should distinguish between what we may call common or garden emotions, the sorts of feeling that may be provoked by a great variety of objects, and a specific aesthetic emotion, a kind of feeling directly related to works of art as such. If there is such a specific feeling, then there seems little doubt that it is a response to equally specific aesthetic qualities: and if so, it is those qualities, rather than the related emotion, that we should take as a standard of aesthetic judgement. But if we are thinking of common or garden emotions, it is very hard to see why we should value a work of art on the ground of its tendency to evoke them. This criterion seems at any rate to be quite unsuitable for the judging of architecture, or novels, or drama, or even painting or sculpture. It is most plausible when applied to certain kinds of music, but even there it would seem on its own to be a very inadequate standard. It may seem plausible as a standard for lyric poetry, but again our analogy between lyric poetry and rhetoric seems relevant. A poem, like a debating speech, may *employ* emotion: but it employs it in order to make some further point effectively, not as an end in itself.

(viii)   Organic Unity

All the criteria that I have so far mentioned have one thing in common: they are all *relational* criteria. In each case the suggested standard of merit consists in some relation between the work of art and something else—the audience or the spectator, the object portrayed, or the historical development of society. This has as a consequence that one and the same work may be good in relation to one audience but bad in relation to another, good in relation to one historical context but bad in relation to another. If we use any such relational criterion, whether a work is valued highly depends not only on the work itself, but also on the other term in the relation. We may be dissatisfied on this account with all the criteria mentioned so far: we may feel that artistic merit should be based on qualities that are intrinsic to the work of art, that belong purely and simply to the work itself.

It has been suggested that there is at least one intrinsic property that can be taken as an aesthetic standard, the property of being a complex unity. Some writers, indeed, argue that this is the only proper aesthetic criterion, and identify it with beauty itself. Thus Harold Osborne says that 'the beautiful is the organisation of perceptual material into an organic whole' (*Theory of Beauty* (London, 1952), p. 126), and adds that the degree of beauty will be a resultant of two factors: 'the richness, complexity, or subtlety of the configurational organisation' and 'the completeness or compactness of the organisation for experience'. Much the same concept is indicated if we speak about the working out of a theme. However we express it, the point is that the work of art exhibits both unity and diversity. A single theme is expanded or developed in a number of phases: the different phases are united not only by being instances of a single principle or theme, but also by fitting together in a structural complex: in philosophical terms, they are not only instances of a universal but also parts of a whole.

These ways of speaking may seem obscure, but there is no great difficulty in explaining what is meant at least in very simple instances. Some of the simplest examples are found in natural objects: the pattern of the bare stems of a deciduous tree often has this sort of organic unity, simply because from the longest branches down to the smallest twigs we find similar shapes and similar styles of branching, and there is also a systematic progression from large to small. A novel may be a far more complex organic whole: here the unity may be given both by the characters and their situation which together determine the development, and by the fact that some problem is both built up and resolved. By contrast, it is fairly easy to detect items that intrude irrelevantly into what would be more of an organic whole without them: in architecture, features of a building that are discordant because they have no visual connection with the rest (even if they have a utilitarian connection), or ornament which is not only functionally but also visually irrelevant; in a novel or a drama the intrusion of sheer coincidences or a *contrived* resolution of the problem. The *Philoctetes* of Sophocles is a good example. The human drama reaches a perfectly satisfactory conclusion: but this conclusion happens not to be in agreement with the traditional story on which the play was based. So Sophocles brings in at the end what is quite literally a *deus ex machina*: the deified hero Heracles comes down from Olympus, swung over the stage by a crane, to rearrange the ending.

This property of being an organic whole is one that can itself take many different forms. But there need not be anything obscure or mysterious about it. It can be progressively clarified by close and comparative study of works of art, so that we can learn to decide quite objectively whether, or to what extent and in what respects, this property is present in a particular work. It is, of course, a resultant feature: an object has this organic unity in virtue of the simpler characteristics and relations of its parts, but it is still a natural feature and an objective one. (In this respect it resembles symmetry, which is a simpler formal feature and one which has only occasionally, or for very restricted purposes, been taken as an aesthetic criterion.) To recognize organic wholeness is not in itself to make any sort of evaluation, though we may *take* this property as an aesthetic criterion and so value works in relation to it.

A great deal has been written about this property under one name or another; but I think we are much more likely to specify it unambiguously, and to identify its different forms, if we take certain precautions. First, we should not try to expand this into a single universal criterion for artistic merit as a whole: if we do, we shall be forced to re-define it so widely and so loosely that our terms lose all meaning and the criterion ceases to discriminate. Secondly, we should not try to identify this property with beauty in the sense mentioned at the beginning, a property which is supposed to have a *necessary* connection with admiration and enjoyment. Thirdly, we should not mix up *feeling* or *expression* with our account of organic wholeness. This sort of unity may perhaps be felt, and the perceiving of it may evoke feeling, either a specific aesthetic feeling or a common or garden one. But it is not a unity which is made such by feeling, or a unity in which feeling itself is a component: this line of thought, which stems from the idealist aesthetic concept of the true work of art as a mental entity, leads only to confusion and obscurity. It is worth noting that one of the objections to sentimentalism in art is that it uses connections of feeling as a substitute for organic unity: sentiment is a sort of glue which patches together items that are formally incoherent.

These three precautions are connected with one another: I believe that writers on aesthetics have been tempted to mix feeling into their account of organic wholeness because they were looking for a property which could apply to all works that have been recognized as having any sort of artistic merit, and for a property which should somehow *necessitate* appreciation.

5 CONCLUSIONS

There are, then, several possible criteria of artistic merit, but not all are equally applicable to the different arts. There is no question of establishing that one or more than one of these standards *ought* to be adopted. Aesthetic criteria cannot be laid down by any *a priori* metaphysical deduction. They cannot be inferred from any sweeping thesis about the nature and purpose of art in general. Nor can they be justified by any empirical process of, say, making a statistical survey of popular responses to art. There is an irreducible element of choice in the adopting of anything as a standard of value. There are in fact three aspects or three phases of critical work which can be sharply distinguished from one another: the choice of criteria, the elucidation of criteria, and the judging of particular works in relation to criteria that have been chosen and elucidated. In practice critical work will often combine these three aspects and run them together: nevertheless, it is vital that we should be able to *distinguish* them, just because they are tasks of such radically different kinds. The choice of criteria is quite literally a matter of *choice*: it does not either admit of, or require any systematic defence or justification. The task of clarifying criteria, of elaborating them and making them precise, is essentially one of explanation; it will include the learning or constructing and teaching of a language, the developing a precise and meaningful way of using words: this is something that can be done well or can be done badly; what a critic does in this phase of his work cannot be defended on the ground that it is a matter of free choice, and yet it does not in itself raise questions of truth or falsehood either. The third phase, that of applying the criteria, is quite different again: once criteria have been chosen and adequately clarified and made precise, it is a question of hard objective fact whether a given work satisfies the chosen criteria or not, or how well it satisfies them. *Now* we come to issues of truth and falsehood, and in this phase critical judgements both are open to, and need, just as solid substantiation as descriptive factual statements in any other field. Once we have the standards, an evaluation of a particular work in relation to those standards can be true, or can be false, in a perfectly simple, literal, down-to-earth sense. This does not mean that aesthetic evaluation ever becomes an easy or mechanical matter: the features in question will often be difficult to detect accurately, and constant effort will be needed to attend to the chosen criteria and not to let one's perception of them become confused or distorted: but it does mean that aesthetic judgements, in this third phase, will be checkable, it will be possible to substantiate them in a straight-forward, non-mysterious way. And in consequence the work of the critic himself, with respect to the second and third phases, will be susceptible of objective, non-mysterious assessment: we can ask how far a critic has succeeded in making clear and precise the standards of judgement that he is using, and whether he has then applied them honestly, consistently, and accurately.

It is worth noting that while on this view aesthetic evaluation is always relative to criteria, those criteria themselves need not be relational. Several of those that I have mentioned are relational, but the formal feature which was mentioned under the name of organic wholeness is a qualitative feature, an intrinsic property which does not depend on anything outside the work of art itself. Similarly, while the choice of criteria can be called subjective, a judgement that applies criteria can be a fully objective one. This account, therefore, enables us to avoid both extreme relativism and extreme absolutism, and equally it avoids both the extreme objec-tivism which attempts to lay down *a priori*, perhaps metaphysical, requirements for art, and the extreme subjectivism that interprets every aesthetic judgement as a mere expression of a direct emo-tional response.

VI

SIDGWICK'S PESSIMISM

BUT the fundamental opposition between the principle of Rational Egoism and that on which such a system of duty is constructed, only comes out more sharp and clear after the reconciliation between the other methods. The old immoral paradox, 'that my performance of Social Duty is good not for me but for others', cannot be completely refuted by empirical arguments: nay, the more we study these arguments the more we are forced to admit, that if we have these alone to rely on, there must be some cases in which the paradox is true. And yet we cannot but admit with Butler, that it is ultimately reasonable to seek one's own happiness. Hence the whole system of our beliefs as to the intrinsic reasonableness of conduct must fall, without a hypothesis unverifiable by experience reconciling the Individual with the Universal Reason, without a belief, in some form or other, that the moral order which we see imperfectly realized in this actual world is yet actually perfect. If we reject this belief, we may perhaps still find in the non-moral universe an adequate object for the Speculative Reason, capable of being in some sense ultimately understood. But the Cosmos of Duty is thus really reduced to a Chaos: and the prolonged effort of the human intellect to frame a perfect ideal of rational conduct is seen to have been foredoomed to inevitable failure.

This splendid passage concludes the first (1874) edition of *The Methods of Ethics*. (Was Sidgwick thinking partly of the prolonged effort of his own 473 pages?) Taken by itself it is, of course, ambivalent. It asserts merely the conditional statement that *if* we reject the belief in a moral government of the universe, something like a God who will reward utilitarian virtue, *then* there will be an irreducible conflict within the rational principles of conduct, between rational egoism and social duty. And this conditional could be part either of a *modus ponens* or of a *modus tollens* argument: the implied continuation could be either 'We must reject this belief, so the cosmos of duty is reduced to chaos' or 'The cosmos of duty cannot be a chaos, so we must not reject this belief'. Sidgwick himself seems also to have been ambivalent. A few pages earlier he says that although 'it is ... a matter of life and death to the Practical Reason that this premiss [that the performance of duty will be

Reprinted from *The Philosophical Quarterly*, Vol. 26, No. 105 (October 1976).

adequately rewarded and its violation punished] should be somehow obtained', none the less 'the mere fact that I cannot act
rationally without assuming a certain proposition, does not appear
to me—as it does to some minds,—a sufficient ground for believing
it to be true', and he rejects even more vehemently 'the Kantian
resource of thinking myself under a moral necessity to regard all my
duties *as if they were* commandments of God, although not entitled
to hold speculatively that any such Supreme Being exists "as
Real"'. Sidgwick 'cannot even conceive the state of mind which
these words seem to describe, except as a momentary half-wilful
irrationality, committed in a violent access of philosophic despair'.
All this suggests the *modus ponens* continuation. But on the second
last page of the book, after speaking of 'an hypothesis logically
necessary to avoid a fundamental contradiction in a vast system of
Beliefs: a contradiction so fundamental that if it cannot be over-
come the whole system must fall to the ground and scepticism be
triumphant over one chief department of our thought', he goes on,
rather lamely, 'The exact weight to be attached to this consideration, I cannot here pretend adequately to estimate. To do so would
require a complete discussion of the Theory of Method, and of the
ultimate basis of philosophic certainty.' This suggests, though only
very faintly, the *modus tollens* continuation. In the second (1877)
and later editions this point is made more explicit. 'Those who hold
that the edifice of physical science is really constructed of conclusions logically inferred from self-evident premises, may reasonably
demand that any practical judgments claiming philosophic certainty should be based on an equally firm foundation. If on the
other hand we find that in our supposed knowledge of the world
of nature propositions are commonly taken to be universally true,
which yet seem to rest on no other grounds than that we have a
strong disposition to accept them, and that they are indispensable
to the systematic coherence of our beliefs, it will be more difficult
to reject a similarly supported assumption in ethics, without opening the door to universal scepticism' (seventh edition, p. 509).
Moreover, the concluding passage quoted at the beginning of this
article was itself suppressed in the second and later editions, and in
the Preface to the second edition Sidgwick explains that in these
and associated changes 'I have yielded as far as I could to the
objections that have been strongly urged against the concluding
chapter ...' (seventh edition, p. viii). But in this Preface he makes

it clear that he still adheres to the 'Dualism of the Practical Reason', and since, as he says, he learnt it from 'Butler's well-known Sermons', he is surprised that his critics are surprised by it (seventh edition, pp. x–xi). I shall discuss later the argument faintly hinted at in the first edition and more explicitly stated in the second; but for the present it is enough to note that in his earlier and, I think, better thoughts, before he yielded even partly to the pressure of his critics, Sidgwick was inclining towards the pessimistic or sceptical side.

These questions are raised in a chapter which in the first edition was entitled 'The Sanctions of Utilitarianism', though the reorientation in the second and later editions changed this to 'The Mutual Relations of the Three Methods'. In Book IV, Sidgwick is echoing at least the headings of Mill's chapters; not surprisingly, there are also two chapters entitled 'The Proof of Utilitarianism' (II and III in the first edition: Chapter III was re-titled in later editions). But his stress in Chapter VI on the 'Sanctions' is due partly to what he regarded as the inconclusiveness of the 'Proof'. He takes account of the view of 'others' who 'will maintain that the proof offered in ch. 2 does not really convert them from Egoistic to Universalistic Hedonism; but only convinces them that, unless the two can be shown to coincide, Practical Reason is divided against itself'. Since this position 'is certainly very difficult to assail with argument', he is 'led to examine the Egoistic inducements to conform to Utilitarian rules in order to see whether an Egoist who remains obstinately impervious to what we have called Proof may be persuaded into practical Utilitarianism by a consideration of Sanctions' (first edition, pp. 460–1). Similarly the final chapter in later editions begins by noting that '[the Egoist] may avoid the proof of Utilitarianism by declining to affirm [that his own happiness is not merely the rational ultimate end for himself, but a part of Universal Good]' (seventh edition, pp. 497–8).

But what exactly is wrong with the 'Proof'? With his usual combination of acuteness and honesty, Sidgwick has here got right something that many other moral thinkers have got wrong. I quote the key passage as it is given in the first edition. Referring to an argument addressed to egoism, Sidgwick says:

It should be observed that the applicability of this argument depends on the manner in which the Egoistic first principle is formulated. If the Egoist strictly confines himself to stating his conviction that he ought to take his own happiness or pleasure as his ultimate end, there seems no opening for any line of reasoning to lead him to Universalistic Hedonism as a first principle. In this case all that the Utilitarian can do is to effect as far as possible a reconciliation between the two principles: by expounding to the Egoist the *sanctions* (as they are usually called) of rules deduced from the Universalistic principle: that is, the pleasures and pains that will accrue to himself from their observance and violation respectively. It is obvious that such an exposition has no tendency to make him accept the greatest happiness of the greatest number as his ultimate end: but only as a means to the end of his own happiness. It is therefore totally different from a *proof* (as above explained) of Universalistic Hedonism. When, however, the Egoist offers, either as a reason for his Egoistic principle, or as another form of stating it, the proposition that his happiness or pleasure is objectively desirable or Good; he gives the ground needed for such a proof. For we can then point out to him that *his* happiness cannot be more objectively desirable or more a good than the similar happiness of any other person: the mere fact (if I may so put it) that *he* is *he* can have nothing to do with its objective desirability or goodness. Hence, starting with his own principle, he must accept the wider notion of Universal happiness or pleasure as representing the real end of Reason, the absolutely Good or Desirable: as the end, therefore, to which the action of a reasonable agent as such ought to be directed.

This is not changed substantially in later editions. At the end of the second sentence there is added 'it cannot be proved that the difference between his own happiness and another's happiness is not *for him* all-important'; in the sixth sentence 'objectively desirable or Good' becomes 'Good, not only *for him* but from the point of view of the Universe,—as (e.g.) by saying that "nature designed him to seek his own happiness"'; below 'more objectively desirable or more a good' becomes 'a more important part of Good, taken universally', and, regrettably, the very telling remark 'the mere fact (if I may so put it) that *he* is *he* can have nothing to do with its objective desirability or goodness' is deleted. Other changes are minor and merely verbal. (See seventh edition, pp. 420-1). Sidgwick is saying that a cogent *ad hominem* argument against the egoist can be constructed if, and only if, the egoist introduces into his view the notion of something's being objectively good, that is objectively desirable, or 'Good ... from the point of view of the Universe'. Once the egoist has claimed not merely that his own happiness is relatively good for him, something that it is reasonable for him to pursue, but that his being happy is intrinsically good—and perhaps that his desiring it, or his seeing it to be reasonable for him to pursue it, is evidence for its intrinsic goodness, being an apprehension of that goodness, then and only then can the utilitarian step in and point out the irrelevance, to such intrinsic goodness, of the happiness being *his*. This universalization follows the introduction of objective or intrinsic goodness-as-an-end. But, as Sidgwick sees, this move is not one which the egoist needs to make: in introducing objective goodness he is gratuitously compromising his position. Moreover, it is not ethical objectivity in general that has this effect, but specifically the objectivity of *good*. The objectivity of rightness or oughtness would not have the same effect. The egoist can assert that he absolutely and objectively ought to take his own happiness as his end, and there will still be no cogent *ad hominem* argument to make him adopt utilitarianism. In fact Sidgwick assumes from the start the objectivity of oughtness, and claims general agreement with this assumption. 'That there is in any given circumstances some one thing which ought to be done and that this can be known, is a fundamental assumption, made not by philosophers only, but by all men who perform any processes of moral reasoning' (first edition, p. 6). And he argues that such ought-propositions are not merely hypothetical imperatives or counsels of prudence: most of us would think that a man *ought* to seek his own happiness (first edition, p. 8). But he is more cautious about assuming the objectivity of goodness, partly because many moralists, including many intuitionists, 'hold that our obligation to obey moral rules is not conditional on our knowledge of the end ...' (first edition, p. 3). 'Hence it seems best not to assume at the outset that Ethics investigates an end at all, but rather to define it as the study of what ought to be done ...' (p. 4).

But why is there this curious difference between goodness on the one hand and either rightness or oughtness on the other? This Sidgwick does not explain; but it is a consequence of their formal logical features, essentially that '... is good' is a one-place predicate whereas '... is right for ...' or '... ought to ...' are two-place predicates. Whatever is objective must be universalizable over relevantly similar cases, but universalization works differently with one-place and with two-place predicates. If we start with '*A*'s being happy is (objectively) good', and universalize this with respect to all persons, or perhaps all sentient beings, relevantly similar to *A*, we can infer that B's being happy is good, and C's, and so on; in fact that for all X, X's being happy is good—where 'for all X' is simply a quantifier: this is not to be read as saying that X's happiness is good merely for X. It is in this way that, as Sidgwick says, the egoist can be brought to acknowledge that the happiness of others is good. On the other hand, if we start with the premiss 'A ought to seek A's happiness' there are four ways in which universal quantification can be introduced: (1) For all X, X ought to seek X's happiness; (2) For all X, A ought to seek X's happiness; (3) For all X, X ought to seek A's happiness; and (4) For all X and for all Y, X ought to seek Y's happiness. Of these, only the first would be a valid universal generalization in modern formal logic: (4) would be a valid generalization from either (2) or (3), but neither (2) nor (3) would be a valid generalization from the premiss. But the important question is whether they are morally cogent. If the identity of the seeker with the person whose happiness is sought is, or may be, a morally relevant feature of what the premiss prescribes, the derivation of (2) or (3), and hence of (4), is non-cogent; it will be cogent only if it can be claimed confidently that this identity is irrelevant. But to claim this irrelevance is in effect to treat either '... ought to seek A's happiness' or 'A ought to seek ...' as a one-place predicate; it is to say that A's happiness is intrinsically seekable, that is, objectively good. As long as we keep consistently to a two-place predicate interpretation of the 'ought' in the premiss we must allow that the identity of the seeker and the person whose happiness is sought may be morally relevant, and then (1) will be the only morally cogent universalization. And this, so far from refuting egoism, endorses a form of it. Equally if we use the two-place predicate '... is good for ...', its universalization will be powerless to defeat the egoist. But when Sidgwick speaks of 'objectively desirable or Good' or of 'Good not only *for him* but from the point of view of the Universe', it is distinctively the one-place predicate that he is introducing.

Sidgwick's correct analysis here throws light on several less accurate discussions. Mill, in his notorious 'proof' of the principle of utility, says

No reason can be given why the general happiness is desirable, except that each person ... desires his own happiness. This, however, being a fact, we have not only all the proof which the case admits of, but all which it is possible to require, that happiness is a good: that each person's happi-

ness is a good to that person, and the general happiness, therefore, a good
to the aggregate of all persons (*Utilitarianism*, Chapter IV).

This looks like an argument in two steps, from 'Each person desires
his own happiness' to 'Each person's happiness is desirable for that
person' and then from the latter to 'The general happiness is desirable for every person'. The first step seems to move without war-
rant from 'is' to 'ought', while the second seems to involve a fallacy
of composition. To yield a utilitarian conclusion, we must take 'the
aggregate of all persons' as equivalent to 'every person' read dis-
tributively; but then the conclusion will not follow. Even with just
two persons '*A*'s happiness and *B*'s happiness are desirable for *A*,
and are also desirable for *B*' does not follow from '*A*'s happiness
is desirable for *A* and *B*'s happiness for *B*'. The word 'aggregate'
would most naturally suggest a collective reading; for example,
with two persons. 'The happiness of the *A-B* collective is desirable
for the *A-B* collective'. This is plausibly analogous with '*A*'s
happiness is desirable for *A*'. But what it is for something to be
desirable for a two-person or for a multi-person collective is
obscure, and in any case this is not what a utilitarian is trying to
establish.

Read thus, Mill's argument seems to be riddled with fallacies.
But it can be read more charitably. Perhaps what he had at the
back of his mind was that each person desires his own happiness
because he realizes, or believes, that his own happiness is good—
not just for him, but objectively—and that we can take each person's desiring of his own happiness as evidence that that happiness
is good objectively. Then Mill's first step is not an invalid move
from 'is' to 'ought' but a fairly plausible inference from the fact
that judgements, of a certain sort, of objective value are widely
believed to the truth of those judgements and hence to the corresponding evaluations—*A*'s happiness *is* objectively good, and so on.
Then the second step becomes either the justifiable universalization
from each of these evaluations to all the others—if *A*'s happiness
is good, so is *B*'s, and so on—or else (as Mill himself claimed in a
letter) it merely sums up all these separate evaluations so as to
conclude that the general happiness, comprising the happinesses of
A, of *B*, and so on, is also good. This would, no doubt, be too
charitable as a reading of what Mill actually says. But it is more
plausible to suppose that he had something of this sort in mind

than that he committed the blatant fallacies of which critics have
been too eager to accuse him.

G.E. Moore's criticism of egoism (*Principia Ethica*, pp.
97–104) turns upon the allegation that there is a confusion in the conception
of 'my own good':

> It is obvious ... that the only thing which can belong to me, which can be
> *mine*, is something which is good, and not the fact that it is good ... I
> must mean either that the thing I get is good or that my possessing it is
> good ... The only reason I can have for aiming at 'my own good', is that
> it is *good absolutely* that what I so call should belong to me.

Here Moore is simply asserting that any being good that can constitute a reason for anyone's aiming at something must be 'absolute'—that is, that 'good' must be a one-place predicate. But he has
nothing to support this assertion except his extraordinarily limited
views about the possible forms of meaningful linguistic construc-
tions. Quoting from the passage in *The Methods of Ethics*, Book
IV, Chapter II, which I have quoted above, he asks: 'What does
Prof. Sidgwick mean by the phrases "the ultimate rational end for
himself" and "*for him* all-important"'? He does not attempt to
define them; and it is largely the use of such undefined phrases
which causes absurdities to be committed in philosophy' (p. 99).
This, from the man who is best remembered as the defender of the
view that 'good' is indefinable! What effrontery! Or rather, what
naïvety, for Moore clearly thinks that an undefined one-place predicate 'good' can be straightforwardly meaningful, but a two-place
predicate 'good for' or 'all-important for' cannot. In fact Sidgwick
would have had rather less difficulty in explaining these relations
than Moore would have had in explaining his non-natural quality.
However, it is clear that if we assume, with Moore, that the only
reason anyone can have for aiming at anything is that that thing
is absolutely good, then we shall find egoism self-contradictory,
whether it is expressed as 'It is reasonable for everyone to aim only
at his own happiness' or as 'Each person's happiness is the sole
good for him'. But it is equally clear that this assumption is one
which the egoist has no need to grant.

Moore also criticizes the suggestion in Sidgwick's final chapter
that divine sanctions might avoid a contradiction in our apparent
intuitions about what is reasonable:

> Prof. Sidgwick here commits the characteristic fallacy of Empiricism—the
> fallacy of thinking that an alteration in *facts* could make a contradiction

cease to be a contradiction. That a single man's happiness should be the *sole good*, and that also everybody's happiness should be the *sole good*, is a contradiction which cannot be solved by the assumption that the same conduct will secure both (*Principia Ethica*, p. 103).

This is true, but Sidgwick never said it could. Sidgwick sees as clearly as Moore that if it were just a question about a sole (absolute) good, there would be no contradiction to solve, because egoism would have been refuted; but he also sees, as Moore does not, that the issue cannot be thus simplified, and that we are left with the competing apparent intuitions that it is rational for a man to seek his own happiness and that it is rational for a man to seek the general happiness. These are not in themselves contradictory: a contradiction arises only when we add to these two intuitions the factual statement that what best promotes a man's own happiness does not always coincide with what best promotes the general happiness. It is the facts that decide whether the two intuitions come into practical conflict or not. Moore fails to see that Sidgwick is keeping the questions of 'proof' and of 'sanctions' apart. Divine sanctions may come in not to complete a proof or to solve a contradiction between two intuitions, but to resolve a contradiction that would otherwise arise from the conjunction of these intuitions with a factual truth.

Thomas Nagel recognizes the weakness of Moore's position:

nothing resembling an argument is offered for these claims ... They seem to him self-evident because he regards it as already established that 'good' is a one-place predicate denoting a simple, non-natural property. But that would not be granted by an egoist, whose fundamental evaluative concept would be a *relation:* '*X* is good for *Y* '.[1]

But Nagel proposes to 'explain exactly what [Moore] assumes: that in order to accept something as a goal for oneself, one must be able to regard its achievement by oneself as an *objective* good'. I cannot discuss Nagel's argument adequately, because its intricacies and obscurities make it hard to pin down. But it attempts to do what Sidgwick says cannot be done, that is refute the egoist without first getting him to talk about objective good. Nagel deals not with good but with reasons for action. His crucial claim is that if we are to avoid 'practical solipsism'—and the reasons for doing this are essentially those that support universalizability—we must be able

[1] T. Nagel, *The Possibility of Altruism* (Oxford, 1970), p. 86 and note.

to frame our practical judgements impersonally but 'with motivational content': objective principles, he thinks, will meet this requirement whereas subjective principles will not:

> If I merely consider in impersonal terms the individual who I in fact am, I can conclude that there is, for him, subjective reason to do this or that, but this does not involve, and cannot even explain, any desire that he do so. The motivational content which forms an essential part of a first-person practical judgement is therefore missing entirely from an impersonal judgement about the same individual, if that judgement derives from a subjective principle (p. 117).

But what in concrete terms does this mean? What Nagel calls a subjective principle would be, for example, the egoistic one that a man has reason to do what will avoid pain for himself. A derived impersonal judgement would be, say, that J.M. has reason for keeping his hand out of the fire. Nagel's thesis is that even though I am J.M. this judgement *qua* impersonal gives *me* no motive for keeping my hand out of the fire. This seems absurd. This judgement gives J.M. a motive, and since I *am* J.M., it gives *me* a motive. But presumably this obvious move violates Nagel's standard of impersonality. But then his demand for impersonality plus motivational content is equivalent to the demand that practical judgements should be of the form 'For all X, X has reason to do S'—where S is some specific act such as 'keep J.M.'s hand out of the fire'—or of some more general form from which this would follow, such as 'For all Y and for all X, X has reason to do what will avoid pain for Y'. He is dissatisfied with judgements of the form 'For all X, X has reason to do what will avoid pain for X' because when the act component is instantiated to 'keep J.M.'s hand out of the fire' the agent component will be correspondingly instantiated to 'J.M.' and we shall lose impersonal motivational content. But what ground is there for insisting on impersonality plus motivation thus interpreted? No general considerations in favour of the action-guidingness and universalizability of rational practical judgements will support this insistence, for they will be met by the obvious action-guidingness for J.M. of 'J.M. has reason to keep J.M.'s hand out of the fire' and such universalizations of it as 'For all X, X has reason to do what will avoid pain for X'. In being dissatisfied with these, Nagel is just insisting on using the one-place predicate 'For all X, X has reason to do ...' which, for all its apparent difference in form, is equivalent to Moore's '... is good'; and Nagel has no more of an argument for this than Moore has.

R.M. Hare has endeavoured to 'establish a point of contact between utilitarianism' and his own universal prescriptivism, in effect to show that the latter method of moral argument will lead to some sort of utilitarianism:

The logical character of moral language, as I have claimed it to be, is the formal foundation of any such [utilitarian] theory. It is in the endeavour to find lines of conduct which we can prescribe universally in a given situation that we find ourselves bound to give equal weight to the desires of all parties (the foundation of distributive justice); and this, in turn, leads to such views as that we should seek to maximize satisfactions.[2]

But the phrase 'lines of conduct which we can prescribe universally' conceals a vital ambiguity. Are these to be policies defined with reference to the agent—such as 'X is to avoid pain for X', or 'X is to look after X's children'—or are they to be attempts, by all the agents involved in some situation, to achieve some unitary goal? It is only with the latter interpretation that the endeavour to prescribe universally will lead towards some kind of utilitarianism. But there is nothing in the logical character of moral language to rule out the former interpretation. Even if egoism is suspect, what C.D. Broad has called self-referential altruism is not—that is, the doctrine that 'each of us has specially strong obligations to benefit certain persons and groups of persons who stand in certain special relations to *himself*', such as parents, children, friends, benefactors, and fellow-countrymen.[3] Self-referential altruism forms, and always has formed, a large part of common sense morality. When William Godwin argued against its most central doctrines and in favour of utilitarianism—for example, that one should rescue Archbishop Fénelon from a fire rather than one's own mother—it was his views that seemed paradoxical or even outrageous (*Political Justice*, Book II, Chapter 2).[4] It would be quite implausible to say that the logical character of moral language excludes the universal prescription of such self-referentially altruistic principles. This shows at once that universal prescriptivism will not in itself lead to any kind of utili-

[2] R.M. Hare, *Freedom and Reason* (Oxford, 1963), pp. 122–3.

[3] See 'Moore's Ethical Doctrines' in *The Philosophy of G.E. Moore*, edited by P.A. Schilpp (La Salle, Illinois, 1942), pp. 53–5.

[4] Quoted and discussed by D.H. Monro, *Empiricism and Ethics* (Cambridge, 1967), pp. 197–9.

tarianism. Further, once self-referential altruism is allowed, egoism cannot be excluded by any appeal to the logical character of moral language: 'For all X, X ought to avoid pain for X' is universally prescribable in the sense required by the logic of moral language. In order to arrive by this route at some kind of utilitarian conclusion we need to add some further restriction, for example that what is to be prescribed universally is a single goal which all the agents involved should try to achieve, or some agreed distribution of benefits. Any such appropriate restriction will be a counterpart, within universal prescriptivism, of Moore's insistence on the one-place predicate 'good'; but the egoist, or the self-referential altruist, is no more bound to accept such a restriction than, as Sidgwick shows, he is bound to talk in terms of an objective good.

I conclude, then, that Sidgwick was right to query the cogency of his own argument against egoism, and that various arguments produced by other moralists, before and after him, are not stronger than his. Rather these thinkers have failed to bring out as clearly as he did the special assumptions or restrictions that are needed to make such arguments cogent. I shall therefore return to the argument about sanctions which, Sidgwick thought, arose naturally from the noted inadequacy of the 'Proof'. Briefly, this runs as follows. It is rational for each man to seek his own happiness. It is also rational for each man to seek the general happiness. In the natural course of events, the actions most fitted to promote the agent's own happiness will not always coincide with those most fitted to promote the general happiness. For perfect coincidence, therefore, we must postulate a moral government of the universe, something like a God who will adequately reward the performance of duty and adequately punish its violation. This hypothesis is 'logically necessary to avoid a fundamental contradiction in one chief department of our thought', namely practical reason. The question is whether this avoidance is an adequate ground for adopting this hypothesis.

An argument from two moral or practical premisses to a factual conclusion is unusual, but there is nothing wrong with its logic. Similarly there are valid arguments with two imperative premisses and a factual conclusion—indeed, there must be, if there are, as is more commonly recognized, valid arguments with one imperative

and one factual premiss and an imperative conclusion. If 'Do everything that father says' follows from 'Do everything that mother
says' in conjunction with 'Everything that father says mother says
too', then equally from the conjunction of 'Do everything that
mother says' with 'Don't do everything that father says' it will
follow that father says some things that mother does not. But
though such arguments can be made formally valid, moral or practical premisses seem to provide not merely insufficient but also
inappropriate grounds for factual beliefs. In the last sentence of the
second and later editions Sidgwick suggests that factual and scientific 'truths' 'rest on no other grounds than that we have a strong
disposition to accept them, and that they are indispensable to the
systematic coherence of our beliefs'; if so, may not the systematic
coherence of our practical judgements supply an equally respectable basis for factual (theological) truths? I think not. This sort of
argument is back to front. What it is rational to do depends on
how the facts are; we cannot take what we are inclined to think
that it is rational to do as evidence that the facts are one way rather
than another. As Sidgwick says in the first edition, 'the mere fact
that I cannot act rationally without assuming a certain proposition,
does not appear to me ... a sufficient ground for believing it to be
true'.

What, then, is the outcome of our discussion? Starting with a
variety of apparent intuitions about rational conduct, Sidgwick
thought that those of common sense and intuitionistic morality
could be reconciled with and absorbed into a utilitarian view, but
that this left unresolved the duality of egoist and utilitarian principles. He considered two procedures for reconciliation, 'Proof' and
'Sanctions'. Whether or not we had a sanction, the objectivity of
goodness would provide a proof; and so likewise would the centring
of a moral system on some other appropriate one-place predicate,
some counterpart of an objective good, for example within a theory
of good reasons for action or within universal prescriptivism. But
egoism can coherently resist any such proof by adhering to the use
of such two-place predicates as 'right', 'ought', and 'good for':
objectivity and universalization with respect to these are powerless
against it. Again, the existence of a moral government of the universe, of something like a God, would provide a sanction whether
or not we had a proof; but there is no adequate independent case

Persons and Values

for this, and it is not reasonable to use these apparent moral intuitions themselves as evidence in favour of the hypothesis that would reconcile them. So, in the end, we have neither a proof nor a sanction: the fundamental apparent intuitions of practical reason remain obstinately unreconciled: the Cosmos of Duty is indeed a Chaos.

VII

THE DISUTILITY OF
ACT-UTILITARIANISM

'The principle of utility, (I have heard it said) is a dangerous principle: it is dangerous on certain occasions to consult it.' This is as much as to say, what? that it is not consonant with utility to consult utility: in short, that it is *not* consulting it, to consult it.

In these words Jeremy Bentham dismisses an attack on the principle of utility by Alexander Wedderburn, then Attorney or Solicitor General, later Chief Justice of the Common Pleas and Chancellor of England under the successive titles of Lord Loughborough and Earl of Rosslyn. But Bentham admits that the principle is indeed a dangerous one to the interest of anyone like Alexander Wedderburn and to any government that has for its object the greatest happiness of some small number of privileged individuals.

In a Government which had for its end in view the greatest happiness of the greatest number, Alexander Wedderburn might have been Attorney General and then Chancellor: but he would not have been Attorney General with £15,000 a year, nor Chancellor, with a peerage, with a veto upon all justice, with £25,000 a year, and with 500 sinecures at his disposal, under the name of Ecclesiastical Benefices, besides *et caeteras* (*Principles of Morals and Legislation*, Ch. I, § 13, footnote).

Regrettably, such brisk treatment for the critics of utility is no longer in order: the view that utilitarianism may itself have disutility is put forward soberly today by philosophers who cannot be suspected of defending sinister interests and who are not likely to enjoy even nominal incomes, after two centuries of inflation, as large as Alexander Wedderburn's.[1]

Though we cannot impugn the motives of such men as Warnock and Hodgson, it remains true that what they say is paradoxical. How *could* it be contrary to utility to aim at utility? Of course,

Reprinted from *The Philosophical Quarterly*, Vol. 23, No. 93 (October 1973)
[1] E.g., D.H. Hodgson, *Consequences of Utilitarianism* (Oxford, 1967), Chapter 2; and G.J. Warnock, *The Object of Morality* (London, 1971), Chapter 3.

people can make mistakes: the pursuit of utility by inappropriate means may indeed produce disutility, or at any rate less utility than obedience to any number of alternative guides to conduct. That is not in dispute. But what is alleged is that even the most enlightened and well-informed pursuit of utility—however this is interpreted— may, or even must, produce disutility; and this is a paradox.

Hodgson's argument for this surprising conclusion is rather complex. But the first and most vital step is what purports to be a proof that a society in which everyone is an act-utilitarian and is highly rational, and everyone knows that everyone else is an act-utilitarian and is highly rational, 'would be at a disadvantage as compared with almost any society that has ever existed'.[2] This proof itself rests on the thesis that in such a society there could be no making of promises and no communicating of information, and therefore 'no human relationships as we know them', whereas 'so much that is of value, on any criteria, is bound up with human relationships'.[3]

Warnock's thesis is more sweeping.

> Can one say that what simple Utilitarianism essentially defeats is the possibility of *co-operation?* It seems that, if two or more persons are effectively to co-operate, in wars, in professional pursuits, in business, or even in conversation, there must be such a thing as being prepared to be, and recognized as being, *bound* to specific requirements of the co-operative 'ethics', or to specific undertakings. It is not ... essential that such bonds should ... never ... be broken; but it is essential that they should not in general make absolutely no difference. ... But if general beneficence is to be our sole criterion, they would inevitably count for nothing.[4]

It is easy to show that this at any rate is *too* sweeping. We can describe situations in which two or more act-utilitarians would be able to co-operate and to reap the benefits of co-operation. Let us start with just two, say Alf and Bill, and let us represent a situation in which each of the two can act in any one of several ways on a three-dimensional graph, letting the x-axis represent various possible actions of Alf, the y-axis various possible actions of Bill, and the third dimension represent the amounts of utility or disutility that will result from each combination of an action of Alf with an

[2] *Consequences of Utilitarianism* (hereafter *CU*), p. 45.
[3] *CU*, p. 45.
[4] *The Object of Morality*, p. 34.

action of Bill. We shall then have a perhaps pretty irregular surface, with hills and valleys. Alternatively, we can show the same information on a two-dimensional diagram by writing in plus and minus utility values to replace the heights and depths. Diagram (i) indicates one such possible utility situation. Here if Alf does action 1 while Bill does action 1, the result will have considerable disutility, namely a utility of -4, but if Alf does action 1 while Bill does action 3, the result will have a utility of $+4$, and so on.

Now suppose that there is a unique highest point on the graph, a unique utility maximum, e.g., things are as in Diagram (i) leaving out the fifth column, so that the result of Alf's doing action 2 while Bill does action 3 is a utility of $+6$, while any other combination of actions whatever will result in a lower utility than this. If both agents know exactly what the graph is, that is, if they know that this combination of actions will uniquely maximize utility, and if each is aiming simply at maximizing utility, and each knows both that the other is doing so, and that the other knows that he himself is doing so, then clearly Alf will choose action 2 and Bill will choose action 3. Of course, Alf can choose action 2 only because he can rely on Bill to choose action 3: if Bill did anything else the results would be very bad.

$$
\begin{array}{c}
\text{Bill's} \\
\text{actions}
\end{array}
\left\{
\begin{array}{c|ccccc}
4 & +3 & -2 & +2 & +3 & [-4] \\
3 & +4 & +6 & -1 & 0 & [-1] \\
2 & 0 & -3 & +1 & +2 & [+6] \\
1 & -4 & 0 & +2 & +3 & [+4] \\
\hline
 & 1 & 2 & 3 & 4 & 5
\end{array}
\right.
$$

Diagram (i)

Alf's actions

And similarly Bill can choose action 3 only because he can rely on Alf to choose action 2. There is a kind of circularity here, but it is not vicious. Assuming simply rationality, goodwill, and knowledge both of the causal connections between action-combinations and utility and of each other's rationality, goodwill, and knowledge, Alf and Bill will each so act that their combined action will maximize utility. The situation is radically different from those commonly discussed in games theory where the players are playing *against* each other, and where each, to guard against the greatest risks, chooses a maximin or minimax strategy, and the result is not a peak but a saddle-point. Here the two players are on the same side, and knowing this, they will rationally choose actions that will lead to a utility peak. They will act, even independently, as if their choices were concerted. And if this is not co-operation, it is as near to it as makes no difference.

Admittedly the situation is changed if there are, say, two equal maxima on the graph, e.g., if we now bring in the fifth column in Diagram (i). A utility of +6 is now reached not only if Alf does action 2 while Bill does action 3, but also if Alf does action 5 while Bill does action 2, whereas any other combination of actions would produce lower utility. Then, indeed, each is in a dilemma. Alf doesn't know whether to do 2 or 5 because he doesn't know whether Bill will do 3 or 2, and Bill is similarly perplexed.

There is in fact a classic situation of this form, that in which two people meet face to face when walking in opposite directions along a pavement. If each goes to his own left utility will be maximized: they will pass one another safely. But utility has an equal maximum if each goes to his own right. But if one goes to his left while the other goes to his right, the result will have a high degree of disutility. So neither person, however rational and well-intentioned, even with complete confidence in the other's rationality and good intentions, knows which way to go. The dilemma appears insoluble. And yet most of us solve it in practice every day, just occasionally with a little difficulty and a few false starts. Moreover, we do so without calling into play any of the extra machinery which it has been doubted whether an act-utiltarian society could possess— without making bargains or promises, without communicating information, and without relying on any conventional rule. It is no harder to avoid running head on into other pedestrians in a foreign country than in one's own. An attempt has been made to introduce 'Walk on the right' as a conventional rule, but observation any day in any city in England will show that the attempt has not yet succeeded. Then how do we solve this apparently insoluble problem? (It does not matter whether, when we solve it, we are behaving as act-utilitarians or as rational egoists, since in this special situation the interests of both parties coincide.) The answer is, of course, that one person happens to move to his left, or to his right, a moment or two before the other has made a deviation either way; the second person then adapts his own movement to fit in with that of the first. This procedure, which is natural and rational, not conventional, fails only if they both move, one to his right and one to his left, simultaneously, and then both correct their moves simultaneously in the light of what each sees the other start to do, and so on. But it takes remarkably good and continuingly good synchronization to maintain an undamped oscillation, and in fact this never persists for long. In this paradigmatic situation, the failure of co-operation is not the universal and inevitable result of a twin-peaked utility graph, but an unusual special case.

We can generalize from this: whatever the nature of the choices Alf and Bill have to make, it will be reasonable for each to start to act in the direction of one—either one—of the utility maxima and at the same time to keep an eye on what the other is doing. If both happen to start towards the same maximum, they will carry on and reach it. If one starts towards one maximum before the other has moved, the second will notice this and go towards the same maximum. Only if the two happen to start simultaneously towards different maxima is there a risk of a self-defeating series of corrections, and even if this starts it is not likely to persist for long.

We can further generalize these points for any number of agents. If there is a unique utility maximum, each will rationally choose that action of his own which will contribute to it, in the assurance that the others will do likewise. If there is more than one equal utility maximum, there is some risk of temporary hesitation and confusion, but it is likely to sort itself out. Indeed it would be *harder* to maintain an undamped oscillation of the self-frustrating kind with more than two agents: if there are, say, two utility maxima, the chance that initial choices will be equally divided between them is smaller if there is any number of agents greater than two, while if one maximum happens to be initially chosen by a majority, members of the minority are more likely to adjust their actions to this goal than are members of the majority to switch to the goal initially chosen by the minority.

In other words, Warnock has underestimated the possibilities of automatic harmonization of effort among two or more agents, given only a common ultimate purpose (the maximization of whatever is taken as utility), rationality, and knowledge about the situation and about each other, and leaving out any bargaining, communication, or conventional rules.

There is, however, no need to assume that an act-utilitarian society would in fact have to get along without communication.

Hodgson has denied the possibility of the communication of information, and I shall consider this issue later. But whether this is allowed or not, there seems no reason why our act-utilitarians should not engage in imperative discourse. Why could I not, when about to run into a fellow English speaker on the pavement, call out, say, 'Go to your left!'? Knowing that my sole object in the situation is to get past him safely, and that this agrees with his own sole object of getting safely past me, he will obey my instruction with mutually satisfactory results unless, unluckily, he happens to be calling out at just the same moment 'Go to your right!'. Similarly Alf can tell Bill to choose action 3 at the same time that he himself embarks on action 2, and Bill, knowing that Alf is trying, just as he himself is, to maximize utility, will have good reason to comply. And in general imperative communication will help to sort out any initial confusions that may occur when any number of agents is confronted with a multiplicity of equal utility maxima.

Simple (or act-) utilitarianism, then, does not defeat the possibility of co-operation. But does it, as Hodgson maintains, defeat the possibilities of promising and of communicating information? Hodgson's arguments on these points have been forcefully criticized by Peter Singer,[5] but it may be worth while to look at them in another way. Singer has concentrated on the argument about communication, so let us start with that about promising.

Hodgson's argument runs thus. In our hypothetical act-utilitarian society the fact that a certain action would be the fulfilment of a promise will not make the agent perform it if some alternative action would have better consequences. The fact that a promise has been made will have no influence on action, everyone will know this, and so promising would be entirely ineffective. But, the utilitarian will reply, the fact that a promise has been made may bring it about that the action that fulfils it will have greater utility, and any alternative actions will have less utility, than they would have had if no promise had been made. Why? Because the promisee, the person to whom the promise is made, will be expecting its fulfilment. His satisfaction, and the fitting in with whatever he may have done in reliance on the promise, will raise the utility of the promise-fulfilling action, and contrarily his dissatisfaction, and the

---

[5] 'Is Act-Utilitarianism Self-Defeating?', *Philosophical Review*, Vol. 81, No. 1 (January 1972), pp. 94-104.

frustration of whatever he may have done in reliance on the promise, will lower the utility of any alternative courses of action. But, says Hodgson, this will work only if the promisee expects an act which has been promised more than he would have expected it if it had not been promised; but, knowing that the promisor is an act-utilitarian, he cannot have this greater expectation. For the promisor would be more likely to do this act only if doing it would have better consequences as compared with failure to do it than it would have had if it had not been promised.[6]

Essentially Hodgson's argument is that there is a vicious circularity in the attempt to justify promise-keeping not in opposition to, but as a case of, act-utilitarian choice. On the assumption that the parties are act-utilitarians and recognize no conventional rules and even respond to no conventional pressures, the promisor will have an extra reason for doing the promised act only if the promisee has an extra expectation of its being done, and the promisee will have this extra expectation only if the promisor has an extra reason for doing the act.

But it is not certain that the circularity is vicious. Let us consider four cases. In the first the promised act would be, apart from the promise, the promisor's contribution to a unique maximum of utility. In the second it would be, apart from the promise, his contribution to one of two equal maxima of utility. In the third it would be, apart from his promise, his contribution to a combined action which would have less utility than some alternative combinations. In all these three cases it is assumed that there is no ignorance or uncertainty; in the fourth case this assumption is relaxed, and the promised act is a contribution to a combined action about which neither party knows whether it would or would not have at least as much utility as any alternative.

In the first case the promised act will be performed anyway, for reasons already given: the promise will be fulfilled, and the promisee can expect this; but the promising will have been idle, since he could have expected the same action even if it had not been promised.

In the second case, the making of the promise could express the promisor's intention to do what would be his contribution to one rather than the other of the equal utility maxima. Then, unless it can be shown independently that in an act-utilitarian society no

[6] *CU*, p. 40.

one ever has reason to believe what anyone else says, the promisee will expect the promisor to act as he has said he intends to, and will therefore act in reliance on this, e.g., will make his own contribution to the same, not to any other, utility maximum, and this maximum will be in fact achieved. When the promisor finally has to act, he will now have act-utilitarian reasons for fulfilling the promise rather than choosing what would have been a different but equal utility maximum, which he would not have had if the promise had not been made and believed.

Much the same applies to the fourth case. The promisor states his intention to choose one alternative from a set in which it is not known whether this, or some other alternative would, apart from the promise, maximize utility. The promisee will expect him to do so and act in reliance on his doing so, and then when it comes to the point the promisor will have decisive act-utilitarian reasons for actually choosing the alternative he had promised to choose, which he would not have had if no promise had been made. There is, in the second and fourth cases, a kind of circularity, but it is not vicious. Provided that the promisor's statement of intention has some primary slightly greater chance of being true than of being false, the promisee can *in these cases* begin to rely on it, this will then give the promisor a further reason for fulfilling it, which in turn gives the promisee a stronger ground for relying on it, and so on.[7] The full force of the act-utilitarian obligation to keep a promise does indeed arise from this reciprocal relation between the promisor's reasons for acting and the promisee's reasons for expecting; but once the promising can be seen as raising even slightly the likelihood that the promisor will act accordingly we have a virtuous spiral rather than a vicious circle.

It may be objected that what we have here found room for is not *promising* but only *statements of intention*. It is true (as we shall see in a moment) that some of the characteristic point of promising must be absent where interests coincide. But it is still important that the promisor's reason in the end for doing what he has said he will do is not merely that he has said so, but also that the promisee is relying on him, and has acted in accordance with that reliance. The deliberate creation of this special relation, and hence a special reason for acting, gives to what we have here at least part of the character of what we ordinarily call a promise.

[7] Cf. Singer, *op. cit.*, p. 98.

In the third case, on the other hand, the circularity does seem to be vicious. Any slight tendency in the promisee to expect the promisor to fulfil his statement of intention would be outweighed by the promisee's knowledge that the promisor is an act-utilitarian and that there are alternatives to the promised act which have clearly greater utility. Here, then, the spiral cannot get started. Alf's saying that he will perform some act which would contribute only to combined acts of less than maximum utility would be utterly mysterious to Bill: given that they are both act-utilitarians, what could be the point of performing this act or of saying that one would perform it? Even if Bill did come to expect this act of Alf's, and himself acted so as to make the best of a bad job, so that when Alf came to act it was *then* right on utilitarian grounds for him to fulfil his promise, the total performance would have had less utility than if Alf had opted for the, or a, utility maximum and, if there were more than one, had told Bill which one he was opting for. So promising would not work in this third case: nor should it. To go back to our paradigm situation, it would be as if, approaching Bill on the pavement and foreseeing the danger of collision, Alf were to say: 'I shall lie down right across the pavement and roll; you take a running jump to try to get over me'. Bill would be rightly bewildered by this crazy proposal, and would not know whether to believe Alf or not.

It seems, then, that in our act-utilitarian society promising will work only in two special kinds of situation, to assist choice between equal utility maxima or between alternatives none of which is known to have better consequences than all the rest. Hodgson practically admits this exception, though he thinks it arises only if we add to the act-utilitarian principle accepted in our hypothetical society *rules* requiring its members to keep promises, and to tell the truth, unless it would have 'best consequences'—i.e., consequences at least as good as those of any alternative—not to do so.[8] But I have argued that no additional rules are required. Hodgson's main comment on this possibility is that such rules 'would not be very effective instruments for co-ordinating plans', just because they would come into play only in these special kinds of situation, that

---

[8] *CU*, pp. 49–50. I think the rules are not quite correctly stated: the proviso should surely be 'unless not doing so would have better consequences than doing so'.

is, because promising, for example, would not work in the third case we have considered.

I concede that promising would have a very restricted role in our hypothetical act-utilitarian society. But Hodgson is wrong in inferring that because promising is at present such an important ingredient in valuable or useful human relationships, any society which almost completely lacks it will be comparatively in a bad way. The main point of promising in our present society is that it enables people with divergent aims to co-operate to some extent. The point of a promise is that it helps to construct a compromise. Alf, say, would like best to get his work done and not pay any wages for it; Bill would like best to be paid wages and do no work; but Alf would rather pay wages and get the work done than not get the work done and pay no wages, and Bill would rather work and be paid than neither work nor be paid. They can reach a compromise between their divergent interests if Alf promises to pay Bill if he first does the work, and Bill trusts this promise, and does the work, and Alf then keeps his promise and pays Bill. But if there had been no divergence between their aims, if they had each been concerned only for their common welfare, no promising or promise-keeping would have been needed. One is reminded of what Humbert Wolfe said about the British journalist:

> You cannot hope to bribe or twist,
> Thank God, the British journalist;
> But seeing what the man will do
> Unbribed, there's no occasion to.

In much the same way, you cannot hope to bind, by a promise, an act-utilitarian to perform an act that will have, or even one that apart from the promise would have had, less than the maximum possible utility. But seeing that what he in any case will do is what you, as a fellow act-utilitarian, want him to do, you have no occasion so to bind him.

Let us next consider whether Hodgson is right in saying that in an act-utilitarian society there could be no communicating of information. Hodgson's argument again turns upon an accusation of circularity: telling the truth will have 'very best consequences' only if it is believed, but (in the hypothetical society) it will be believed only if the hearer has reason to expect the speaker to tell the truth. And giving false information could be equally supported by a circular train of reasoning; this will have good consequences if the hearer takes the information to be false, as he may if he has reason to expect the speaker to give false information. So the act-utilitarian reasons for telling truth and falsehood are exactly alike, so a hearer has no way of deciding which a speaker is likely to follow, and correspondingly a speaker cannot tell how he is likely to be understood.[9] Now Singer has shown that the two cases are not exactly alike, and therefore that the circularity is not vicious.[10] But if we have admitted the possibility of the use of imperatives, we can perhaps take a short cut here. Suppose that Alf addresses to Bill what we may call a belief-imperative, 'Believe that p'. Then Bill, knowing that (since both are act-utilitarians) Alf's purpose is identical with his own, and that Alf is in general well-informed, knows that it is likely to be in accordance with his, Bill's, own purpose that he, Bill, should believe that p, and he will therefore be willing to do so. Nor need he have any great psychological difficulty in doing so. For most things that it is in accordance with utility for people to believe are truths, so it is, as Bill can see, very likely that it is true that p. Hence the engendering of beliefs by the use of belief-imperatives between members of an act-utilitarian society will work. Secondly, a simple statement 'p' could and would function in that society as shorthand for the corresponding belief-imperative. If Alf said to Bill simply 'p', Bill would know that Alf thought, and was probably right in thinking, that it would be useful (in terms of their common standard of utility) for Bill to believe that p, probably though not necessarily because it was true that p, so Bill would try to believe, and on the whole would be likely to succeed in believing, that p. In this rather curious way the communicating of information would go on in our hypothetical society: it would rest not on a conventional rule of truth-telling, but on an automatic consequence of act-utilitarianism that all members will be agreed in fostering useful beliefs in themselves and in their fellows.

But is this argument still exposed to Hodgson's objection? Does the recipient of a belief-imperative have to wonder 'Does he really want me to believe that p, or is he telling me to believe that p in the hope that I will take this imperative as misleading and so come to believe that not-p?'? Is this uncertainty to be blocked only by the recognition of a non-act-utilitarian moral rule 'Don't use literally-misleading imperatives'? Surely not. It is a conventional matter that imperative sentences mean what they do, that is, that they are *prima facie* aimed at bringing about compliance, and without this convention our style of communication could not get off the ground. But this is only a linguistic convention, a rule of meaning, not a conventional moral rule that would be in competition with act-utilitarian principles.

This use and acceptance of belief-imperatives may not be exactly what we ordinarily call the communicating of information, but it is practically equivalent to this, and in some ways superior to what we have in all actual societies. For though we have conventional rules of truth-telling, we well know that they are often violated, occasionally for benevolent reasons but more often in support of divergent interests. Would it not be better to be sure that your neighbour was always telling you to believe what it would be best for you to believe than to be uncertain whether he was telling you the truth or deceiving you for the sake of his private ends and against your interests?

Summing up then: although an act-utilitarian society would not have promising—except in certain special types of situation—or truth-telling quite as we know them, and therefore would not have human relationships quite as we know them, it would not on that account be at a disadvantage as compared with actual societies: it would have something better.

Hodgson, and Warnock still more so, have made the mistake of not considering their own hypothesis in a sufficiently thorough-going way: they have not seen that the move to an act-utilitarian society, in which there are no conflicts of interest or purpose, does away with the need for our ordinary conventional rules at the same time that it does away with both conventional and utilitarian reasons for observing them. Such a society could enjoy the benefits of co-operation as it arises from an automatic harmonization of effort without requiring the devices that we now need if we are to erect some measure of mutually beneficial co-operation on a foundation of divergent purposes.

But this, though a mistake, is a very understandable one. The hypothesis of a society of pure act-utilitarians is so fantastic, so far removed from anything within our experience, that it is very hard to envisage it consistently and thoroughly. And there is just no possibility of its being realized. Discussion of what would happen in it is purely academic, and has no direct bearing on any policies of practical importance. The societies which it is of practical importance to consider are those whose members have to a great extent divergent and conflicting purposes.

Hodgson also examines the much more practical situation of a single act-utilitarian in an ordinary, non-act-utilitarian society. Will this man's efforts to maximize utility necessarily frustrate themselves, so that he will produce less utility than would certain kinds of non-utilitarian agents?

It is quite true, as Hodgson argues, that if he shows his hand and makes it plain to everyone that he will act, on every occasion, so as to maximize utility, then he will be unable to enter into bargains with his fellow citizens, and they may well not believe what he says, since they will reasonably suspect him of deceiving individuals in order to promote the common good, for which these individuals have no concern. He may therefore be frustrated in most of his efforts to promote utility, and achieve less in this direction than would some agent who was not even aiming at utility. This must be conceded, but this is hardly paradoxical. It is not surprising if the efforts of too candid a saint are frustrated in a wicked world.

But if our isolated act-utilitarian is prepared to conceal his own motives, then—mistakes of judgement apart—there can be no reason why he should fail to achieve whatever maximum utility the circumstances allow. Since we are, as Hodgson stresses throughout, assuming that utilitarianism is not being misapplied, that there are no mistakes of judgement, nothing can prevent our act-utilitarian from asking himself, and answering correctly, the question, 'What course of action, step by step, will produce at least as good results as any possible alternative course of action?', and, having answered it, acting accordingly. This course of action may well include quite a lot of promising, making of bargains—and keeping them often enough not to lower one's credit rating—and various other procedures of ordinary life, apologizing, praising, blaming, and so on. Hodgson stresses that all these activities would be insincere: the act-utilitarian must expect his fellows to interpret him as being guided by motives other than those which really guide him, that is, as feeling *bound* by promises, as feeling that he *ought* to respond to conventional moral pressures, ought not to tell beneficent lies, and so on.[11] Hodgson therefore admits that the act-utilitarian can consistently succeed in choosing the act which would have the best consequences possible *in the circumstances of his being an act-utilitarian*, but thinks that this will fall short of what he might have achieved had he been say, not an act-utilitarian but an honest man. But why? Surely only on the assumption that the honest man would be at peace with his own conscience whereas the act-utilitarian would not. But this is just not so. A thorough-going act-utilitarian would be impervious to the social pressures that condemn even benevolent deceit; knowing that he is deceiving his fellows only for the sake of the common good, he will feel a glow of conscious virtue each time he takes them in.

Of course this hypothesis puts a strain on our imaginations, and once again Hodgson has fallen into error by failing to allow *completely* for the consequences of a possibility that he professes to examine. In practice, of course, we have learned to be on our guard against people who aim so single-mindedly at what they take to be the welfare of the community, or of the human race, that they regard veracity, the keeping of bargains, and what are commonly called the rights of individuals as of no importance. But this is because we either do not share their concept of welfare, or aim obstinately at more limited goals, or think that these well-meaning fanatics are very likely to make mistakes. If we take seriously the hypothesis that none of these qualifications is in order, then we can no longer argue that an act-utilitarian will necessarily fail to maximize utility in his dealings with a non-act-utilitarian society.

In other words, Bentham was right to dismiss the possibility that his modern critics have developed so elaborately, even if he was wrong to dismiss it so abruptly. It is, after all, absurd to say that it is not consonant with utility to consult utility, *except in so far as mistakes of judgement are likely to be made*. This danger, together with the difficulty of reaching agreement about what constitutes welfare or utility, is the source of the real objections to utilitarianism as an immediate practical guide to conduct.

[11] *CU*, pp. 56–8.

VIII

CAN THERE BE A
RIGHT-BASED MORAL THEORY?

IN the course of a discussion of Rawls's theory of justice, Ronald Dworkin suggests a 'tentative initial classification' of political theories into goal-based, right-based, and duty-based theories.[1] Though he describes this, too modestly, as superficial and trivial ideological sociology, it in fact raises interesting questions. In particular, does some such classification hold for moral as well as for political theories? We are familiar with goal-based or consequentialist moral views and with duty-based or deontological ones; but it is not so easy to find right-based examples, and in discussions of consequentialism and deontology this third possibility is commonly ignored. Dworkin's own example of a right-based theory is Tom Paine's theory of revolution; another, recent, example might be Robert Nozick's theory of the minimal state.[2] But each of these is a political theory; the scope of each is restricted to the criticism of some political structures and policies and the support of others; neither is a fully developed general moral theory. If Rawls's view is, as Dworkin argues, fundamentally right-based, it may be the only member of this class. Moreover, it is only for Rawls's 'deep theory' that Dworkin can propose this identification: as explicitly formulated, Rawls's moral philosophy is not right-based. The lack of any convincing and decisive example leaves us free to ask the abstract question, 'Could there be a right-based general moral theory, and, if there were one, what would it be like?'

It is obvious that most ordinary moral theories include theses about items of all three kinds, goals, duties and rights, or, equivalently, about what is good as an end, about what is obligatory or

Reprinted from *Midwest Studies in Philosophy*, Vol. III (1978), copyright by University of Minnesota, Morris.

[1] R. Dworkin, *Taking Rights Seriously* (London, 1977), Chapter 6 ('Justice and Rights'), esp. pp. 171-2. This chapter appeared first as an article, 'The Original Position', in the *University of Chicago Law Review*, Vol. 4, No. 2 (Spring 1973); reprinted as Chapter 2 in *Reading Rawls*, edited by N. Daniels (Oxford, 1975).

[2] R. Nozick, *Anarchy, State, and Utopia* (New York and Oxford, 1974).

about what ought or ought not to be done or must or must not be done, and about what people are entitled to have or receive or do. But it is also obvious that moral theories commonly try to derive items of some of these sorts from items of another of them. It is easy to see how a consequentialist, say a utilitarian, may derive duties and rights from his basic goal. There are certain things that people must or must not do if the general happiness is to be maximized. Equally, the securing for people of certain entitlements and protections, and therefore of areas of freedom in which they can act as they choose, is, as Mill says, something which concerns the essentials of human well-being more nearly, and is therefore of more absolute obligation, than any other rules for the guidance of life.[3]

Again, it is possible to derive both goals and rights from duties. Trivially, there could just be a duty to pursue a certain end or to respect and defend a certain right. More interestingly, though more obscurely, it is conceivable that sets of goals and rights should follow from a single fundamental duty. Kant, for example, attempts to derive the principle of treating humanity as an end from the categorical imperative, 'Act only on that maxim through which you can at the same time will that it should become a universal law.'[4] Taken as literally as it can be taken, the principle of treating humanity—that is, persons, or more generally rational beings—as an end would seem to set up a goal. But it could well be interpreted as assigning rights to persons. Alternatively it could be argued that some general assignment of rights would follow directly from the choice of maxims which one could will to be universal. In either of these ways rights might be derived from duties.

But is it possible similarly to derive goals and duties from rights? And, if we are seeking a systematic moral theory, is it possible to derive a multiplicity of rights from a single fundamental one or from some small number of basic rights?

A right, in the most important sense, is the conjunction of a freedom and a claim-right. That is, if someone, A, has the moral right to do X, not only is he entitled to do X if he chooses—he is not morally required not to do X—but he is also protected in his doing of X—others are morally required not to interfere or prevent

---

[3] J.S. Mill, *Utilitarianism*, Chapter 5.
[4] I. Kant, *Groundwork of the Metaphysic of Morals*, Section 2.

him. This way of putting it suggests that duties are at least logically prior to rights: this sort of right is built up out of two facts about duties, that A does not have a duty not to do X and that others have a duty not to interfere with A's doing of X. But we could look at it the other way round: what is primary is A's having this right in a sense indicated by the prescription 'Let A be able to do X if he chooses', and the duty of others not to interfere follows from this (as does the absence of a duty for A not to do X). Here we have one way, at least, in which duties (and negations of duties) may be derived from rights.

I cannot see any way in which the mere fact of someone's having a certain right would in itself entail that anyone should take something as a goal. Nor does someone's having a right in itself require the achievement or realization of any goal. But the achievement of certain things as goals, or of things that may be taken as goals, may well be a necessary condition for the exercise of a right. Things must be thus-and-so if A is really to be able to do X; his merely having the right is not in itself sufficient. In this way a goal may be derived from a right, as a necessary condition of its exercise.

Rights can be derived from other rights in fairly obvious logical ways. For example, if I have a right to walk from my home to my place of work by the most direct route, and the most direct route is across Farmer Jones's potato field, then I have a right to walk across Farmer Jones's potato field. Again, there may be a right to create rights—in Hohfeld's terminology, a power. If someone has a certain power, and exercises it appropriately, then it follows that there will be the rights he has thus created. But what may be of more interest is a causal derivation of rights from rights. Suppose that A has a right to do X, but it is causally impossible for him to do X unless he does Y. It does not follow from this alone that he has a right to do Y, and in many cases we may have other grounds for denying him the right to do Y. But at least a *prima facie* case for his having the right to do Y could be based on the fact that doing Y is causally necessary for doing X, which he already has the right to do.

It seems, then, to be at least formally possible to have a system of moral ideas in which some rights are fundamental and other rights, and also goals and duties, are derived from these. But is it substantially possible? Are rights really the sort of thing that could be fundamental?

It is true that rights are not plausible candidates for objective existence. But neither are goods or intrinsic goals, conceived as things whose nature in itself requires that they should be pursued, or duties taken as intrinsic requirements, as constituting something like commands for which there need be, and is, no commander, which issue from no source. A belief in objective prescriptivity has flourished within the tradition of moral thinking, but it cannot in the end be defended.[5] So we are not looking for objective truth or reality in a moral system. Moral entities—values or standards or whatever they may be—belong within human thinking and practice: they are either explicitly or implicitly posited, adopted, or laid down. And the positing of rights is no more obscure or questionable than the positing of goals or obligations.

We might, then, go on to consider what rights to posit as fundamental. But it will be better, before we do this, to consider the comparative merits of right-based, goal-based, and duty-based theories. When we know what advantages a right-based theory might secure, we shall be better able to specify the rights that would secure them.

Rights have obvious advantages over duties as the basis and ground of morality. Rights are something that we may well want to have; duties are irksome. We may be glad that duties are imposed on others, but only (unless we are thoroughly bloody-minded) for the sake of the freedom, protection, or other advantages that other people's duties secure for us and our friends. The point of there being duties must lie elsewhere. Duty for duty's sake is absurd, but rights for their own sake are not. Duty is, as Wordsworth says, the stern daughter of the voice of God, and if we deny that there is a god, her parentage becomes highly dubious. Even if we accepted a god, we should expect his commands to have some further point, though possibly one not known to us; pointless commands, even from a god, would be gratuitous tyranny. Morality so far as we understand it might conceivably be thus based on divine commands, and therefore have, for us, a duty-based form; but if we reject this mythology and see morality as a human product we cannot intelligibly take duties as its starting point. Despite Kant, giving laws to oneself is not in itself a rational procedure. For a group to give laws to its members may be, but not for the sake of

[5] This is argued at length in Chapter 1 of my *Ethics, Inventing Right and Wrong* (Harmondsworth, 1977).

the restrictions they impose, or even for the sake of the similarity of those restrictions, but only for the sake of the correlative rights they create or the products of the co-operation they maintain. However, such points as these can be and commonly are made against duty-based theories on behalf of goal-based ones. When duties have been eliminated from the contest, is there anything to be said for rights as against goals?

A central embarrassment for the best known goal-based theories, the various forms of utilitarianism, is that they not merely allow but positively require, in certain circumstances, that the well-being of one individual should be sacrificed, without limits, for the well-being of others. It is not that these theories are collectivist in principle; it is not that the claims of individual welfare are overridden by those of some unitary communal welfare. They can and usually do take utility to be purely a resultant of individual satisfactions and frustrations. It is, quite literally, to other individuals that they allow one individual to be sacrificed. If some procedure produces a greater sum of happiness made up of the enjoyments experienced separately by B and C and D and so on than the happiness that this procedure takes away from A—or a sum greater than that needed to balance the misery that this procedure imposes on A— then, at least on a simple utilitarian view, that procedure is to be followed. And of course this holds whether the quantity to be maximized is total or average utility.

I have called this an embarrassment for utilitarianism, and it is no more than this. There are at least three well known possible reactions to it. The tough-minded act-utilitarian simply accepts this consequence of his principles, and is prepared to dismiss any contrary 'intuitions'. Indirect utilitarianism, of which rule-utilitarianism is only one variety, distinguishes two levels of moral thinking.[6] At the level of ordinary practical day-to-day thinking, actions and choices are to be guided by rules, principles, dispositions (virtues), and so on, which will indeed protect the welfare of each individual against the claims of the greater happiness of others: rights, in fact, will be recognized at this level. But at a higher level of critical or philosophical thinking these various provisions are to be called in question, tested, explained, justified, amended, or rejected by con-

---

[6] For example, R.M. Hare, 'Ethical Theory and Utilitarianism', in *Contemporary British Philosophy—Personal Statements*, Fourth Series, edited by H.D. Lewis (London, 1976).

sidering how well practical thinking that is guided by them is likely to promote the general happiness. Such intermediate devices, interposed between practical choices and the utilitarian goal, may for various reasons do more for that goal than the direct application of utility calculations to everyday choices. But in this goal itself, the general happiness which constitutes the ultimate moral aim and the final test in critical moral thought, the well-being of all individuals is simply aggregated, and the happiness of some can indeed compensate for the misery (even the undeserved misery) or others. This, then, is the second possible reaction. The third says that the difficulty or embarrassment results, not because utilitarianism is a goal-based theory, but because it is a purely aggregative one, and that what is required is the addition to it of a distributive principle that prescribes fairness in the distribution of happiness. It is not fair to sacrifice one individual to others.

Of these three reactions, the first would be attractive only if there were some strong *prima facie* case for adopting a simple utilitarian morality; but there is not.[7] The indirect view also has to assume that there are good general grounds for taking a sheer aggregate of happiness as the ultimate moral aim. But its great difficulty lies in maintaining the two levels of thinking while keeping them insulated from one another. There is, I admit, no difficulty in distinguishing them. The problem is rather the practical difficulty, for someone who is for part of the time a critical moral philosopher in this utilitarian style, to keep this from infecting his everyday moral thought and conduct. It cannot be easy for him to retain practical dispositions of honesty, justice, and loyalty if in his heart of hearts he feels that these don't really matter, and sees them merely as devices to compensate for the inability of everyone, himself included, to calculate reliably and without bias in terms of aggregate utility. And a thinker who does achieve this is still exposed to the converse danger that his practical morality may weaken his critical thinking. He will be tempted to believe that the virtues built into his own character, the principles to which he automatically appeals in practice, are the very ones that will best promote the general happiness, not because he has reached this conclusion by cogent reasoning, but just because this belief reconciles his theory with his practice. He may come to cultivate a quite artificial distrust of his

---

[7] I have tried to show this in Chapter 6 of *Ethics, Inventing Right and Wrong*, appealing to radical weaknesses in anything like Mill's proof of utility.

own ability to work out the consequences of actions for the general happiness. And what happens if the two levels cannot be kept apart? If the critical thinkers let their higher level thinking modify their own day-to-day conduct, the division will cease to be between two levels of thinking for at least some people, and become a division between two classes of people, those who follow a practical morality devised for them by others, and those who devise this but themselves follow a different, more directly utilitarian, morality. If, alternatively, the critical thinkers let their practical morality dominate their criticism, there can indeed be the same moral system for everyone, but it will have ceased to be a goal-based one. The derivation of the working principles from utility will have become a mere rationalization. Altogether, then, indirect utilitarianism is a rather unhappy compromise. And it is inadequately motivated. Why should it not be a *fundamental* moral principle that the well-being of one person cannot be simply replaced by that of another? There is no cogent proof of purely aggregative consequentialism at any level.[8]

Is the remedy, then, to add a distributive principle? This is still not quite what we need. If one individual is sacrificed for advantages accruing to others, what is deplorable is the ill-treatment of this individual, the invasion of his rights, rather than the relational matter of the unfairness of his treatment in comparison with others. Again, how are we to understand fairness itself? Within a purely goal-based theory it would have to be taken as an end or good, presumably a collective good, a feature of multi-person distributions which it is good to have in a group, or perhaps good for the group, though not good for any one member. And this would be rather mysterious. Further, within a goal-based theory it would be natural to take fairness, if it were recognized, as one additional constituent of utility, and then, unless it were given an infinite utility value, it is turn could be outweighed by a sufficient aggregate of individual satisfactions. There could still be a moral case for sacrificing not only A's welfare but also fairness along with it to the greater utility summed up in the welfare of B and C and so on.

Fairness as a distributive principle, added to an otherwise aggregative theory, would prescribe some distribution of utility. But what distribution? Presumably an equal one would be the ideal, to which distributions in practice would be expected to approximate

[8] The discussion referred to in note 7 applies here also.

as closely as was reasonably possible. But though extreme inequalities of satisfaction are deplorable, it is not clear that simple equality of satisfaction is the ideal. We surely want to leave it open to people to make what they can of their lives. But then it is inevitable that some will do better for themselves than others. This same point can be made about groups rather than individuals. Consider a society containing two groups, A and B, where the members of each group are in contact mainly with co-members of their own group. Suppose that the members of A are more co-operative, less quarrelsome, and so more successful in co-ordinating various activities than the members of B. Then the members of A are likely to do better, achieve more satisfaction, than the members of B. And why shouldn't they? Would there be any good reason for requiring an equal distribution of welfare in such circumstances? There is, of course, no need to adopt the extravagances and the myths of sturdy individualism, above all no ground for supposing that all actual inequalities of satisfaction result from some kind of merit and are therefore justified. All I am suggesting is that inequalities may be justified, and in particular that we should think of protecting each individual in an opportunity to do things rather than of distributing satisfactions.

Perhaps when fairness is added to an otherwise goal-based theory it should be thought of as a duty-based element. But then the arguments against duty-based systems apply to this element. What merit has even the duty to be fair for its own sake? It would be easier to endorse something like fairness as a right-based element, giving us a partly goal-based and partly right-based system.

But even this is not enough. A plausible goal, or good for man, would have to be something like Aristotle's *eudaimonia*: it would be in the category of activity. It could not be just an end, a possession, a termination of pursuit. The absurdity of taking satisfaction in the sense in which it is such a termination as the moral goal is brought out by the science-fictional pleasure machine described by Smart.[9] But Aristotle went wrong in thinking that moral philosophy could determine that a particular sort of activity constitutes the good for man in general, and is objectively and intrinsically the best way of life. People differ radically about the kinds of life that they choose to pursue. Even this way of putting it is misleading: in

[9] J.J.C. Smart and B. Williams, *Utilitarianism, For and Against* (Cambridge, 1973), pp. 18–21.

general people do not and cannot make an overall choice of a total plan of life. They choose successively to pursue various activities from time to time, not once and for all. And while there is room for other sorts of evaluation of human activities, morality as a source of constraints on conduct cannot be based on such comparative evaluation.[10] I suggest that if we set out to formulate a goal-based moral theory, but in identifying the goal try to take adequate account of these three factors, namely that the 'goal' must belong to the category of activity, that there is not one goal but indefinitely many diverse goals, and that they are the objects of progressive (not once-for-all or conclusive) choices, then our theory will change insensibly into a right-based one. We shall have to take as central the right of persons progressively to choose how they shall live.

This suggestion is dramatically illustrated by some of the writings of the best known of utilitarian moralists, John Stuart Mill. When he reiterates, in *On Liberty*, that he regards utility 'as the ultimate appeal on all ethical questions', he hastens to add that 'it must be utility in the largest sense, grounded on the permanent interests of a man as a progressive being'. Not, as it is sometimes misquoted, 'of man as a progressive being': that would imply a collectivist view, but here the stress is on the claims of each individual. 'These interests, I contend, authorize the subjection of individual spontaneity to external control, only in respect to those actions of each, which concern the interest of other people.' And the next few lines make it clear that he is thinking not of *any* interests of other people, but particularly of their rights and the defence of their rights. It is at least as plausible to say that the deep theory of *On Liberty* is right-based as that this holds of Rawls's *A Theory of Justice*.[11] The same point emerges from a close examination of the last chapter of *Utilitarianism*, 'On the Connection between Justice and Utility'. There Mill argues that what is morally required or obligatory is included in but not coextensive with what is expedient or worthy, and that what is just (or rather, what is required for justice) is similarly a proper sub-class of what is obligatory. By 'justice' he makes it clear that he means the body of rules which

[10] I am speaking here of what I call morality in the narrow sense in *Ethics, Inventing Right and Wrong*, Chapter 5.
[11] Dworkin makes this point, at least implicitly, in Chapter 11 ('Liberty and Liberalism') of *Taking Rights Seriously*.

protect rights which 'reside in persons'. They are 'The moral rules which forbid mankind to hurt one another (in which we must never forget to include wrongful interference with each other's freedom)' and 'are more vital to human well-being than any maxims, however important, which only point out the best way of managing some department of human affairs'. And though he still says that general utility is the reason why society ought to defend me in the possession of these rights, he explains that it is an 'extraordinarily important and impressive kind of utility which is concerned'. 'Our notion, therefore, of the claim we have on our fellow-creatures to join in making safe for us the very groundwork of our existence, fathers feelings around it so much more intense than those concerned in any of the more common cases of utility, that the difference in degree ... becomes a real difference in kind.' In such passages as these we can see Mill, while still working within the framework of a goal-based theory, moving towards a right-based treatment of at least the central part of morality.

When we think it out, therefore, we see that not only can there be a right-based moral theory, there cannot be an acceptable moral theory that is not right-based. Also, in learning why this approach is superior to those based either on duties or on goals, we have at least roughly identified what we may take as the fundamental right. If we assume that, from the point of view of the morality we are constructing, what matters in human life is activity, but diverse activities determined by successive choices, we shall, as I have said, take as central the right of persons progressively to choose how they shall live. But this is only a rough specification, and at once raises problems. Who is to have this right? Let us make what is admittedly a further decision and say that all persons are to have it, and all equally. It is true that this leaves in a twilight zone sentient and even human beings that are not and never will be persons; let us simply admit that there are problems here, but postpone them to another occasion.[12] Other problems are more pressing. The rights we have assigned to all persons will in practice come into conflict with one another. One person's choice of how to live will constantly be interfering with the choices of others. We have come close to Jefferson's formulation of fundamental rights to life, liberty, and the pursuit of happiness. But one person's

---

[12] I have touched on it in Chapter 8, Section 8, of *Ethics, Inventing Right and Wrong*.

pursuit of happiness will obstruct another's, and diverse liberties, and even the similar liberties of different people, are notoriously incompatible. Liberty is an all-purpose slogan: in all wars and all revolutions both sides have been fighting for freedom. This means that the rights we have called fundamental can be no more than *prima facie* rights: the rights that in the end people have, their final rights, must result from compromises between their initially conflicting rights. These compromises will have to be worked out in practice, but will be morally defensible only in so far as they reflect the equality of the *prima facie* rights. This will not allow the vital interests of any to be sacrificed for the advantage of others, to be outweighed by an aggregate of less vital interests. Rather we might think in terms of a model in which each person is represented by a point-centre of force, and the forces (representing *prima facie* rights) obey an inverse square law, so that a right decreases in weight with the remoteness of the matter on which it bears from the person whose right it is. There will be some matters so close to each person that, with respect to them, his rights will nearly always outweigh any aggregate of other rights, though admittedly it will sometimes happen that issues arise in which the equally vital interests of two or more people clash.

In discussing what rights we have, Dworkin has argued against any general right to liberty and in favour of a fundamental right to equal concern and respect.[13] The latter has, indeed, the advantage that it could be a final, not merely a *prima facie*, right: one person's possession or enjoyment of it does not conflict with another's. But it will not serve as the foundation of a right-based moral theory. Dworkin is, indeed, putting it forward as a fundamental *political* right: it is governments that must treat those whom they govern with equal concern and respect, or, more generally, social and economic arrangements that must represent these in a concrete form. But this cannot be what is morally fundamental. The right to be treated in a certain way rests on a prior, even if somewhat indeterminate, right to certain opportunities of living. Dworkin's main reason for rejecting a general right to liberty is that it cannot explain or justify the discriminations we want between legitimate and illegitimate restrictions of freedom, or the special stress liberals place on freedom of speech and political activity. But we can discriminate in terms of how closely a certain freedom is bound up

[13] *Taking Rights Seriously*, Chapter 12 ('What Rights Do We Have?').

with a person's vital central interests—but, of course, it may tell against a freedom which is fairly vital in this sense to someone if his exercise of it tends to affect adversely at least equally central interests of some others. The specifically political liberties may not be thus vital to many people, but they are important, far more widely, in an indirect way, as providing means for the defence of more central freedoms. That their importance is, morally speaking, thus derivative, and therefore contingent and relative to circumstances, is a conclusion which we should accept.

Dworkin is unwilling to recognize a general right to liberty also because this supposed right is commonly used to support a right to the free use of property. However, on the view I am putting forward such a right would be qualified and restricted by the consideration of how the ways in which this or that kind of property was acquired and used affect the central interests not only of the owner but of other people as well. I believe that a right to some sorts of property and some uses of it would be supported by such consideration; but by no means all the kinds and uses of property that are current in 'bourgeois' society.

Any right-based moral or political theory has to face the issue whether the rights it endorses are 'natural' or 'human' rights, universally valid and determinable *a priori* by some kind of reason, or are historically determined in and by the concrete institutions of a particular society, to be found out by analysis of its actual laws and practices. However, the view I am suggesting straddles this division. The fundamental right is put forward as universal. On the other hand I am not claiming that it is objectively valid, or that its validity can be found out by reason: I am merely adopting it and recommending it for general adoption as a moral principle. Also, I have argued that this fundamental right has to be formulated only as a *prima facie* right. Derived specific rights (which can be final, not merely *prima facie*) will be historically determined and contingent upon concrete circumstances and upon the interplay of the actual interests and preferences that people have. But the fact that something is an institutional right, recognized and defended by the laws and practices of a particular society, does not necessarily establish it as a moral right. It can be criticized from the moral point of view by considering how far the social interactions which have generated and maintain this institutional right express the fundamental right of persons progressively to choose how they shall live, interpreted along the lines of our model of centres of force, and to what extent they violate it. Our theory could have conservative implications in some contexts, but equally it could have reforming or revolutionary implications in others.

It may be asked whether this theory is individualist, perhaps too individualist. It is indeed individualist in that individual persons are the primary bearers of rights, and the sole bearers of fundamental rights, and one of its chief merits is that, unlike aggregate goal-based theories, it offers a persistent defence of some interests of each individual. It is, however, in no way committed to seeing individuals as spontaneous originators of their thoughts and desires. It can recognize that the inheritance of cultural traditions and being caught up in movements help to make each individual what he is, and that even the most independent individuals constitute their distinctive characters not by isolating themselves or by making 'existential' choices but by working with and through inherited traditions. Nor need it be opposed to co-operation or collective action. I believe that Rousseau's description of a community with a general will, general 'both in its object and in its essence', that is, bearing in its expression upon all members alike and located in every member of the community, provides a model of a conceivable form of association, and there is nothing in our theory that would be hostile to such genuine co-operation. But I do not believe that there could actually be a community with a genuine, not fictitious, general will of this sort of the size of an independent political unit, a sovereign state. The fundamental individual rights could, however, be expressed in joint activity or communal life on a smaller scale, and organizations of all sorts can have derived, though not fundamental, moral rights. Our theory, therefore, is not anti-collectivist, but it will discriminate among collectivities, between those which express and realize the rights of their members and those which sacrifice some or even most of their members to a supposed collective interest, or to the real interest of some members, or even to some maximized aggregate of interests.

I hope I have not given the impression that I think it an easy matter to resolve conflicts of rights and to determine, in concrete cases, what the implications of our theory will be. What I have offered is not an algorithm or decision procedure, but only, as I said, a model, an indication of a framework of ideas within which the discussion of actual specific issues might go on. And in general this paper is no more than a tentative initial sketch of a right-based moral theory. I hope that others will think it worth further investigation.

This paper has been read at a number of universities in the United States and Canada, and has met with some acute and forceful criticisms. I do not know how to cope with all of them, but at least some further clarifications are needed.

It has been asked whether this right-based theory is extensionally equivalent to some form of utilitarianism, yielding exactly the same output of practical prescriptions, and whether it is even just a notational variant of some form of utilitarianism. This question has, as yet, no determinate answer, because the right-based theory has not yet been made sufficiently precise. I hope that it will not turn out to be an extensional equivalent, let alone a mere notational variant, of any form of utilitarianism. But even if it does, there may be some merit in the formulation in terms of rights. It may be easier to keep this distinct from other forms of utilitarianism. And there would be no reason for preferring to formulate it in a utilitarian style unless there were some general presumption that *some* version of utilitarianism must be correct, that moral thinking ought somehow to be cast in a utilitarian mould, and I would argue that there is no ground for such a presumption.

It may also be asked just what is it to *base* a moral theory on goals or duties or rights. One possible view is that an X-based theory is one which takes 'X' as its only undefined term, and defines other moral terms in relation to 'X'. In this sense G.E. Moore's moral system is good-based. Since I have allowed that statements about rights can be analysed into conjunctions of affirmative and negative statements about duties, my account seems not to be right-based in this sense, but rather duty-based. However, this is not what I find most important. Another interpretation is that a moral theory is X-based if it forms a system in which some statements about Xs are taken as basic and the other statements in the theory are derived from them, perhaps with the help of non-moral, purely factual, premises. But what would make a theory X-based in the most important sense is that it should be such a system not merely formally but in its purpose, that the basic statements about

Xs should be seen as capturing what gives point to the whole moral theory. The possibility into which I am enquiring is that of a theory which is right-based in this most important sense.

The greatest difficulties concern the suggestions about how to deal with conflicts of *prima facie* rights. One question is whether each agent can say, authoritatively, how vital some matter is to him. If we were working out a detailed theory, we would want to give considerable weight to sincere claims of this sort, but not complete authority: we may have to tell a busybody that something is not as vital to him, from the point of view of this moral theory, as he thinks it is. Another problem is that a model of point-centres of force seems to offer no solution at all to conflicts of equally vital interests. This difficulty is partly met by the reflection that the proposed theory calls for compromises worked out in practice, for the historical development of institutional rights as derivatives from and realizations of the *prima facie* rights, rather than for direct solution of conflicts as they arise at any moment by reference to the general theory alone. Institutional rights may resolve what would be insoluble conflicts of claims. The suggested theory is only right-*based*; it does not make rights, let alone fundamental *prima facie* rights, the only moral elements; it provides for the derivation of goals and duties from those fundamental rights. But this reply leads to a further difficulty: will not an indirect right-based theory be open to objections similar to those pressed against indirect utilitarianism? I think it will be less open to such objections, because the protection of rights can be seen throughout as what gives force to the derived moral judgements: there is less need to detach them from this source than there is to detach the working principles of an indirect utilitarianism from a purely aggregative basic theory. Whatever problems there are about adjusting conflicts of rights, this theory is not saddled with the embarrassing presumption that one person's well-being can be simply replaced by that of another.

Finally, it does not seem to me to be a reasonable requirement for a moral theory that it should, even when fully developed, be able to resolve all conflicts. But my main thesis is that this right-based approach is worth some further study, similar to that which has been lavished on various forms of utilitarianism.

IX

THE LAW OF THE JUNGLE:
MORAL ALTERNATIVES AND
PRINCIPLES OF EVOLUTION

WHEN people speak of 'the law of the jungle', they usually mean unrestrained and ruthless competition, with everyone out solely for his own advantage. But the phrase was coined by Rudyard Kipling, in *The Second Jungle Book*, and he meant something very different. His law of the jungle is a law that wolves in a pack are supposed to obey. His poem says that 'the strength of the Pack is the Wolf, and the strength of the Wolf is the Pack', and it states the basic principles of social co-operation. Its provisions are a judicious mixture of individualism and collectivism, prescribing graduated and qualified rights for fathers of families, mothers with cubs, and young wolves, which constitute an elementary system of welfare services. Of course, Kipling meant his poem to give moral instruction to human children, but he probably thought it was at least roughly correct as a description of the social behaviour of wolves and other wild animals. Was he right, or is the natural world the scene of unrestrained competition, of an individualistic struggle for existence?

Views not unlike those of Kipling have been presented by some recent writers on ethology, notably Robert Ardrey and Konrad Lorenz. These writers connect their accounts with a view about the process of evolution that has brought this behaviour, as well as the animals themselves, into existence. They hold that the important thing in evolution is the good of the species, or the group, rather than the good of the individual. Natural selection favours those groups and species whose members tend, no doubt through some instinctive programming, to co-operate for a common good; this would, of course, explain why wolves, for example, behave co-operatively and generously towards members of their own pack, if indeed they do.

Reprinted from *Philosophy*, Vol. 53, No. 206 (October 1978).

However, this recently popular view has been keenly attacked by Richard Dawkins in his admirable and fascinating book, *The Selfish Gene*.[1] He defends an up-to-date version of the orthodox Darwinian theory of evolution, with special reference to 'the biology of selfishness and altruism'. One of his main theses is that there is no such thing as group selection, and that Lorenz and others who have used this as an explanation are simply wrong. This is a question of some interest to moral philosophers, particularly those who have been inclined to see human morality itself as the product of some kind of natural evolution.[2]

It is well, however, to be clear about the issue. It is not whether animals ever behave for the good of the group in the sense that this is their conscious subjective goal, that they *aim* at the well-being or survival of the whole tribe or pack: the question of motives in this conscious sense does not arise. Nor is the issue whether animals ever behave in ways which do in fact promote the well-being of the group to which they belong, or which help the species of which they are members to survive: of course they do. The controversial issue is different from both of these: it is whether the good of the group or the species would ever figure in a correct evolutionary account. That is, would any correct evolutionary account take either of the following forms?

(i) The members of this species tend to do these things which assist the survival of this species because their ancestors were members of a sub-species whose members had an inheritable tendency to do these things, and as a result that sub-species survived, whereas other sub-species of the ancestral species at that time had members who tended not to do these things and as a result their sub-species did not survive.

(ii) The members of this species tend to do these things which help the group of which they are members to flourish because some ancestral groups happened to have members who tended to do these things and these groups, as a result, survived better than related groups of the ancestral species whose members tended not to do these things.

In other words, the issue is this: is there natural selection by and for group survival or species survival as opposed to selection by

[1] R. Dawkins, *The Selfish Gene* (Oxford, 1976).
[2] I am among these: see p. 113 of my *Ethics, Inventing Right and Wrong* (Harmondsworth, 1977).

and for individual survival (or, as we shall see, gene survival)? Is behaviour that helps the group or the species, rather than the individual animal, rewarded by the natural selection which determines the course of evolution?

However, when Dawkins denies that there is selection by and for group or species survival, it is not selection by and for individual survival that he puts in its place. Rather it is selection by and for the survival of each single gene—the genes being the unit factors of inheritance, the portions of chromosomes which replicate themselves, copy themselves as cells divide and multiply. Genes, he argues, came into existence right back at the beginning of life on earth, and all more complex organisms are to be seen as their products. We are, as he picturesquely puts it, gene-machines: our biological function is just to protect our genes, carry them around, and enable them to reproduce themselves. Hence the title of his book, *The Selfish Gene*. Of course what survives is not a token gene: each of these perishes with the cell of which it is a part. What survives is a gene-type, or rather what we might call a gene-clone, the members of a family of token genes related to one another by simple direct descent, by replication. The popularity of the notions of species selection and group selection may be due partly to confusion on this point. Since clearly it is only types united by descent, not individual organisms, that survive long enough to be of biological interest, it is easy to think that selection must be by and for species survival. But this is a mistake: genes, not species, are the types which primarily replicate themselves and are selected. Since Dawkins roughly defines the gene as 'a genetic unit which is small enough to last for a number of generations and to be distributed around in the form of many copies', it is (as he admits) practically a tautology that the gene is the basic unit of natural selection and therefore, as he puts it, 'the fundamental unit of self-interest', or, as we might put it less picturesquely, the primary beneficiary of natural selection. But behind this near-tautology is a synthetic truth, that this basic unit, this primary beneficiary, is a small bit of a chromosome. The reason why this is so, why what is differentially effective and therefore subject to selection is a small bit of a chromosome, lies in the mechanism of sexual reproduction by way of meiosis, with crossing over between chromosomes. When male and female cells each divide before uniting at fertilization, it is not chromosomes as a whole that are randomly distributed between the parts, but sections of chromosomes. So sections of chromosomes can be separately inherited, and therefore can be differentially selected by natural selection.

The issue between gene selection, individual selection, group selection, and species selection might seem to raise some stock questions in the philosophy of science. Many thinkers have favoured reductionism of several sorts, including methodological individualism. Wholes are made up of parts, and therefore in principle whatever happens in any larger thing depends upon and is explainable in terms of what happens in and between its smaller components. But though this metaphysical individualism is correct, methodological individualism does not follow from it. It does not follow that we must always conduct our investigations and construct our explanations in terms of component parts, such as the individual members of a group or society. Scientific accounts need not be indefinitely reductive. Some wholes are obviously more accessible to us than their components. We can understand what a human being does without analysing this in terms of how each single cell in his body or his brain behaves. Equally we can often understand what a human society does without analysing this in terms of the behaviour of each of its individual members. And the same holds quite generally: we can often understand complex wholes as units, without analysing them into their parts. So if, in the account of evolution, Dawkins's concentration upon genes were just a piece of methodological individualism or reductionism, it would be inadequately motivated. But it is not: there is a special reason for it. Dawkins's key argument is that species, populations, and groups, and individual organisms too, are as genetic units too temporary to qualify for natural selection. 'They are not stable through evolutionary time. Populations ... are constantly blending with other populations and so losing their identity', and, what is vitally important, 'are also subject to evolutionary change from within' (p. 36).

This abstract general proposition may seem obscure. But it is illustrated by a simple example which Dawkins gives (pp. 197–201).

A species of birds is parasitized by dangerous ticks. A bird can remove the ticks from most parts of its own body, but, having only a beak and no hands, it cannot get them out of the top of its own head. But one bird can remove ticks from another bird's head: there can be mutual grooming. Clearly if there were an inherited tendency for each bird to take the ticks out of any other bird's head, this would help the survival of any group in which that tendency happened to arise—for the ticks are dangerous: they can cause death. Someone who believed in group selection would, therefore, expect this tendency to be favoured and to evolve and spread for this reason. But Dawkins shows that it would not. He gives appropriate names to the different 'strategies', that is, the different inheritable behavioural tendencies. The strategy of grooming anyone who needs it he labels 'Sucker'. The strategy of accepting grooming from anyone, but never grooming anyone else, even someone who has previously groomed you, is called 'Cheat'. Now if in some population both these tendencies or strategies, and only these two, happen to arise, it is easy to see that the cheats will always do better than the suckers. They will be groomed when they need it, and since they will not waste their time pecking out other birds' ticks, they will have more time and energy to spare for finding food, attracting mates, building nests, and so on. Consequently the gene for the Sucker strategy will gradually die out. So the population will come to consist wholly of cheats, despite the fact that this is likely to lead to the population itself becoming extinct, if the parasites are common enough and dangerous enough, whereas a population consisting wholly of suckers would have survived. The fact that the group is open to evolutionary change from within, because of the way the internal competition between Cheat and Sucker genes works out, prevents the group from developing or even retaining a feature which would have helped the group as a whole.

   This is just one illustration among many, and Dawkins's arguments on this point seem pretty conclusive. We need, as he shows, the concept of an *evolutionarily stable strategy* or ESS (p. 74 *et passim*). A strategy is evolutionarily stable, in relation to some alternative strategy or strategies, if it will survive indefinitely in a group in competition with those alternatives. We have just seen that where Cheat and Sucker alone are in competition, Cheat is an ESS but Sucker is not. We have also seen, from this example, that an ESS may not help a group, or the whole species, to survive and multiply. Of course we must not leap to the conclusion that an ESS never helps a group or a species: if that were so we could not explain much of the behaviour that actually occurs. Parents sacrifice themselves for their children, occasionally siblings for their siblings, and with the social insects, bees and ants and termites, their whole life is a system of communal service. But the point is that these results are not to be explained in terms of group selection. They can and must be explained as consequences of the self-ishness of genes, that is, of the fact that gene-clones are selected for whatever helps each gene-clone itself to survive and multiply.

But now we come to another remarkable fact. Although the gene is the hero of Dawkins's book, it is not unique either in principle or in fact. It is not the only possible subject of evolutionary natural selection, nor is it the only actual one. What is important about the gene is just that it has a certain combination of logical features. It is a replicator: in the right environment it is capable of producing multiple copies of itself; but in this process of copying some mistakes occur; and these mistaken copies—mutations—will also produce copies of themselves; and, finally, the copies produced may either survive or fail to survive. Anything that has these formal, logical, features is a possible subject of evolution by natural selection. As we have seen, individual organisms, groups, and species do not have the required formal features, though many thinkers have supposed that they do. They cannot reproduce themselves with sufficient constancy of characteristics. But Dawkins, in his last chapter, introduces another sort of replicators. These are what are often called cultural items or traits; Dawkins christens them *memes*—to make a term a bit like 'genes'—because they replicate by memory and imitation (mimesis). Memes include tunes, ideas, fashions, and techniques. They require, as the environment in which they can replicate, a collection of minds, that is, brains that have the powers of imitation and memory. These brains (particularly though not exclusively human ones) are themselves the products of evolution by gene selection. But once the brains are there gene selection has done its work: given that environment, memes can themselves evolve and multiply in much the same way as genes do, in accordance with logically similar laws. But they can do so more quickly. Cultural evolution may be much faster than biological evolution. But the basic laws are the same. Memes are selfish in the same sense as genes. The explanation of the wide-spread flourishing of a certain meme, such as the idea of a god or the belief in hell fire, may be simply that it is an efficiently selfish meme. Something about it makes it well able to infect human minds, to take root and spread in and among them, in the same way that something about the smallpox virus makes it well able to take root and spread in human bodies. There is no need to explain the success of a meme in terms of any benefit it confers on individuals or groups; it is a replicator in its own right. Contrary to the optimistic view often taken of cultural evolution, this analogy shows that a cultural trait can evolve, not because it is advantageous to society, but simply because it is advantageous to itself. It is ironical that Kipling's phrase 'the law of the jungle' has proved itself a more efficient meme than the doctrine he tried to use it to propagate.

So far I have been merely summarizing Dawkins's argument. We can now use it to answer the question from which I started. Who is right about the law of the jungle? Kipling, or those who have twisted his phrase to mean almost the opposite of what he intended? The answer is that neither party is right. The law by which nature works is not unrestrained and ruthless competition between individual organisms. But neither does it turn upon the advantages to a group, and its members, of group solidarity, mutual care and respect, and co-operation. It turns upon the self-preservation of gene-clones. This has a strong tendency to express itself in individually selfish behaviour, simply because each agent's genes are more certainly located in him than in anyone else. But it can and does express itself also in certain forms of what Broad called self-referential altruism, including special care for one's own children and perhaps one's siblings, and, as we shall see, reciprocal altruism, helping those (and only those) who help you.

But now I come to what seems to be an exception to Dawkins's main thesis, though it is generated by his own argument and illustrated by one of his own examples. We saw how, in the example of mutual grooming, if there are only suckers and cheats around, the strategy Cheat is evolutionarily stable, while the strategy Sucker is not. But Dawkins introduces a third strategy, Grudger. A grudger is rather like you and me. A grudger grooms anyone who has previously groomed him, and any stranger, but he remembers and bears a grudge against anyone who cheats him—who refuses to groom him in return for having been groomed—and the grudger refuses to groom the cheat ever again. Now when all three strategies are in play, both Cheat and Grudger are evolutionarily stable. In a population consisting largely of cheats, the cheats will do better than the others, and both suckers and grudgers will die out.

But in a population that starts off with more than a certain critical proportion of grudgers, the cheats will first wipe out the suckers, but will then themselves become rare and eventually extinct: cheats can flourish only while they have suckers to take advantage of, and yet by doing so they tend to eliminate those suckers.

It is obvious, by the way, that a population containing only suckers and grudgers, in any proportions, but no cheats, would simply continue as it was. Suckers and grudgers behave exactly like one another as long as there are no cheats around, so there would be no tendency for either the Sucker or the Grudger gene to do better than the other. But if there is any risk of an invasion of Cheat genes, either through mutation or through immigration, such a pattern is not evolutionarily stable, and the higher the proportion of suckers, the more rapidly the cheats would multiply.

So we have two ESSs, Cheat and Grudger. But there is a difference between these two stable strategies. If the parasites are common enough and dangerous enough, the population of cheats will itself die out, having no defence against ticks in their heads, whereas a separate population of grudgers will flourish indefinitely. Dawkins says, 'If a population arrives at an ESS which drives it extinct, then it goes extinct, and that is just too bad' (p. 200). True: *but is this not group selection after all?* Of course, this will operate only if the populations are somehow isolated. But if the birds in question were distributed in geographically isolated regions, and Sucker, Cheat and Grudger tendencies appeared (after the parasites became plentiful) in randomly different proportions in these different regions, then some populations would become pure grudger populations, and others would become pure cheat populations, but then the pure cheat populations would die out, so that eventually all surviving birds would be grudgers. And they would be able to re-colonize the areas where cheat populations had perished.

Another name for grudgers is 'reciprocal altruists'. They act as if on the maxim 'Be done by as you did'. One implication of this story is that this strategy is not only evolutionarily stable within a population, it is also viable for a population as a whole. The explanation of the final situation, where all birds of this species are grudgers, lies partly in the non-viability of a population of pure cheats. So this is, as I said, a bit of group selection after all.

It is worth noting how and why this case escapes Dawkins's key argument that a population is 'not a discrete enough entity to be a unit of natural selection, not stable and unitary enough to be "selected" in preference to another population' (p. 36). Populations can be made discrete by geographical (or other) isolation, and can be made stable and unitary precisely by the emergence of an ESS in each, but perhaps different ESSs in the different regional populations of the same species. This case of group selection is necessarily a second order phenomenon: it arises where gene selection has produced the ESSs which are then persisting selectable features of groups. In other words, an ESS may be a third variety of replicator, along with genes and memes; it is a self-reproducing feature *of groups.*

Someone might reply that this is not really group selection because it all rests ultimately on gene selection, and a full explanation can be given in terms of the long-run self-extinction of the Cheat gene, despite the fact that within a population it is evolutionarily stable in competition with the two rival genes. But this would be a weak reply. The monopoly of cheating *over a population* is an essential part of the causal story that explains the extinction. Also, an account at the group level, though admittedly incomplete, is here correct as far as it goes. The reason why all ultimately surviving birds of this species are grudgers is partly that *populations* of grudgers can survive whereas *populations* of cheats cannot, though it is also partly that although a population of suckers could survive—it would be favoured by group selection, if this possibility arose, just as much as a population of grudgers—internal changes due to gene selection after an invasion of Cheat genes would prevent there being a population of suckers. In special circumstances group selection (or population selection) can occur and could be observed and explained as such, without going down to the gene selection level. It would be unwarranted methodological individualism or reductionism to insist that we not merely can but must go down to the gene selection level here. We must not fall back on this weak general argument when Dawkins's key argument against group selection fails.

I conclude, then, that there can be genuine cases of group selection. But I admit that they are exceptional. They require rather special conditions, in particular geographical isolation, or some other kind of isolation, to keep the populations that are being differentially selected apart. For if genes from one could infiltrate another, the selection of populations might be interfered with.

(Though in fact in our example *complete* isolation is not required: since what matters is whether there is more or less than a certain critical proportion of grudgers, small-scale infiltrations would only delay, not prevent, the establishing of pure populations.) And since special conditions are required, there is no valid general principle that features which would enable a group to flourish will be selected. And even these exceptional cases conform thoroughly to the general logic of Dawkins's doctrine. Sometimes, but only sometimes, group characteristics have the formal features of replicators that are open to natural selection.

Commenting on an earlier version of this paper, Dawkins agreed that there could be group selection in the sort of case I suggested, but stressed the importance of the condition of geographical (or other) isolation. He also mentioned a possible example, that the prevalence of sexual reproduction itself may be a result of group selection. For if there were a mutation by which asexual females, producing offspring by parthenogenesis, occurred in a species, this clone of asexual females would be at once genetically isolated from the rest of the species, though still geographically mixed with them. Also, in most species males contribute little to the nourishment or care of their offspring, so from a genetic point of view males are wasters: resources would be more economically used if devoted only to females. So the genetically isolated population of asexual females would out-compete the normal sexually reproducing population with roughly equal numbers of males and females. So the species would in time consist only of asexual females. But then, precisely because all its members were genetically identical, it would not have the capacity for rapid adaptation by selection to changing conditions that an ordinary sexual population has. So when conditions changed, it would be unable to adapt, and would die out. Thus there would in time be species selection against any species that produced an asexual female mutation. Which would explain why nearly all existing species go in for what, in the short run, is the economically wasteful business of sexual reproduction.[3]

What implications for human morality have such biological facts about selfishness and altruism? One is that the possibility that mor-

---

[3] This suggestion is made in a section entitled 'The paradox of sex and the cost of paternal neglect' of the following article: R. Dawkins, 'The Value Judgments of Evolution', in *Animal Economics*, edited by M.A.H. Dempster and D.J. McFarland (London and New York, forthcoming).

ality is itself a product of natural selection is not ruled out, but care would be needed in formulating a plausible speculative account of how it might have been favoured. Another is that the notion of an ESS may be a useful one for discussing questions of practical morality. Moral philosophers have already found illumination in such simple items of game theory as the Prisoners' Dilemma; perhaps these rather more complicated evolutionary 'games' will prove equally instructive. Of course there is no simple transition from 'is' to 'ought', no direct argument from what goes on in the natural world and among non-human animals to what human beings ought to do. Dawkins himself explicitly warns against any simple transfer of conclusions. At the very end of the book he suggests that conscious foresight may enable us to develop radically new kinds of behaviour. 'We are built as gene machines and cultured as meme machines, but we have the power to turn against our creators. We, alone on earth, can rebel against the tyranny of the selfish replicators' (p. 215). This optimistic suggestion needs fuller investigation. It must be remembered that the human race as a whole cannot act as a unit with conscious foresight. Arrow's Theorem shows that even quite small groups of rational individuals may be unable to form coherently rational preferences, let alone to act rationally. Internal competition, which in general prevents a group from being a possible subject of natural selection, is even more of an obstacle to its being a rational agent. And while we can turn against some memes, it will be only with the help and under the guidance of other memes.

This is an enormous problematic area. For the moment I turn to a smaller point. In the mutual grooming model, we saw that the Grudger strategy was, of the three strategies considered, the only one that was healthy in the long run. Now something closely resembling this strategy, reciprocal altruism, is a well known and long established tendency in human life. It is expressed in such formulae as that justice consists in giving everyone his due, interpreted, as Polemarchus interprets it in the first book of Plato's *Republic*, as doing good to one's friends and harm to one's enemies, or repaying good with good and evil with evil. Morality itself has been seen, for example by Edward Westermarck, as an outgrowth from the retributive emotions. But some moralists, including Socrates and Jesus, have recommended something very different from this, turning the other cheek and repaying evil with good. They have tried to substitute 'Do as you would be done by' for 'Be done by as you did'. Now this, which in human life we characterize as a Christian spirit or perhaps as saintliness, is roughly equivalent to the strategy Dawkins has unkindly labelled 'Sucker'. Suckers are saints, just as grudgers are reciprocal altruists, while cheats are a hundred per cent selfish. And as Dawkins points out, the presence of suckers endangers the healthy Grudger strategy. It allows cheats to prosper, and could make them multiply to the point where they would wipe out the grudgers, and ultimately bring about the extinction of the whole population. This seems to provide fresh support for Nietzsche's view of the deplorable influence of moralities of the Christian type. But in practice there may be little danger. After two thousand years of contrary moral teaching, reciprocal altruism is still dominant in all human societies; thoroughgoing cheats and thoroughgoing saints (or suckers) are distinctly rare. The sucker slogan is an efficient meme, but the sucker behaviour pattern far less so. Saintliness is an attractive topic for preaching, but with little practical persuasive force. Whether in the long run this is to be deplored or welcomed, and whether it is alterable or not, is a larger question. To answer it we should have carefully to examine our specifically human capacities and the structure of human societies, and also many further alternative strategies. We cannot simply apply to the human situation conclusions drawn from biological models. Nevertheless they are significant and challenging as models; it will need to be shown how and where human life diverges from them.

X

THE THIRD THEORY OF LAW

I HAVE resisted the temptation to entitle this paper 'Taking Rights Seriously and Playing Fast and Loose with the Law'. But it will become plain, as I go on, why I was tempted.

Professor Dworkin's theory of law is now well known, especially since the publication of his book, *Taking Rights Seriously*.[1] But it may be as well to review it, and show how some of his main theses fit together.

I call it the third theory of law because it contrasts both with legal positivism and with the doctrine of natural law, and is in some ways intermediate between the two. The natural law doctrine is well summarized by Blackstone: 'This law of nature being coeval with mankind and dictated by God himself is of course superior in obligation to any other. It is binding over the whole globe, in all countries and at all times. No human laws are of any validity if contrary to this, and such of them as are valid derive their force and all their authority, mediately or immediately, from this original.'[2] This entails that a judge, relying on his rational knowledge of natural law, may overrule even what appears to be the settled law of the land—unambiguous and regularly enacted statutes or clearly relevant and unopposed precedents—and declare that the apparently settled law is not the law. Against this, I think that Professor Dworkin would concede that all law is made somehow by human beings, and that the (detailed) question, What is the law? makes sense only if construed as asking, What is at a certain time the law of England, or of France, or of the United States, or of South Dakota? The validity of a law is wholly relative to the legal system to which it belongs. Consequently the finding out of what is the law is an empirical task, not a matter of *a priori* reasoning. But, this being conceded, Professor Dworkin stresses a

Reprinted from *Philosophy and Public Affairs*, Vol. 7, No. 1 (Fall 1977), copyright by Princeton University Press.

[1] Ronald Dworkin, *Taking Rights Seriously* (London, 1977), hereafter referred to as *TRS*.

[2] *Commentaries*, quoted by Julius Stone, *The Province and Function of Law* (Sydney, 1946), p. 227.

series of contrasts between his view and legal positivism, even such a cautious form of positivism as Professor Hart's.

First, he holds that the law consists not only of rules but also of principles, the distinction between these being logical: 'Rules are applicable in an all-or-nothing fashion', whereas principles have the extra dimension of weight (*TRS*, pp. 22-8).

Secondly, he rejects the positivist notion of a single ultimate or fundamental test for law, such as Professor Hart's 'rule of recognition'. In its place he puts the sort of reasoning that he ascribes, in 'Hard Cases', to his imaginary judge, Hercules. Some parts of the law in a certain jurisdiction are settled and relatively uncontroversial, in the constitution or statutes or precedents. Hercules uses these as data, seeking the theory, in terms of further rights and principles, which best explains and justifies this settled law. Having developed this theory, he then applies it to the hard case (*TRS*, pp. 105-23).

Thirdly, and as a result of this method, Professor Dworkin holds that in any sufficiently rich legal system (notably in that of England no less than in that of the United States) the question, What is the law on this issue? always has a right answer, discoverable in principle, and it is the duty of the judge to try to discover it. One of the parties will always have a right to a decision in his favour. 'Judicial decisions enforce existing political rights.' There is a theoretical possibility of a tie, a dead heat, between competing sets of principles when all relevant considerations have been taken into account, but this is so unlikely that it may in practice be ignored. (See *TRS*, pp. 81, 279-90, esp. 286-7.)

Consequently, and fourthly, though judges in hard or controversial cases have discretion in the weak sense that they are called upon to exercise judgement—they are not supplied with any cut and dried decision procedure—they never have discretion in the strong sense which would exclude a duty to decide the case one way rather than the other (*TRS*, pp. 31-5, 68-71).

Fifthly, though it is really only another way of making the same point, Professor Dworkin holds that even in a hard case one does not reach a stage where the law has run out before it has yielded a decision, and the judge has to make some new law to deal with a new problem. Judges never need to act, even surreptitiously, as legislators, though he has allowed that they may in fact do so as they sometimes do when they make a mistake or when they prospectively overrule a clear precedent.[3]

A sixth point is a further consequence of this. If judges were in effect legislating, it would be appropriate for them to do so in the light of considerations of policy—in particular, of utility or the general welfare of the community or the known will of the majority of the people. But if they are not legislating but still discovering an already existing law, they must confine themselves to considerations of principle; if they let policy outweigh principle, they will be sacrificing someone's rights in order to benefit or satisfy others, and this is unjust. There is, however, an exception to this point. It holds uniformly in civil cases, Professor Dworkin says, but only asymmetrically in criminal cases. The accused may have a right to be acquitted, but the prosecution never has a right to a conviction. So a court may sometimes justly acquit, for reasons of policy, someone who is in fact guilty (*TRS*, pp. 82–100).

Seventhly, Professor Dworkin rejects the traditional positivist separation of law from morality. However, this is a tricky issue. The legal positivism he has explicitly taken as his main target is that of Professor Hart, and Professor Hart recognizes many ways in which law and morality are closely linked. For example, he says, 'In some systems, as in the United States, the ultimate criteria of legal validity explicitly incorporate principles of justice or substantive moral values ...' '... statutes may be a mere legal shell and demand by their express terms to be filled out with the aid of moral principles; the range of enforceable contracts may be limited by reference to conceptions of morality and fairness ...' and 'Judicial decision, especially on matters of high constitutional import, often involves a choice between moral values....' But one point on which Professor Hart stands firm is that we can sometimes say, 'This is law but too iniquitous to obey or apply', rather than, 'Because this is iniquitous it is not law'. He argues (against supporters of natural law) that it is both more clear-headed and morally better to allow that something can be valid law and yet evil.[4] It is not clear to me whether Professor Dworkin would deny

---

[3] *TRS*, pp. 82–4. Professor Dworkin gave this clarification in reply to a question from Professor Sir Rupert Cross at a seminar on Hard Cases in Oxford, 12 May 1976.

[4] H.L.A.Hart, *The Concept of Law* (Oxford, 1961), pp. 181–207, esp. 199–200 and 205–7.

this. But he makes the following important point. The task which he assigns to Hercules in 'Hard Cases' is to find the theory that best explains and justifies the settled law, and to use this theory to decide otherwise unsettled issues. He construes the phrase 'best explains and justifies' as including a moral dimension; Hercules has to find the morally best justification of the constitution, statutes, practices, and so on which are not in dispute. In doing this, Hercules must himself make substantive moral judgements, and not merely take account of conventional morality, of widely accepted social rules (*TRS*, pp. 123–8; cf. pp. 206–22).

This third theory of law combines descriptive with prescriptive elements. On the one hand, Professor Dworkin is claiming that it gives the best theoretical understanding of legal procedures and legal reasoning actually at work in such systems as those of England and the United States. But on the other, he wants it to be more explicitly accepted and more consciously followed. He wants it to become a truer description than it yet is, whereas some views that might count as interpretations of the positivist model—for example, the 'strict constructionist' view favoured by ex-President Nixon—would, he thinks, have deplorable results (*TRS*, pp. 131–49).

It follows that discussion of this theory must also be on more than one level. We are concerned with both its truth as a description and its merit as a recommendation. Let us consider it first as a description. Professor Dworkin argues that courts do, in fact, appeal to principles as distinct from rules and that no coherent description of their procedures can be given by a theory which recognizes only rules as constituting the law. This must, I think, be conceded. But he further maintains that the way in which judges reason in hard cases is some approximation to that which he ascribes to his superhuman judge, Hercules; and such a view is much more controversial. Along with other aspects of his descriptive theory it needs to be checked empirically and in detail. But some general preliminary comments can be made.

First, there is a distinction—and there may be a divergence—between what judges say they are doing, what they think they are doing, and the most accurate objective description of what they actually are doing. They may say and even believe that they are discovering and applying an already existing law, they may be following procedures which assume this as their aim, and yet they may in fact be making new law. Such a divergence is not even improbable, because even where new law is being made, it will seem fairer if this fact is concealed and the decision is believed to enforce only presently existing rights; and because the making of new law will usually mean only that existing rules or principles are extended somewhat beyond their previous field of application.

Secondly, even though legal reasoning in hard cases involves appeals to principles and rights and is affected by 'the 'gravitational force of precedents', it does not follow that it does or must or even should work in terms of a complete theory of the underlying law for the jurisdiction in question. The superhuman Hercules is, as his name indicates, a mythical figure, and human judges will always operate in a more limited way. However, the practical force of Professor Dworkin's account is that it allows and encourages judges to bring to bear upon a controversial case general considerations and notions about rights which are supported by elements in the settled law that are remote from the case in hand. We may or may not want this; but I would stress that this holistic treatment of the law is in no way required by the admission that legal reasoning appeals to principles as well as to rules. That admission allows such remote control, but does not require it.

Thirdly, though legal reasoning in hard cases refers to rights, this does not entail that it can take no account of interests. Admittedly, to take rights seriously is to see them as having some resistance to interests; in particular, it is to recognize that the rights of an individual will often justify a decision in his favour which is against the interests of the community as a whole. However, Professor Dworkin himself does not regard all rights as absolute, but admits that they may sometimes be overruled by community interest. And when rights conflict with one another, interests may help to determine which right is the stronger in the particular circumstances.

There is no doubt that judges sometimes argue in this way, as in *Miller* v. *Jackson and Another*, heard in the British Court of Appeal—reported in *The Times*, 7 April 1977. The plaintiff lived in a house built in 1972 near a village cricket ground which had been used for over seventy years. He sought an injunction to prevent the club members from playing cricket unless they took adequate steps to prevent stray balls from hitting his house and garden. There is a conflict of rights here: *prima facie* the club has a right to go on playing cricket and the plaintiff has a right to enjoy his home and garden in safety. The court refused, by two to one, to grant the injunction. The judges on the majority side spoke of the public interest and also stressed that the injunction sought was a discretionary remedy. Lord Denning said that the public interest lay in protecting the environment by preserving playing fields in the face of mounting development and enabling our youth to enjoy the benefits of outdoor games, in contrast to the private interest, which lay in securing the privacy of a home and garden without intrusion or interference. Lord Justice Cumming-Bruce said that in considering whether to exercise a judicial discretion to grant an injunction the court was under a duty to consider the interests of the public. That is, they seemed to think that while each party had a *prima facie* right, when these rights came into conflict the importance of the public interest made the cricket club's right the stronger. Professor Dworkin may deplore such reasoning, but he can hardly deny that it occurs, nor can he argue that it should not occur merely because in a hard case there are appeals to principles and rights.

Fourthly, it would be a mere fallacy (which I want to guard against, but do not accuse Professor Dworkin of committing) to argue from the premiss that hard cases should be reasoned (partly) in terms of rights—including *prima facie*, non-absolute rights—to the conclusion that in such a case one party must have a (final or resultant) right to a decision in his favour.

Fifthly, there is a weakness in the argument that an exactly equal balance between the considerations on either side is so unlikely that it is almost certain that one party will have an antecedent right to win (*TRS*, pp. 286-7). This argument assumes too simple a metric for the strength of considerations, that such strengths are always commensurable on a linear scale, so that the strength of the case for one side must be either greater than that of the case for the other side, or less, or else they must be equal in the sense of being so finely balanced that even the slightest additional force on either side would make it the stronger. But in fact considerations may be imperfectly commensurable, so that neither of the opposing cases is stronger than the other, and yet they are not finely balanced. Consider the analogous question about three brothers: Is Peter more like James than he is like John? There may be an objectively right and determinable answer to this question, but again there may not. It may be that the only correct reply is that Peter is more

like James in some ways and more like John in others, and that
there is no objective reason for putting more weight on the former
points of resemblance than on the latter or vice versa. While we
might say that Peter's likeness to James is equal to his likeness to
John (because neither is determinately the greater), this does not
mean that any slight additional resemblance to either would decide
the issue; hence, it does not mean that this equality expresses an
improbably exact balance.

Sixthly, we must note an implication of Professor Dworkin's inclusion of a moral dimension in the reasoning he assigns to Hercules. Hercules' judgement about what the law is on some sepcific
issue depends on what he finds to be the best explanatory and
justificatory theory of the settled law. So what the law is, on Professor Dworkin's view, may crucially depend on what is morally
best—what is best, not what is conventionally regarded as best in
that society. Now I would argue, though I cannot do so here, that
moral judgements of this kind have an irreducibly subjective element.[5] If so, then Professor Dworkin's theory automatically injects
a corresponding subjectivity into statements about what the law is.
Of course, Professor Dworkin is right in arguing that the moral
judgements people make—and this may also be true for those that
Hercules can be presumed to make—are not, in general, reports of
socially established rules or even such reports conjoined with the
speaker's acceptance or endorsement of those rules (*TRS* 45–58).
Moral judgements typically include what I call a claim to objectivity and to the objectivity precisely of their prescriptive authority.
But these claims, I maintain, are always false. Prescriptive moral
judgements are really subjective, though those who make them
commonly think that they are objectively valid and mean them to
be objectively valid. Suppose Hercules and another judge in the
same jurisdiction, both following Professor Dworkin's methods,
reach different conclusions about what the law on some issue is
because each has reasoned coherently in the light of his own moral
views. Though each of them will sincerely and consistently believe
that the law already is as he determines it, I maintain that they will
both be wrong. The grounds on which they rely fail to determine
an objective pre-existing law. Whichever judge's opinion wins the
day in the final court of appeal will become the law and will then

---

[5] I have argued for this view in Chapter 1 of my *Ethics, Inventing Right and
Wrong* (Harmondsworth, 1977).

be the law. The judges who finally decide the case will have been legislating, though they will sincerely, consistently, and rationally believe that they have not. By making a choice determined by their subjective moral judgements for which they honestly but mistakenly claim objective validity, they will have been making law on an issue on which there was previously no determinate law, on which they had no antecedent duty to decide one way rather than the other, and on which neither party had a right to a decision in his favour.

These six general points cast doubt on some parts of Professor Dworkin's descriptive theory, but they should be tested along with the theory, against actual examples of hard cases. I now want to leave the question of description and consider the merits of the third theory as a recommendation. I can do this best by going straight to a concrete example, taken from the legal history of the United States. Professor Dworkin, in a review of Robert M. Cover's book *Justice Accused*, applies his theory to cases which arose before the American Civil War under the Fugitive Slave Acts.[6]

He finds it puzzling that such judges as Joseph Story and Lemuel Shaw, though themselves strongly opposed to slavery, enforced these Acts, sending alleged runaway slaves back from states in which slavery was not permitted to states where it still existed and from which they were alleged to have escaped. But why is there a puzzle? Were these judges not, as they themselves said, simply doing their legal duty of enforcing what was then the law of the land, despite the fact that it conflicted with their own moral views? Professor Dworkin argues that it is not so simple. The relevant law was not settled: these cases were controversial. Though the judges in question explicitly denied this, in their deeper thinking they admitted it. But then, being legal positivists, they concluded that they had to legislate, to make new law by their findings. But why, then, did they not make the law in accordance with their moral convictions and their sense of justice? Because, says Professor Dworkin, following Cover, they saw themselves as subordinate legislators only, bound to make the law in harmony with the discoverable intentions of the superior legislators in Congress and, earlier, in the Constitutional Convention. These legislators had, in their several enactments, created and maintained a compromise between the slave states and the non-slave states; therefore, sending

6 *The Times Literary Supplement*, 5 December 1975.

an alleged slave back to the state from which he had come was the natural fulfilment of that compromise.

According to Professor Dworkin, the reasoning of these judges was a 'failure of jurisprudence'. If they had been adherents, not of positivism, but of the third theory, they could have found in the general structure of the American Constitution 'a conception of individual freedom antagonistic to slavery, a conception of procedural justice that condemned the procedures established by the Fugitive Slave Acts, and a conception of federalism inconsistent with the idea that the State of Massachusetts had no power to supervise the capture of men and women within its territory'. These principles were 'more central to the law than were the particular and transitory policies of the slavery compromise'.

It is not in dispute that if these judges had been adherents of the natural law doctrine—as evidently they were not—they might have refused to enforce the Fugitive Slave Acts. Then the judges would have held that even if the Acts were settled law in the sense of being unambiguous and regularly enacted statutes, they were not genuine law because they violated principles of justice and natural right which were prior to any man-made system of law. The problem is whether the third theory would have yielded the same result.

First, was the law really not settled? Professor Dworkin says that the (federal) Fugitive Slave Acts 'left open many questions of procedure, particularly about the power of the free states themselves to impose restrictions on the process in the interests of the alleged slave'. And Massachusetts had enacted such restrictions. However, the judges held that these restrictions were overruled by the federal laws, and this seems to follow from a straightforward interpretation of Article VI of the United States Constitution: 'This Constitution, and the laws of the United States which shall be made in pursuance thereof,... shall be the supreme law of the land; and the judges in every State shall be bound thereby, anything in the constitution or laws of any State notwithstanding.' Professor Dworkin refers also to 'narrowly legalistic and verbal arguments' on behalf of the alleged slaves, but arguments of that description, too easily produced, will not show that the law was not, for all that, settled. The only ground on which he can claim, in a way that is even initially plausible, that the law was not settled, is that the procedures laid down in these Acts 'offended ordinary notions of due process'. The federal official who returned the alleged slave to his purported master was 'a mere commissioner who received a higher fee if the alleged slave was sent back than if he was not, there was no question of a jury trial, and the defendant was not allowed to contest whether he was in fact a slave, that issue being left to be decided in the slave state after his return'.

But it is far from clear that these provisions offend against due process. They would be defended on the ground that these proceedings were only preliminary: the legal issue about the fugitive's status was still to be decided in the state from which he had come, and that, surely, was where witnesses to his identity and status would be available. He was not being deprived of liberty without due process of law; the due process would take place in, say, Virginia. This argument could be rebutted only by casting doubt on the legal respectability of the Virginia courts, and whatever private doubts the Massachusetts judges may have had about this, it was an essential part of the federal compromise that they should not be guided by such doubts in their legal decisions. Article IV, Section I, of the Constitution says that 'full faith and credit shall be given in each State to the public acts, records, and judicial proceedings of any other State'. The Virginian slave-owner could have argued that if he were not allowed to get his slave back without bringing a large number of witnesses five hundred miles so as to have his claim heard before a Massachusetts jury which was likely to be hostile to the very institution of slavery on which his claim was based, he would be, in effect, being deprived of his property, namely the slave, without due process of law. Article IV, Section 2, of the Constitution is quite explicit: 'No person held to service or labor in one State, under the laws thereof, escaping into another, shall, in consequence of any law or regulation therein, be discharged from such service or labor, but shall be delivered up on claim of the party to whom such service or labour may be due.'

That, in the face of all this, Professor Dworkin can hold that the law was not settled brings out an important characteristic of his theory, highly relevant to the assessment of its merits as a recommendation: the third theory often takes as unsettled issues which on a legal positivist view belong clearly to the realm of settled law.

But suppose that the law was not settled, and that a judge at the time had tried to decide these cases by Professor Dworkin's method. What conclusion would he have reached? Hercules, being a product of Professor Dworkin's imagination, would no doubt have argued as Professor Dworkin does. But let us invent another mythical judge, say Rhadamanthus.[7] He might have argued as follows:

What principles that are relevant to this case are implicit in the settled law? The fundamental fact is the Union itself, which arose out of an alliance, against Britain, of thirteen separate and very different colonies. It was recognized from the start that these colonies, and the states which they have become, have diverse institutions and ways of life. The Union exists and can survive only through compromises on issues where these differing institutions and ways of life come into conflict. One salient principle, then, enshrined as clearly as anything could be in the federal Constitution and in various statutes, is that the rights which individuals have by virtue of the institutions of the states in which they live are to be protected throughout the Union. A Virginian slave-owner's property in his slaves is one of these rights; the clear intention of Article IV, Section 2, of the Constitution and of the Fugitive Slave Acts is to protect this right. Therefore, whatever merely technical defects may be found in them the law of the land, as determined by the third theory of law which I hold, is that the alleged slave should be returned from Massachusetts to Virginia, where it can be properly decided, by the evidence of many witnesses, whether he is in fact the slave of the man who claims him.

The contrary view, that the Constitution presupposes a conception of freedom antagonistic to slavery, cannot be upheld. Jefferson, who actually wrote the Declaration of Independence, and who later was mainly responsible for the amendments which most strongly assert individual rights, was himself a slave-owner. The individual freedom which the Constitution presupposes was never intended to apply to slaves. Nor will the requirements of procedural justice, which can indeed be seen as principles enshrined in the settled law, support a finding in favour of the alleged slave. On the presumption that slave-owners have legally valid property rights in their slaves, procedural justice will best be secured by

---

[7] Cf. Plato, *The Apology of Socrates* 40ᶜ-41ᵃ: 'Would it be such a bad journey if one arrived in Hades, having got rid of the self-styled judges here, and found the true judges who are said to have jurisdiction there, Minos and Rhadamanthus and Aeacus and Triptolemus and such other demigods as were just during their lives?'

sending the alleged slave back. The conception of federalism does no doubt give the state of Massachusetts the power to supervise the capture of men and women in its territory, but this power must be exercised in ways that respect the institutions of Virginia and the rights of citizens of Virginia, especially as these are further protected by federal law.

Even if Joseph Story and Lemuel Shaw had shared Professor Dworkin's theory of jurisprudence, they might still have followed Rhadamanthus rather than Hercules and, without for a moment abandoning their reliance on principles or their concern for rights, might have reached just those decisions they did reach by a more positivistic route. This brings out a second characteristic of the third theory, highly relevant to the assessment of its merits as a recommendation: the rights thesis, like the natural law doctrine that it in some ways resembles, is a two-edged weapon. It is particularly risky for an opponent of slavery and of racial discrimination to appeal to states' rights within a federal system. The special importance which Professor Dworkin, in his essays on applied jurisprudence (*TRS*, pp. 206–58), gives to the right to equality is not a necessary consequence of the rights thesis as such.

A third important characteristic of Professor Dworkin's theory is that its adoption would tend to make the law not only less certain but also less determinate than it would be on the rival positivist view. Of course, it is never completely determinate. Reasonable judges may well disagree on hard cases, whatever theory of jurisprudence they hold. But the third theory introduces a further source of indeterminacy. It is well known that the inference from a precedent to a general rule supposed to be implicit in it is not watertight; but a much larger degree of freedom is introduced if the judge has to frame hypotheses, not merely about rules which apply directly to cases, but also about far more general and abstract principles of justice and their implications.

Professor Dworkin would deny this. He would say that it is legal positivism that would make the law in hard cases indeterminate, since it envisages situations in which the law as a whole, not merely the settled law, has run out. Judges are then called upon to legislate, bringing in considerations of policy as well as morality, and it tells judges that they thus have discretion in the strong sense. His theory, on the other hand, holds that there is on every issue a determinate and, in principle, discoverable, though perhaps not settled or certain, law.

This is why I am tempted to speak of Professor Dworkin playing fast and loose with the law.[8] The alleged determinacy of the law in hard cases is a myth, and the practical effect of the acceptance of this myth would be to give, in three ways, a larger scope for what is in reality judicial legislation. First, it would shift the boundary between the settled and the unsettled law, it would make what on another view would be easy cases into hard ones. Secondly, this approach would encourage a holistic treatment of the law, letting very general principles and remote parts of the law bear upon each specific issue. Thirdly, it would encourage judges, in this holistic treatment, to rely upon their necessarily subjective views about a supposedly objective morality.

The third theory of law is thus a plea for a more speculative and enterprising handling by judges of their traditional materials and data. Like the natural law doctrine, this theory allows the consciences and the speculations of judges to intervene more significantly between what the legislative and executive branches try to do—or, for whatever reason, leave undone—and the law as it actually operates. We know well that people's prejudices, training, and social position—the movements in which they are caught up and the ideologies linked with these—strongly influence their consciences and their speculations. Whether we consider this a merit or a demerit depends upon our judgement of the judges, and particularly upon comparative judgements we make between them, the legislators, and the holders of executive office. Which of these three, with their characteristic methods and the influences to which they are exposed or from which they are sheltered, are the more to be trusted with the opportunity for partly independent decision in the making and remaking of the law? Should we give up some certainty and determinacy about what the law is, and some freedom for legislators to decide what it shall be, in order to give greater weight to what judges will see as people's rights or just claims? I do not know what answer to give, but I want it to be clear that this is the choice.

---

[8] Cf. *Oxford English Dictionary:* 'Fast and loose: A cheating game played with a stick and a belt or string, so arranged that a spectator would think he could make the latter fast by placing a stick through its intricate folds, whereas the operator could detach it at once.'

XI

BOOTSTRAPS ENTERPRISES

I NEUTRALITY

There was some obscurity about the ways in which external and internal scepticism were said to be related to neutrality. Let us take an example. A says that lions are more handsome than tigers, and therefore aesthetically superior to them. B says the opposite, that tigers are more handsome than lions. C says that there are aesthetic truths about some matters, e.g. paintings, but that the looks of lions and tigers are outside this area, so he is neutral as between the views of A and B—he rejects them both. D is a global internal sceptic about aesthetics. He says, perhaps, that if there had been a convergence in the reactions of people (in certain controlled conditions) this would have been evidence for aesthetic merits and demerits, but there is no such convergence and equally no other appropriate evidence, and concludes that nothing has any aesthetic merit or demerit. E is an external sceptic who says that the whole

'Bootstraps Enterprises' was written in reply to a paper of Professor Dworkin's and read to the same group that is referred to in the footnotes to Chapters XVII and XVIII. It is included in this collection because, although only the second half of an exchange, it is the only record that we have of any direct confrontation between Mackie and Dworkin on the basic issue of subjectivism versus objectivism in ethics (see Mackie's reference on p. 138 in the preceding chapter).

Of the paper read by Professor Dworkin no summary or account is available, but its content is readily inferred from 'Bootstraps Enterprises' itself taken in conjunction with pages 73-84 of Dworkin's own 'No Right Answer?' in *Law, Morality, and Society*, edited by P.M.S. Hacker and J. Raz (Oxford, 1977) or pages 19-32 of the revised and expanded version of this essay in the *New York University Law Review*, Vol. 53, No. 1 (1978)—or simply with the summary of the argument from 'No Right Answer?' that is provided in pages 331-5 of the revised edition of *Taking Rights Seriously* (London, 1978).

'Bootstraps Enterprises' has not been published previously. Mackie preserved the original (manuscript) draft which he read to the group and from which he subsequently made a typescript dated 6 June 1980, adding one or two sentences but otherwise making only minor changes here and there in the wording. It is, of course, this final version that is printed here, but for the sake of clarity the past tense used in the manuscript to refer to the previous meeting has been restored in the opening sentence (where in the typescript Mackie had substituted the present tense). No other alterations have been made to the author's typescript.

aesthetic enterprise is mistaken; let us assume that his reason is the crude one that aesthetics is a bootstraps enterprise, so that no aesthetic questions are effectively decidable. Now the thesis of the neutrality of external scepticism *might* be taken as meaning that the external sceptic has to be neutral (for example) between the views of A and B, but this would push E into agreement with C, that is, into adopting a specific judgement within the enterprise. Alternatively, it might be taken as meaning that E has to be neutral between all judgements within the enterprise, in that he rejects them all equally. Thirdly, it might be taken as meaning that external scepticism has no bearing on the choice between judgements within the enterprise, so that E is free to agree with A or with B or with C. Dworkin thinks that those who put forward the neutrality thesis (about second vis-à-vis first order judgements) will try to defend this third interpretation, but he argues against the thesis with that interpretation, on the ground that E cannot agree with A or B (and in that sense is neutral between them) but must agree with C: he (E) must say that lions are not more handsome than tigers, nor tigers more handsome than lions, and that they are not equally handsome either.

Now it is true that E must say this, and to that extent must agree with C. But he is still disagreeing with C on a related issue. C says that there is a genuine relation (with actual instances) *aesthetically superior to* (and perhaps *more handsome than*), but it just doesn't have the great cats within its domain. D, too, says that there is a genuine relation *aesthetically superior to* in that this relation would supervene upon some possible ordinary facts, but that this relation has no actual instances because what it would supervene upon is never realized. E, I take it, disagrees with D in that he denies that there are any principles of supervenience such as the one to which D is pointing. D would say that there are aesthetic truths in some possible worlds, though not in the actual world, whereas E (as identified above) would say that there are no aesthetic truths in any possible world, if it is a defining characteristic of aesthetic truths that they should be the objects of a bootstraps enterprise. But E as identified above is not the only conceivable kind of external sceptic. Another would be F, whose views about aesthetics were like mine about morals. F would say that the objects of a bootstraps enterprise are not automatically incoherent, so that there are presumably some possible worlds in which they occur, but that these worlds are more remote from the actual world than are the ones in which, on D's view, aesthetic relations are realized, since they do not even have principles of supervenience in common with the actual world.

Can what I say here about E be reconciled with what I say in my book (p. 16)† about the complete independence of first and second order views? Yes, because the first order views referred to there were conceived more widely than the views internal to a bootstraps enterprise as considered here. The first order moral views with which any second order view is compatible are identified simply as approval of and support for certain things and condemnation of others. A similar relaxed interpretation of aesthetic views—as not necessarily the objects of a bootstraps enterprise—would allow the external sceptic to be neutral in the third of the senses distinguished above between aesthetic views. Thus E could say this:

> Though the whole aesthetic enterprise, with its bootstraps character and its pretence of discovering aesthetic facts of the matter, is mistaken, yet there are aesthetic sentiments, and I myself have some, and in fact I like tigers (to look at) much more than lions, so much so that I can't stand people who prefer lions to tigers. So there is a sense in which I agree with B about first order aesthetic judgements, though I disagree with him about their status. Also, it happens that there are other external sceptics who like lions more than tigers to look at, and others again who prefer Rubens to Picasso but who don't care aesthetically one way or the other about lions and tigers. That is, there is a sense in which other external sceptics agree with A and others again with C in their first order judgements. But of course their view of what they are doing in making these first order judgements is different from the view of these that A, B, C, and even D all share with one another.

2   EXTERNAL AND GLOBAL INTERNAL SCEPTICISM

The example in 1 shows how E can (and must) agree with C about the non-application of the bootstraps enterprise of aesthetics to the

† *Ethics, Inventing Right and Wrong.*

great cats, without thereby becoming a participant in that enterprise. He is also agreeing with D about this, but not thereby collapsing into global internal scepticism. It is true that it is difficult to construct plausibly distinct external and global internal sceptical positions, but this is because it is so hard to find a plausible global internal view. However, I think the one ascribed to D in 1 does fill the bill, though in order to keep it internal D has to say that the convergence is only evidence for aesthetic truths, not constitutive of them. But then, Dworkin may object, E must also say this, at least if he uses the argument from relativity in the way that the first year law students do. In reply, I would say that if E is (or the law students are) really externally sceptical, he is (or they are) using the notion of evidence in a different way from D. D has either accepted some principles of supervenience or at least assumed that there are some principles of supervenience and that convergence would reveal people's mastery of them. But E is saying that there are no such principles; he merely concedes that if there had been convergence he would have admitted that there was a *prima facie* case for thinking that there are some principles of supervenience, though he would then have fallen back on other arguments against this view. But it would not be surprising to find that the first year law students are muddled and hold incoherent mixtures of the views of D and E, perhaps also with an admixture of the view that agreement in opinion or attitude would actually constitute truth in whatever the field in question was—which would presumably make it not a bootstraps enterprise.

3   REALISM, SCIENCE, AND LITERARY EXTENSION

Science (in a broad sense) and literary extension are both bootstraps enterprises. Why, then, am I a realist about the one but not the other? I am a realist about science in the broad sense because its job is to discover what is the case (Die Welt ist alles, was der Fall ist) and it seems incoherent to be universally sceptical about this, to say that nothing at all is the case (just as it seems incoherent to be universally relativist about this, to say that things are thus and so only relatively to such and such, and that that they are thus and so relatively is itself so only relatively to something else, and so on for ever). But there is no such threat of incoherence in any local scepticism (or any partial relativism), so that scepticism about literary extension is at least an option. But there are also positive reasons of two sorts for such scepticism. First, any statement of the surface form 'Hamlet (or his mother, or Claudius, or Ophelia, or Laertes, etc.) did x' must be shorthand for something like 'It is part of the story of Shakespeare's play *Hamlet* that the character Hamlet (etc.) in it did x'. With any such interpretation, there are many things that Hamlet certainly did—e.g., he thought he saw his father's ghost—for they are explicitly revealed in the text. But other things are problematic—e.g., did his father's ghost really come and speak to him? This is problematic, because even though the text says 'Enter ghost' and assigns speeches to the ghost, it is still disputable whether it is part of the story that the ghost really comes in and speaks. Now we cannot argue that because this is problematic there is no right answer. But the logic of the interpretation offered above for statements of the form 'Hamlet (etc.) did x' has the consequence that there can be well-formed and meaningful questions of the form 'Did Hamlet (etc.) do x?' which have no right answer, and corresponding statements that are neither true nor false, whereas simple questions about what is the case, which don't require expansion into any sort of *oratio obliqua*, must have a right answer. Thus the logical form of the only sensible interpretation of statements about what Hamlet (etc.) did positively invites scepticism about some well-formed and meaningful questions in this area; and this interpretation is part (or the whole) of what Dworkin calls the thin conceptual analysis that identifies the enterprise of literary extension. But, secondly, my formula *It is part of the story of Shakespeare's play* was (deliberately and for good reason) loose. It had to be vague enough to accommodate the conflicting more specific interpretations of rival schools of literary criticism, and the disputes between them about *thick* conceptual analysis. This is what makes it a bootstraps enterprise. We not only have to decide whether it is part of the story that the ghost really appeared; we also have to decide what it is for something to be part of the story. Are things part of the story if and only if they are explicitly stated in the text? Or either explicitly stated or entailed by what is explicitly stated? Or if and only if they were intended by Shakespeare to be part of the story? Or if the postulation of them makes the best psychological sense of all that is explicitly stated? Or perhaps of *most* of what is explicitly stated, leaving it open to us to cancel even some things that are explicitly stated? Or if the postulation of them makes the best aesthetic whole out of all or most of what is explicitly stated? And so on. Different answers to these questions may well lead to different answers to the primary question 'Did the ghost really appear and speak?', or may leave it problematic or even with no right answer. Though it is explicitly stated in the text that a ghost comes in and claims to be Hamlet's father's spirit, perhaps Shakespeare did not intend this to be taken literally. The best psychological sense might be made by taking all this as imagined by Hamlet. If so, the further question whether Claudius really did murder his brother may have no right answer: the play makes equally good psychological sense either way. And so on. But if it is asked 'What is the *right* interpretation of the question whether something is *part of the story of Shakespeare's play*?' I see no reason at all why there should be a right answer to *this* question, that is, why there should be a correct interpretation of the task of literary extension. If literary critics think there is, and argue about it—as no doubt they do—this shows only, and unsurprisingly, that they can be confused and can talk at cross purposes. It may be suggested that the correct interpretation of this task will be whatever would contribute most to aesthetic judgement about *Hamlet* and the like. This might shift the issue of scepticism from the field of literary extension to that of aesthetics. But in fact we need not pursue it thither. For even if the aesthetic question has a right answer, there is no reason why this should determine what the task of literary extension is to be.

Thus when we look directly at the enterprise of literary extension we can see both that the logic of its question leaves room for, or rather positively invites, partial scepticism and that the interpretation of the task is itself indeterminate in such a way that there is no reason to suppose that there is a correct interpretation of it. The point is not just that it would be a bootstraps enterprise, but rather that there is no reason to suppose that the enterprise as a whole, as identified only by the thin conceptual analysis, should be the *discovery* of something rather than include an ineliminable element of choice. But the denial of discovery here is quite compatible with the admission that once an interpretation of the task has been chosen—say, that of making the best psychological sense of most of what is explicitly stated—then some questions of the form 'Did Hamlet (etc.) do x?' will have right answers, though these may not be effectively decidable, while other questions of this form, though meaningful, will have no right answers.

How should the doctrine presented here be classified with respect to internal and external scepticism? It is external scepticism about the supposedly determinate and unitary bootstraps enterprise of literary extension. This external scepticism is based on the ground that the enterprise, identified by the thin conceptual analysis, is radically indeterminate, and that there is no reason here, as there is in the case of science in the broad sense, to assume that something must be the case. It also includes partial internal scepticism about any particular chosen form of the enterprise. This internal scepticism is based on the logical form of the question that defines the enterprise, given by the thin analysis and therefore applicable to all particular forms of it. But such a particular form is no longer a bootstraps enterprise. And, finally, there is no incoherence in the doctrine's inclusion of these distinct external and internal scepticisms. Neither collapses into the other, and internal scepticism is not the only game in town.

*

All of this can be translated so as to apply to law considered as a bootstraps enterprise. This is left as an exercise for the student.

XII

CO-OPERATION, COMPETITION, AND MORAL PHILOSOPHY

IT may be thought that the topics discussed in the earlier chapters in this book have no bearing at all on ethics. Ethics, it may be said, is autonomous; there is no way of arguing validly from 'is' to 'ought', from any truths or plausible hypotheses about the 'natural' facts to any moral prescriptions or judgements of value. However, this would be a mistake. All that Hume himself claimed is that what he calls 'reason' cannot alone, by itself, establish moral distinctions, not that it has no bearing on them at all. Although, he says, the 'final sentence' which pronounces moral judgements depends on some feeling or sentiment, much reasoning has to pave the way for that sentiment and give a proper discernment of its object; distinctions have to be made, conclusions drawn, comparisons formed, relations examined, and general facts ascertained.[1] Even actions and passions can be irrational if they are based on false beliefs, either about simple matters of fact or about causal relations.[2] Or, to approach the issue from a different side, even if some ultimate or basic ethical principles are autonomous, the derivation from them of practical moral precepts must take facts and causal relations into account.

Even someone who held, therefore, that there are objectively valid ethical principles, discoverable by some sort of intuition, some independent moral awareness or understanding, would still have to pay attention to the topics of those earlier chapters in working out the details of his moral theory. But their significance is much greater for someone who holds, as I do, that morality is a human product, that it is a system of thought and evaluation and control

Written for *Cooperation and Competition in Humans and Animals*, edited by A.M. Colman (van Nostrand Reinhold, 1982), where it appears as the penultimate chapter, following contributions by biologists and social scientists.

[1] *Enquiry concerning the Principles of Morals*, Section I.

[2] *Treatise of Human Nature*, Book II, Part III, Section iii, and Book III, Part I, Section i.

of conduct into which human feelings and desires and instincts and social interactions and reciprocal pressures enter, along with knowledge and beliefs of various sorts.[3] Sociobiology and the theories of games and of collective action are then relevant to morality in two distinct ways. On the one hand they may help to explain already-existing moralities, by outlining the contexts in which they have arisen and identifying some of the forces and mechanisms that have produced them. On the other hand they may indicate constraints on any workable moral systems, constraints which must be taken into account in any intelligent advocacy of moral principles or any worthwhile proposals for the reform of existing moral attitudes and ideas.

THE EXPLANATION OF EXISTING MORALITIES

Sociobiology is the offspring of a marriage between game theory and the Neo-Darwinian theory of evolution. Genetically determined behavioural features, including elements of social behaviour, will be favoured by evolutionary selection in so far as they help the individuals that display them to propagate the genes which determine those features, typically in situations in which those individuals are in relations of mixed competition and co-operation with other members of the same species. It is important that the key process is gene selection, not group selection: there is no general principle that features which promote the well-being or flourishing of a group will be evolutionarily favoured. Tendencies which, if they became widespread, would thus help a group may well be defeated, in competition within the group, by tendencies that are relatively harmful to the group as a whole but are more likely to enable the individuals that display them to propagate their own genes. Thus altruism directed indiscriminately towards all group members will lose out in competition with more selfish behaviour. Yet it would be almost equally wrong to speak of individual tion, since the characteristics that are favoured are not necessarily ones which help the individuals that have them to flourish: an individual's genes may be propagated best by behaviour in which that individual sacrifices itself in helping its offspring or other near relatives to survive and reproduce. In consequence it is not purely

[3] This view is defended in my *Ethics, Inventing Right and Wrong* (Harmondsworth, 1977) and *Hume's Moral Theory* (London, 1980).

egoistic behaviour that we can expect to result from evolutionary selection, but a mixture of egoism with self-referential altruism— that is, altruism directed towards individuals who are somehow related to the agent. But such altruism need not be directed only towards blood-relations: reciprocal altruism can also be favoured by evolutionary selection.[4] If, conditionally upon A's helping B in some way, B will do something that helps A to flourish and have offspring, then there will be an evolutionary pressure in favour of A's helping B—and B need not even be a member of the same species as A.

Of particular interest in relation to morality is the way in which retributive tendencies can be selectively favoured. This is most obvious for hostile retribution. Suppose that an animal is injured by another, either of the same or of a different species, where the first is able to do some harm to the second which the second can associate with its own initial aggression. The aggressor will then be discouraged from repeating the attack, so the retaliation which discourages it will tend to benefit the retaliator. More generally, where such situations constantly recur there will be two related selective pressures: among the potential victims of aggression, in favour of retaliation, and among the potential aggressors, against aggression towards retaliators. Of course there need not be any calculation or deliberate choice by either party; it is rather that the mechanism of natural selection mimics purposiveness, producing instinctive behaviours which resemble those that might well result from intelligent calculation. Thus we can understand how there could come to be instinctive spontaneous retaliatory tendencies, in much the same way as we can understand the development of reciprocal altruism and instinctive spontaneous mutual assistance. Kindly retributive tendencies—a disposition to display 'gratitude' for benefits, which is not quite the same thing as systematic mutual assistance—could in principle be developed in a corresponding way to hostile ones, but it would not be surprising if hostile retribution were in general stronger and more widespread than kindly retribution, simply because occasions in which it is likely to be beneficial will tend to occur more often. This is particularly significant in so far as morality itself can be seen as an outgrowth from retributive (especially hostile retributive) tendencies, as will be shown below. It is hostile

---

[4] R.L. Trivers, 'The Evolution of Reciprocal Altruism', *Quarterly Review of Biology*, Vol. 46 (1971), pp. 35–57.

retributive *behaviour* that is initially explained in this way; but in creatures that have a high level of consciousness there will naturally also be retributive sentiments, such as anger and resentment, accompanying and sustaining the behaviour.

A central sociobiological concept is that of an evolutionarily stable strategy. A 'strategy'—that is, a genetically determined behavioural tendency—is evolutionarily stable, relative to a certain context and to certain alternative strategies, if in that context it, rather than any of the alternatives, will be favoured by natural selection in the competition between these rival tendencies within a group of members of the same species. As was suggested above, indiscriminate altruism will not, in most contexts, be evolutionarily stable in relation to a more 'selfish' strategy. But what is thus evolutionarily stable may be a mixed strategy or a mixture of strategies rather than a single uniform strategy. Consider a situation where members of the same species repeatedly come into conflict, perhaps over food or mates or territory, and consider just the two alternative strategies of aggression and conciliation.[5] When two aggressors meet, they fight and in general both suffer a certain amount of injury, while only one of them eventually gets the item in dispute. When an aggressor meets a conciliator, the conciliator gives way without fighting and without being hurt, while the aggressor gets the goods. When two conciliators meet, they peaceably share the wanted item. Now while aggressors clearly do better against conciliators than other conciliators do, it may well be that aggressors will do less well against other aggressors than conciliators. This will be so if the damage sustained in fighting is considerable in proportion to the value of the items in dispute—both reckoned in terms of the tendency to decrease or increase the propagation of one's genes. If the average value of a fifty per cent chance of getting the item in question is less than the average disvalue of the injuries, then the average payoff to an aggressor in dispute with another aggressor will be negative, whereas the payoff to a conciliator in dispute with an aggressor is merely zero. Now if this is so, if aggressors do better against conciliators than conciliators do, while conciliators do better against aggressors than aggressors do, then neither of these two strategies on its own will be evolutionarily stable. A population consisting wholly of conci-

---

[5] This example is borrowed from R. Dawkins, *The Selfish Gene* (Oxford, 1976).

liators could be successfully invaded by aggressor genes, but equally one consisting wholly of aggressors could be successfully invaded by conciliator genes. The evolutionarily stable strategy will be some mixture of the two. The precise ratio will depend on the average values and disvalues of the various possible results: for example, if the average disvalue of the injuries sustained in fighting is equal to the average value of getting the item in dispute, the stable ratio will be equality between aggression and conciliation. But this ratio may be realized in either a mixture of strategies or a mixed strategy. That is, it may be sustained either by there being just as many pure aggressors as pure conciliators, or by each individual being disposed to be aggressive half the time and conciliatory half the time, or, indeed, by some combination of these. Of course, this is only a simple illustration; what is evolutionarily stable may well be a more complicated mixture of strategies that are themselves more complicated (for example, by including various conditionalities) than simple conciliation or aggression.

So far we have been thinking of genetically determined behaviour—instinctive, spontaneous, uncalculating. But the formal character of these developments depends solely on the fact that the genes involved are self-replicating items which cause behaviour which in turn reacts favourably or unfavourably on the frequency of their replication, but whose replication is not always perfect: some mistakes in copying—mutations—occur, and these mistaken copies can in turn produce copies of themselves. Anything with these formal features is a possible subject of evolution by natural selection. Now in human (and in some non-human) populations there can arise self-replicators of another sort, cultural traits or, as Dawkins calls them, 'memes', which include tunes, ideas, fashions, and techniques.[6] Provided that such items can reproduce themselves (fairly faithfully, but with occasional variations) by memory and imitation, and can cause behaviour which then reacts on their own propagation, they too and the behaviour they produce will be subject to evolutionary pressures which work in the same way as those that result in gene selection. Memes, no less than genes, will be selected on account of their tendency to produce behaviour that favours their own propagation—which is not necessarily behaviour beneficial either to the individuals or to the societies in which these memes take root. That some idea or belief or practice has a social

[6] Dawkins, *op. cit.*

function is neither necessary nor sufficient in itself to explain its persistence or its spreading. Its performance of a social function may be part of such an explanation, if it can be shown that its having this function helps to propagate it; but a trait which is socially neutral or harmful may also have the power to propagate itself. Just as infectious diseases can spread among the bodies of a population, harmful ideas can flourish and spread among their minds.

One sort of cultural item which both performs a social function and in so doing contributes to its own reproduction is what we can call a convention. Conventions can arise to solve problems of two sorts, of co-ordination and of partial conflict.

A problem of co-ordination arises where the interests of the parties do not diverge, but where their independent choices of action may or may not maximize the fulfilment of their interests. A typical problem of this sort occurs when each of two or more people wants to meet the other(s), but each has to decide independently where and when to go to do so. For example, in a primitive setting, people may want to meet to barter their respective products. A suitable convention might be that they should meet at the foot of a certain tall tree on the morning after each full moon. It is easy to see how such a convention establishing a regular market place and market day could grow up even without any explicit agreement. If by chance two or three people met, with significant advantage to each, at some striking and therefore memorable time and place, they would be likely to associate that success with that time and place, and so tend to return to the same place at a later corresponding time—say, after the next full moon. Once two or three started meeting regularly, others who happened to find out about it would tend to join in: the advantage of the incipient convention to each joiner would provide a force sufficient to spread and maintain it.

Less obviously, a convention can arise to solve a problem of partial conflict—say, something of the form of a prisoners' dilemma. Suppose that there are two families, of which one catches fish and the other collects edible fruit and roots. They are too much afraid of each other to meet and barter, although each would do better if they exchanged some of their products than if each consumed only its own products, and both families know this. But if each family has to decide independently what to do, each will do better by consuming all of its own products, whether or not the other family gives the first some of what it produces. Since neither family can trust the other, it looks as if no exchange can take place. But suppose that some time when the fishermen have had a good catch they say to one another: 'We might just try leaving two or three fish well in view on that rock that the fruit gatherers often pass, and see what happens.' Of course, it may not work; the fruit gatherers may just take the fish and leave nothing, and then it is likely to be some time before the experiment is repeated. On the other hand, the fruit gatherers may take the fish and leave some fruit in return, and then come back to see what the fishermen do the next day. In favourable circumstances a virtuous spiral could be set up, with each family encouraging the other, rewarding it when it repeats or increases its gifts, but reducing its own offering if the other family reduces its. With such reciprocal sanctioning, a convention of regular exchanges of produce could grow up and be maintained without any explicit bargaining or agreement, and without any prior principles of agreement-keeping or mutual trust between these parties. In fact this sort of convention maintained by reciprocal sanctioning is a more basic social relation than agreement or contract: indeed, even in a society where there is full communication the making and keeping of agreements can itself be seen as a particular example of this sort of convention. For the main motive that each party has for keeping an agreement lies in the fact that if it fails to do so it is less likely to be trusted another time. Nor need this be a consciously calculated motive: rather, the tendency to keep rather than break agreements can be automatically 'reinforced' by the rewards of honesty and the penalties for dishonesty, so that each agent develops a spontaneous inclination to keep agreements.

Situations of partial conflict, where the prior interests of the parties diverge to some extent, and yet where each will do better in terms of those prior interests if they co-operate, each making some concessions, than if each pursues his own interests directly, need not be symmetrical: one party may have an initial advantage over another. Such a situation of unequal partial conflict can still be resolved by the growth of a convention in much the same way as one of equal partial conflict, but the convention that emerges is likely to be differentially advantageous to the party that starts in the stronger bargaining position. Conventions that arise in this way and are sustained by reciprocal sanctioning will thus include 'norms of partiality' as well as 'prisoners' dilemma norms'.[7]

In speaking of 'norms' as well as of 'conventions', we are recognizing that what arise in this way are not only patterns of behaviour but also rules or principles of action which are 'internalized' by the participants. The association of moral sentiments with the practices, in particular disapproval of violations, the feeling that they are wrong or not to be done, and a sense of guilt about one's own transgressions, is a major part of such internalization. Only when this stage is reached can we speak properly of a morality, though as we have seen there can be pre-moral tendencies to behave in ways that coincide with or come close to those that are characteristically supported by moral thinking. But where does the notion of wrongness come from? We have already sketched a possible genetic explanation of hostile retribution and resentment of injuries. We have also seen how co-operation can arise and be maintained either by genetic selection or by the corresponding social evolution of a certain kind of meme, namely conventions. Putting these two together, we can understand how there can come to be co-operation in resentment, where all or most members of a group jointly react against injuries to any of them. Among human beings in particular, certain *kinds* of behaviour can be recognized and can become the objects of co-operative resentment. This may be the source of the characteristic 'disinterestedness' and 'apparent impartiality' of the moral sentiments—only apparent impartiality, since the conventions which are 'impartially' observed and enforced may themselves be norms of partiality, differentially more advantageous to some kinds of person than to others. The notion of moral wrongness includes three main elements: what is thought wrong is seen as being harmful generally (not just to this or that particular person), as being intrinsically forbidden (not merely forbidden by this or that authority, but in itself simply not to be done), and as calling for a hostile response (again not merely from a particular person: it is rather that a hostile response from *somewhere* is needed). All three of these elements can be understood in the light of the above-outlined genetic and social mechanisms, as

---

[7] The ways in which prisoners' dilemma norms, co-ordination norms, and norms of partiality arise from the corresponding problem situations are fully discussed in Edna Ullman-Margalit, *The Emergence of Norms* (Oxford, 1977).

projections of the sentiments associated with co-operative resentment and hostile retribution. And this notion of wrongness is the
central moral notion: other moral ideas fall easily into place around
it. A sense of duty, for example, is the feeling that failure to act in
such-and-such a way would be wrong in this sense.[8]

Existing moralities vary between societies and even within one
society. And even one morality will commonly recognize quite a
collection of diverse requirements—for example, such virtues as
courage, temperance, perseverance, honesty with regard to property, veracity, promise-keeping, loyalty to friends, patriotism, mar-
ital fidelity, parental devotion, chastity, modesty (in two different
senses), piety, cheerfulness, compassion, tolerance, fairness, sports-
manship, and so on. And what has to be explained is not only the
recognition of these as virtues but also the fact that people maintain
a partial, but only partial, conformity to them. The content of
moral thought and moral conduct is complex, and an adequate
explanation of morality would have to cover much more than a bit
of general benevolence and some rules about sexual behaviour. But
what I have outlined here is the beginning of such an explanation:
we can see how this sort of approach could account for the complex
reality that we actually find. We have referred both to genetic
(sociobiological) mechanisms and to sociological ones. We have
found possible sources of self-referential altruism and reciprocal
altruism, and of co-operation within groups guided and sustained
by various conventional norms, including co-ordination norms, prisoners' dilemma norms, and norms of partiality. We have traced a
possible development of retributive behaviour and retributive sentiments growing into co-operation in resentment and thence into
the central moral concept of wrongness.[9]

Is there some competition between the genetic and the cultural
accounts? If so, it can be fairly easily resolved. It will be reasonable
to ascribe to biological evolution those pre-moral tendencies to
care for children and close relatives, to enjoy the company of fellow
members of a small group, to display reciprocal altruism and both

---

[8] The view that morality is an outgrowth from the 'retributive emotions' was put
forward in E. Westermarck, *Ethical Relativity* (London, 1932). I have discussed and
developed it in 'Morality and the Retributive Emotions', to be published in a
collection on Westermarck edited by T.D. Stroup. [Now reprinted as Chapter XV
below.—Edd.]

[9] This account of the origin of morality is related to that of Hume in the *Treatise*,
Book III.

kindly and hostile retribution, which we share with many non-human animals, but to ascribe to cultural evolution the more specifically moral virtues which presuppose language and other characteristically human capacities and relations, such as honesty, veracity, promise-keeping, fairness, modesty as opposed to arrogance, and so on, as well as those detailed moral principles which vary from one society to another.

I want to guard especially against two possible misunderstandings, both of which would make my account of morality seem more egoistic than it is.

First, I would stress that none of the above-mentioned mechanisms requires calculation, let alone calculation in terms of self-interest, on the part of the agents concerned. With the 'lower' animals there is no question of motives, but simply of genetically determined behaviour, self-referentially altruistic, retributive, and so on. Even among animals, including humans, to whom we can ascribe motives, altruism, resentment, gratitude, norm-following, moral disapproval, a sense of duty, and the like have been explained as direct motives. From the agent's point of view the corresponding actions are not adopted as means to anything else. It is only that both the genetic and the convention-forming mechanisms can mimic purposiveness, can give the agents direct, spontaneous, motives which lead them to act in ways which in fact promote what we can regard as their pre-existing interests.

Secondly, even those pre-existing interests are not to be taken as being purely egoistic. At the genetic level, what we can describe, speaking behaviourally, as the selfishness of genes is not equivalent, even behaviourally, to the selfishness of individual organisms. And at the social level the pre-existing interests that create the problems of co-ordination or partial conflict, prisoners' dilemmas and the like, from which conventions may emerge, are not necessarily, and in fact will not be, exclusively egoistic. The human individuals enter into these situations already with their various direct motives of self-referential altruism (concern for children, relatives, friends, and so on as well as for themselves) and the joint purposes of already co-operating groups, as well as motives of pride, self-respect, honour, and the like. Prisoners' dilemmas, it must be emphasized, can arise whenever the parties have partly divergent purposes of whatever sort—even if, for example, both parties are aiming at the general happiness, but have different views about how it can best be promoted—and are not produced only by a clash of selfish aims.

A wide variety of moral rules and principles could be understood as having developed by the operation of mechanisms of these sorts in different concrete circumstances, and the fact that what is evolutionarily stable—either genetically or, by analogy, socially—may be a mixture of strategies could explain the coexistence within a single social group, even in a stable environment, of different norms with regard to the same sort of choice, and of different degrees of conformity to a norm. Yet despite such diversity and indeterminacy there are some significant common features of the behavioural tendencies and moral principles that might emerge in these ways.

Except where individuals sacrifice themselves for the sake of their own children or close relatives, we should not expect there to be principles of complete sacrifice of the agent; but there could be principles of joining, when others do so too, in enterprises which carry some risk of the agent's being killed or suffering some other serious harm. We should not expect there to be principles of pure altruism or pure benevolence directed unconditionally towards the well-being of a whole community, of loving all your neighbours literally as yourself; the social insects are a striking exception, but their behaviour is covered by the above-mentioned proviso, since with them all members of the hive or nest are indeed close relatives. Equally, we should not expect to find people guided by the pure abstract principle of doing as you would be done by; we can expect them to follow rather the Hobbesian variant of this, to be willing to co-operate and make concessions *when others are so too*. One is not to do to or for others whatever one *would like* them to do to or for oneself absolutely or unconditionally, but only in so far as there is or can be established such a practice in which others as well as oneself will join. That is, what we should expect to develop and flourish are norms of co-operation and reciprocation, including asymmetrical ones that reflect the unequal bargaining strengths of different kinds of participants, not norms that enjoin that each agent should do whatever is most likely to promote the general happiness. And in fact we find that the norms that really do the work of controlling people's behaviour are of the sorts that this approach would lead us to expect. People generally feel that it is wrong to kill or assault others, and usually refrain from doing so; provided that those others are not a threat to them; they respect private property and keep mutually beneficial agreements; but they do not feel obliged to decide whether each such act or forbearance is likely to do more than its opposite to promote the general happiness. In an election, though one's individual vote is almost always causally inefficacious, one takes credit for having voted for the right party if it wins the election, and one puts a 'Don't blame me ...' sticker on one's car window if it loses; that is, we feel that all those who participate in an activity deserve a share of the praise or blame for its results, even if each person's action on its own was causally irrelevant.

Or consider people's moral feelings with regard to leaving litter at beauty spots. If the place is free from litter when you arrive, there is a fairly strong moral pressure against leaving the first beer can. One does not think 'Just one can won't make a significant difference', but rather 'It wouldn't be fair for me to make a mess when other visitors have taken the trouble to leave it all so clean'. Even if there is rubbish everywhere already, one may well not say 'One more can will make no difference', but rather 'If I throw my can away, I shall share the responsibility for all this filth'.

Thus the norms that do the work include such ones as these:

Join in enterprises that promote public goods in which you will share, and play your part in them.

Join others in refraining from activities that would produce public harms from which you, along with others, would suffer.

Take a share of the credit for any good results of enterprises in which you have joined, and a share of the blame for any bad results of activities in which you have taken part, without calculating the differential effects of your participation; give credit and blame similarly to others.

Such norms as these are different from the utilitarian one:

Act so as to maximize the expected production of general good.

They are also different from the Kantian one:

Act only on a maxim which you can will to be a universal law of nature.

In short, the moral principles which we find flourishing and effective in controlling people's actions are of the sorts which we should expect to find if we assumed that morality has developed through the biological and social mechanisms outlined above; and they are significantly different from the ones recommended by some influential schools of philosophical moralists. The vital differences are that the operative principles involve concrete relations of reciprocity, co-operation, and joint practices whereas the philosophically advocated ones are more abstract or appeal to merely hypothetical considerations, and therefore build less on each agent's pre-moral motives and offer him less chance of a reward.

CONSTRAINTS ON MORAL DEVELOPMENT AND REFORM

If it is agreed that already-existing moral systems can be accounted for in these ways, we may go on to the question whether, and, if so, to what extent, these genetic and social mechanisms generate constraints on any workable and therefore rationally recommendable moral systems.

It is sometimes asked whether we can escape from our own biology. Indeed Dawkins himself, in the final chapter of *The Selfish Gene*, suggests that 'We are built as gene machines and cultured as meme machines, but we have the power to turn against our creators. We, alone on earth, can rebel against the tyranny of the selfish replicators'.[10] But this is a misleading way of putting it. We are, and will remain for the foreseeable future, what biological evolution over millions of years has made us. But on that practically unalterable basis, cultural evolution has already erected a far more complicated set of superstructures: we obviously do not behave *just* in ways that are biologically determined. The interesting question is how much freedom of movement is left for the development of still further superstructures, which will start from and yet may modify the existing culturally-determined ways of behaving and thinking, much as cultural evolution has started from and yet modified the biologically-determined patterns.

For example, we may sensibly enquire whether we could develop a morality of pure altruism or pure rational benevolence, which might replace the existing norms which prescribe more specific kinds of conduct and which are characterized, as we have seen, by reciprocity and (sometimes asymmetrical) co-operation. Such a morality would, of course, require each individual to be ready to sacrifice not only himself but also those close to him for any greater advantage to others, however remote. Such a replacement is most unlikely, for three reasons. First, this morality would frequently have to oppose strong genetically ingrained tendencies of egoism,

---

[10] *The Selfish Gene*, p. 215.

self-referential altruism, reciprocal altruism, and retribution as well as strong culturally developed traits of similar sorts. Secondly, if this kind of morality did begin to flourish among some considerable number or people, it would lay them open to exploitation, to being used by those who diverge not only from this morality but also from the traditional one of reciprocity and conditional co-operation in the direction of pure selfishness. In Dawkins's terms, the more 'suckers' there are, the more 'cheats' will flourish. Or, as Hutcheson said long ago, to do away with reciprocation and a right to the fruits of one's labour 'exposes the industrious as a constant prey to the slothful, and sets self-love against industry'.[11] Thirdly, this sort of morality suffers from a radical indeterminacy in its object. There simply are no natural and obvious ways of measuring the 'general welfare', or of eliciting a 'collective choice' or 'group preference' from the set of divergent preferences of the members of a group. Not even something as apparently neutral and uncontroversial as the Pareto principle is really acceptable in all circumstances.[12] And of course this indeterminacy provides further opportunities for exploitation, for people to represent what are really their own selfish purposes as the promotion of the elusive general welfare.

It is true that we may distinguish between a practical, working, morality which fairly directly guides or controls conduct, and a higher level, critical, moral theory in terms of which philosophers may evaluate and seek to modify the practical, working, morality. All three of our objections tell against the possibility of developing a working morality of pure altruism or general benevolence, but the first two would not tell against the philosophical use of a moral theory based on general benevolence: the points that they make are ones that our critical philosophers would properly take into account in deriving a working morality from their higher level theory. But the third objection tells even against this philosophical use of general benevolence: if there is no satisfactory way of adding up interests or eliciting a collective choice or measuring general welfare then there will be something spurious about any purported derivation of working moral principles from these concepts.

[11] Dawkins, *op. cit.;* F. Hutcheson, *An Inquiry concerning Moral Good and Evil*, in L. A. Selby-Bigge, *British Moralists* (Oxford, 1897), Vol. I, p. 165.

[12] A.K. Sen, *Collective Choice and Social Welfare* (San Francisco and Edinburgh, 1970).

There may, then, be constraints which exclude moralities of the utilitarian type. If there are, I see no reason to regret the fact. As I have argued elsewhere, a morality based on the assigning of rights to each individual would in itself be more attractive, even apart from the fact that it would fit in better with the suggested constraints of reciprocity and conditional co-operation.[13]

Another question is this: do these constraints imply that a workable morality can take account of the interests only of those who are able to compete and to co-operate, and can show no respect for non-human animals, for example, or for seriously and permanently handicapped human beings?

It is true that the mechanisms sketched so far would not in themselves generate moral sentiments in favour of such non-competitors. But they do not positively require that there should *not* be such sentiments, in the way that they do tell against a morality of pure altruism or benevolence. Hume, in referring to this problem, suggested that considerations of 'justice' would not arise between us and creatures, human or non-human, that were permanently unable to compete with us, but that 'we should be bound, by the laws of humanity, to give gentle usage to them'.[14] Hume's use of the word 'justice' to refer only to moral principles of a quasi-contractual sort may be a bit misleading; but we can understand what he meant. But how are we to explain the sentiments of 'humanity'? Surely as Hume himself did, as a product of 'sympathy' and 'imagination'. Once we have developed, in the ways already outlined, a morality that assigns rights to those other human beings who are participators in the mixture of competition and co-operation that is the ordinary and inevitable human condition, and have acquired dispositions to show some respect for their interests and to feel compassion for their sufferings, it is not difficult for us to extend these attitudes to other creatures, human or non-human, in so far as we see them as being like ourselves and like those towards whom we have already developed respect and compassion. It is true that there is no necessity about this. It is perfectly possible for people to combine the finest moral sensitivity in relation to their fellows with extreme inhumanity towards 'brute beasts' and defective human beings, or indeed to non-defective human beings whom they

---

[13] See my 'Can There Be a Right-Based Moral Theory?' in *Midwest Studies in Philosophy*, Vol. III (1978). [Now reprinted as Chapter VIII above.—Edd.]

[14] *Enquiry*, Section III, Part I.

see as in some way alien to themselves and their associates. All that I am saying is that the contrary is also possible, and is the more likely to come about the more people are imaginatively aware of the similarities between themselves and the non-participators. The constraints we have been considering do not rule out a morality that includes an element of humanity in this sense. On the other hand, they do set some limits to its influence. The kind of humanity which we can expect to be effective will fall far short of the equal concern for all sentient beings, proportionate only to their capacity for feeling pain and pleasure, which seems to be a consequence of utilitarian principles. We cannot expect such equal concern for the interests even of other fully active human beings, even those with whom the agent is acquainted. Putting it bluntly, we can expect people in general to display humanity only when they can do so at not too great a cost to themselves and to those close to them, though as I have said, they may be willing to *risk* the final sacrifice.

We have seen that where, in the mixture of competition and co-operation, there are parties with unequal bargaining power, the conventions which resolve such problems are likely to include norms of partiality, rules or principles which are differentially advantageous to what was already the stronger party. Any explanation of existing moralities would have to include such a mechanism, since nearly all actual moral systems have been of this biased sort. Duties and rights have been assigned unequally between peasants and noblemen, slaves and freemen, blacks and whites, brahmins and untouchables, citizens and non-citizens, owners and workers, party-members and non-party-members, men and women. But is this widespread and explainable feature an unavoidable constraint on any workable morality? Must any morality that actually controls human conduct merely reflect and perpetuate differences of strength that arise from other forces and relations in society? Of course there have been and are egalitarian moral *theories;* but the question is whether these can actually operate in practice.

As with our previous problem, we can see how sympathy and imagination can generate egalitarian moral sentiments; but egalitarian, like humanitarian, sentiments are likely to control people's conduct only when the cost to the agents themselves and those close to them is not too great. And, in general, the giving of more equal rights to important classes of those who are fellow participators in the mixture of competition and co-operation would cost more than the displaying of a moderate degree of humanity to non-participators. On the whole, then, we can expect norms of partiality to be replaced by norms of impartiality only in so far as the previously disadvantaged groups find non-moral sources of strength that improve their bargaining position. Otherwise egalitarian moral sentiments will either not arise at all or, if they are generated by sympathy and imagination, will remain largely at the level of theory, and not develop into a genuine working morality. This may seem to be a pessimistic conclusion; but something like it has, I believe, been reached through trial and error by many of those who have been actually engaged in campaigns for racial (etc.) equality. It is also only a generalization of the traditional Marxist thesis that capitalism cannot be reformed by the moral conversion of individual capitalists: as long as the 'relations of production' are unchanged an individual capitalist who attempts to give up exploitation is merely replaced by someone else who plays his social role more efficiently.

In raising this last problem, we have already touched upon the area where there is not only the greatest need for further developments of morality but also the greatest difficulty in devising them, that of the political applications and extensions of morality.[15] Devices for compromise and adjustment of conflicts between individuals have grown up, largely automatically but with some help from deliberate invention, over many thousands of years, and have been widely accepted into moral thinking and into various legal systems. But corresponding devices for compromise and adjustment of conflicts between politically organized groups are relatively rudimentary, and though some principles of international justice are vaguely recognized, they form as yet only a weak system of international morality. Here, I am afraid, I have no specific suggestions to offer, but only a plea that the problems should be considered, and that they should be considered in the light of the understanding of morality in general, and the constraints upon it, that we have been developing. Here, as in all human affairs, the concrete situation is inevitably one of partial conflict, of a mixture of competition and co-operation, of partly coincident and partly divergent interests, but also, and importantly, of unequal and unstable concentrations of power. We cannot reasonably hope for effective principles

---

[15] Cf. my *Ethics, Inventing Right and Wrong*, pp. 235–9 and *Hume's Moral Theory*, pp. 113–18.

of political and international morality based merely on abstract ideals. We need principles of adjustment which both allow for and are themselves sustained by the very forces which they try to control. Hume quotes from Cicero a passage which, as Hume rightly says, anticipates Hobbes's picture of the state of nature, the condition of men in the absence of laws and governments, as a state of war. It concludes:

The difference between this civilized and humane life, and that monstrous one, depends upon nothing so much as upon the difference between law (or justice, *ius*) and force (or violence, *vis*). If we are unwilling to use one of these, then we must use the other. Do we want to eliminate force? Then it is necessary that law should flourish—that is, legal proceedings (*iudicia*) in which all law is contained. Do we not want legal proceedings, or not have them? Then it is necessary that force should rule. Everyone can see this. [16]

This is, however, only part of the truth, We need not only *ius* but also *mores*, morality as well as law, and they must be in reasonable harmony with one another. Besides, we need the right sort of *ius* and the right sort of *mores* to contain the forces that would otherwise break out as *vis*. The problem is to find out what these are. The first step towards solving the problem is to see that this *is* the problem. Regrettably, not everyone has seen this, and many thinkers divert attention from it by posing questions about moral philosophy in less illuminating ways.

[16] Cicero, *Pro Sestio*, 42; quoted in Hume, *Enquiry*, Section III, Part I, note (wrongly named '*Pro Sexto*' in editions of Hume).

XIII

THE THREE STAGES OF UNIVERSALIZATION

How far, in morals, will conceptual and linguistic analysis take us? R.M. Hare, for one, has argued that it will take us a very long way, and that many unsatisfactory moral opinions can be traced largely to neglect of such analysis. My own view is more sceptical. However, I shall not attempt to deal with the whole of this question; I shall confine myself to one part of it, namely, 'What can we get out of the thesis that moral judgements are universalizable?' Even about this my argument will be rather complicated; let me start, therefore, with a very bare summary of my views. First, I stress a distinction between logical or conceptual theses and practical theses. Whatever precise meaning is given to 'universalizable', it will be a logical thesis that moral terms, concepts, and so on are such that every genuinely moral judgement is universalizable; but this will be distinct from the corresponding practical thesis, which would instruct one to act only in ways which one can prescribe to oneself in universalizable judgements. Secondly, I distinguish three stages of universalization and three corresponding degrees of universalizability, and argue that these are not only distinguishable but also coherently separable in practice in the sense that one could adhere to the first stage without the others, or to the second as well as the first without the third. Thirdly, I argue that only the third stage yields any approximation to utilitarian principles; nothing like utilitarian conclusions will follow from the first and second stages without the third. Fourthly, I argue that it is doubtful whether the logical thesis is strictly true for any one stage, let alone for all three, and in particular that the best reason for saying that the logical theses for the first and second stages hold would tell against the best argument for going on from that of the second stage to that of the third, which in any case seems, on direct inspection, to be false.

Putting these four points together, I conclude that nothing like

Previously unpublished: written 1979.

utilitarianism can be established by conceptual analysis by way of the notion of universalizability, for a number of independent reasons, namely

1   Even if moral judgements were, as a matter of conceptual analysis, universalizable in some sense, the 'amoralist' option of refusing to limit oneself to moral choices, and hence of refusing to let one's choices and conduct be constrained by such universalizability, would always be open.

2   Since all of the logical theses are doubtful, and that of the third stage seems plainly to be false, even a decision to act only in ways that could be defended as moral would not commit one to any sort of universalization, and particularly not to that of the third stage.

3   Even if one made the practical decision to act only in ways that conformed to principles which were universalizable in the second as well as in the first degree, no requirements of consistency would lead one on to third stage universalization and so to utilitarian principles of conduct.

I shall also show that the various sorts of universalization are related in a rather complex way to the issue of the objectivity or subjectivity of ethics.

Let me now fill in this sketch.

The distinction between a logical thesis and a practical one is obvious as soon as it has been stated. A practical thesis could, of course, be understood in more than one way. An ethical objectivist would say that there are some objectively valid or authoritative practical theses, whereas a subjectivist would hold that a practical thesis can express only a substantive decision to act in certain ways. It is because I adopt the subjectivist view that I hold that the 'amoralist' position is always open. But there is no disagreement between Hare and me about this.

Let me try to state more accurately than I did in *Ethics, Inventing Right and Wrong* what the three stages of universalization would involve. At the first stage, a judgement is universal if it contains only general terms, but no proper names or indexical expressions. To universalize a judgement would be to replace any such singular terms that it contains with terms containing only predicates—including relational or many-place predicates—logical constants, and

variables, and to bind the appropriate variables with universal
quantifiers. For example, the judgement 'Let Smith pay Jones £5'
would be universalized as follows. We would find some set of
general features, which we can sum up as 'S', possessed by Smith,
and some set, which we can sum up as 'J', possessed by Jones, and
also some set of relations which hold between Smith and Jones,
which we can sum up as 'R', and then say 'For all x and for all y,
if x has S and y has J and x has R to y, then let x pay £5 to y'. To
say that a judgement is universalizable will then have different
meanings according as we consider it as a purportedly objective
truth or as a statement made by a particular speaker. On the first,
objective, interpretation, a judgement will be universalizable if there
is *some* objectively true statement which is in the suggested way a
universalization of the original one. On the second, subjective, interpretation, to say that a judgement is universalizable is to say
something about the person who makes the judgement, namely
that he is willing to universalize it, that is, seriously to make *some*
judgement which is in this way a universalization of the original
one. In either case, the original judgement will of course follow
from the universalization, given the facts that make it an instance
of this, but so will many other instantiations, as a rule, so that
anyone for whom a certain judgement is universalizable is thereby
committed to many other singular judgements, and similarly if an
objectively true judgement were universalizable many other singular judgements would have to be true.

In what follows I shall neglect the objective interpretation and
speak only of the subjective one. But it will be obvious what the
corresponding results for the objective interpretation would be.

For this first stage of universalization, it is enough that the
speaker should endorse some such universal judgement with regard
to the actual world, with everything as it in fact is. For example,
the judgement 'Let *me* be given a special advantage in applications
for jobs, tax exemption, etc.' will be universalizable for me if I am
prepared to endorse the universal judgement 'Let all persons whose
initials are "J.L.M." be given these advantages ...', or any other
universal judgement assigning such advantages to all persons who
share *some* set of features which I happen to have. Consequently,
first stage universalization leaves room for all sorts of special plead-
ing. It does not rule out systematic discriminations which would be
widely recognized to be unfair, so it may be held not to have

captured the moral point of universalization. Indeed, it seems that -the universalizability requirement of this first stage is always trivially satisfied. The second stage may therefore be introduced in an attempt to remedy this defect of the first.

A judgement will be universalizable for a certain speaker in the second degree only if he is prepared to endorse some universalization of it not only with regard to the actual world but also with regard to various possible worlds. But *which* possible worlds? One suggestion is that we should take the set of possible worlds each of which is exactly like the actual world in all general respects, but in which individuals occupy different places and take on general characteristics in all logically possible combinations of ways—that is, the set of worlds which are generically identical with the actual world, though numerically different from it. Then a judgement I make will be universalizable for me if I am prepared to endorse some universalization of it for application to every possible world in which I and other individuals exchange places in any possible way, while the general description of the world remains unaltered. Now this is already a very stringent requirement; it may be difficult to find judgements that are universalizable in this sense. Since almost any practical prescription will work to the disadvantage of someone in the actual world, I may well decline to endorse any universalization of it with regard to a set of possible worlds that includes one or more in which I am the one who suffers this disadvantage. We might, therefore, think of imposing a requirement that the moral judge *must* endorse *some* universal judgement about the point at issue. Let us say that a judgement is universalizable 'under pressure' provided that the person who makes it would endorse some universalization of it with regard to all the possible worlds specified above, if he were compelled to endorse some universalization of some judgement about the case in question for all these possible worlds. A judgement is, then, universalizable under pressure if it is the practical judgement about the case in question the generalization of which, for all interchanges of individuals between places, is (one of) the least unacceptable to the judge of all such generalizations.

But should we thus confine ourselves to the set of possible worlds that are indistinguishable in general terms from the actual world? Or should we say that a judgement is universalizable—still under pressure—only if its maker is (if constrained as above) prepared to endorse some universalization of it for all possible worlds whatever? There are lots of universal judgements which we should ordinarily count as moral ones which would fail this test, which would not be endorsed for all possible worlds. For example, someone might say that children below a certain age should be obedient to their parents in all worlds that are just like the actual one in all general respects, though with individuals occupying different places, and yet not endorse this rule for possible worlds in which children below that age were already wiser than their parents, or for worlds in which parents were so envious of their children that they would often give them harmful or dangerous instructions. Yet it can be argued that underlying any moral judgement that is thus contingent upon some features of the actual world there must be some more basic universal judgement which one would endorse for all possible worlds: perhaps just one in which the previous prescription was made conditional upon whatever the relevant features were, or perhaps some more general principle from which this conditional rule would follow. Hence any genuine moral judgement would seem to pass this test, in that there would be some basic judgement of which it was an instantiation which the maker of the original judgement would endorse for all possible worlds—given, as before, that he was compelled to endorse *some* relevant universal judgement for all possible worlds.

We may, therefore, divide the second stage, calling universalization to all possible worlds which are generically identical with the actual world stage 2a, while stage 2b will be universalization to all possible worlds whatever.

Although stage 2b involves this very thoroughgoing universalization, it still leaves the person whose judgements are being tested with his own distinctive point of view, in particular with his own tastes, preferences, and values. You can still say that poetry is better than pushpin and endorse principles which will differentially encourage poetry, though you must be prepared to endorse their application to situations in which you will have no appreciation of poetry and even no contact with it, indeed in which you will be a frustrated devotee of pushpin. Or, to take the other stock example, if you happen to be a Nazi, you can say that the traits of character and culture which you find prominent in Aryans are more admirable than those which you find prominent in Semites, and endorse principles of action, for all possible worlds, which will tend to foster the former traits and wipe out the latter, even though in some possible worlds not only will you have the latter traits yourself, but, perhaps, the Semites will have all the qualities you find admirable and the Aryans will have all those which you deplore and despise. In short, at the second stage—even at stage 2b—though you are universalizing very thoroughly with respect to the range of situations *for* which you are judging, you are not yet universalizing with respect to the point of view *from* which you are judging: so far that point of view is still firmly your own. It may be thought that this is a defect, that it is a surviving egoistic element which a fully moral way of thinking would exclude. So we may consider a third stage of universalization at which this distinctive point of view is given up, so that we seek judgements which can be endorsed either from every point of view or from some consensus of points of view or perhaps without a point of view at all.

But how shall we formulate the requirement for this third stage? Might we say that a judgement is universalizable to this degree only if the person who makes it will continue (under pressure) to endorse some universalization of it while occupying in turn the point of view of every actual person? This would be equivalent to saying that the universal judgement would be endorsed by every actual person, at least if he were thoroughly well informed and were to work out its implications in full, and if he were compelled to endorse some relevant universal judgement. But it seems that no body of moral judgements precise enough to be a practical guide to action could pass this test. Different points of view just are different, and nothing worth saying can be endorsed as a prescription from all of them. But we might again have recourse to the notion of endorsing something under pressure, and ask whether the judgement would be endorsed by all persons, or by all members of a group of persons representing, between them, every point of view, if they were required to agree in endorsing some principles with regard to the issues in question. Alternatively, we might ask whether it would be endorsed from a point of view which was somehow an average of the points of view of all actual persons. These last two suggestions appear to be effectively equivalent. A further possibility is that this procedure of seeking an agreed or average point of view should be applied not merely to all actual persons but to all possible persons. To avoid the embarrassment of having to choose between these suggestions, and the apparent indeterminacy of the outcome of either of them, it might be better to say that a judgement is universalizable in the third degree only if some universalization of it would be endorsed from a point of view which is devoid of all specificity, which is, in effect, not a point of view at all. That is, to universalize a judgement in this third way is to endorse a principle of which it is an instantiation while having no tastes, no preferences, and no values. All the directive force of a moral judgement thus universalized must come from the situations *for* which one is judging—that is, if it is also universalized at stage 2a, from all the actual preferences of all actual persons taken together and weighted equally, or, if it is also universalized at stage 2b, from all the preferences of all persons in all possible worlds, again taken together and weighted equally.

These distinctions may be illustrated by drawing analogies between different stages of universalization and the corresponding attitudes of an impartial spectator. Stage 2 represents the thought of a spectator who is indeed impartially benevolent, but may still have his own ideas about what constitutes the well-being or the good or proper condition of those about whom he is judging; stage 3 represents the thought of one who is *nothing but* impartially benevolent, who has no such ideas of his own but who interprets well-being simply as all those about whom he is judging severally interpret it.

Once these distinctions have been drawn, it is surely too obvious to need any detailed argument that stage three generates some kind of utilitarianism—exactly what kind will depend on the clearing up of several indeterminacies left by the account so far given—but that universalization which stops short at the second stage (even including 2b) will not.

It also seems plausible to say that one could coherently stop short at the second stage—either at 2a or at 2b—without going on to the third, or, indeed, that one could *coherently* stop at stage 1 and not even go on to stage 2. However, this may be disputed. As we shall see, it can be argued that the three stages are not even logically distinct, and again that even if they are logically distinct there is some other kind of connection between them, that there is some general spirit of universalization which leads us inexorably from one stage to the next. Hare has, indeed, suggested an ingenious argument to show that stage 2 universalization follows automatically from stage 1. The distinction between these stages, we recall, turns upon the contrast between the actual world and various merely possible worlds. In particular, the difference between the actual world to which stage 1 applies and the possible worlds to which stage 2a applies is constituted wholly by the way in which individuals are assigned to places. But even stage 1 eliminates all essential reference to individuals; therefore a thorough stage 1 universalization will carry stage 2a, at least, with it.

Plausible though this may be, it is not correct. The logical description of stage 1 tells us only what form a universalized prescription must have; it says nothing about the range of actual or possible situations to which it is to be applied. One could perfectly well adopt a prescription which contained no singular terms, no essential reference to individuals, and yet apply it only to actual states of affairs. What one is prepared to commit oneself to with regard to merely possible states of affairs is another matter. So stage 1 does not *logically* carry stage 2a with it. But it may be replied that even if stage 2a is thus logically distinguishable, one would be violating the spirit of stage 1 universalization if one refused to go on to 2a. One's only possible reason for such a refusal would be a special attachment to some individuals—notably oneself—in contrast with others. That is true, and if the spirit of universalization is identified as complete non-regard for individuals, then it will indeed commit us at least to 2a. But the fact remains that stage 1 universalization, which fails to embody such complete non-regard, is coherently adoptable; it does not prevent one from having special attachments or from acting in response to them, it only prevents one from expressing such attachments explicitly in the form of the prescriptions one is prepared to endorse.

A similar argument might be used to assimilate stages 2a and 2b. Since the possible worlds over which we universalize in 2a are picked out as those which are generically identical with the actual world, it might seem that we could not distinguish 2a from 2b without mentioning the actual world; and 'the actual world' is either a proper name or an indexical, egocentric, description, such as even stage 1 eliminates. But again there is no such logical collapse. Although for a brief description of 2a it was convenient to mention the actual world, there is no need to use any such singular term. We could draw the distinction equally well by using some such phrase as 'as things are'. Alternatively, we could think of a stage 2a universalization as a conditional prescription, where the antecedent on which it is conditional is a general description of the actual world or some relevant features of it: this will not name or refer to the actual world as such, but merely describe it as it in fact is. However, it is easy to transform this into a 2b universalization where the antecedent is brought inside the prescription itself, and (as I have said) it is natural to suppose that where anyone endorses a prescription with such an antecedent there will be also some more fundamental and more general prescription which gives the reason for the former one, and this will be a straightforward 2b universalization which he is willing to endorse. So nothing turns upon the distinction between 2a and 2b: though the latter does not collapse into the former, the former will in practice carry the latter with it.

There is no such immediate argument to show that stage 2 carries stage 3 with it. But I shall consider later an argument which purports to show that the move to stage 3 cannot be resisted. Let me turn first, however, to the question whether each stage in turn is conceptually necessary, given our basic moral concepts, or the meanings of the central moral terms, or the typical questions which, in moral thinking, we initially seek to answer.

Not even stage 1 is thus conceptually necessary. Although we may be able to rule out as non-moral a judgement which gives some special advantage to the person who makes it, we cannot similarly rule out one which imposes a special *dis*advantage on the person who makes it. 'I must not do X' is perfectly intelligible as a moral judgement even if the judge says that it is all right for others to do X, even for others who are like him in all relevant respects—though we cannot, on pain of circularity, count the mere fact that he makes this judgement a relevant difference. Thus a self-denying judgement is recognizable as moral, but it is not universalizable even in the first degree; the judge need not say that everyone should similarly deny himself. This asymmetry is not surprising if we look primarily not for some logic of moral terms but for the social function of morality. In so far as morality is a system of conventions which enable us to cope with what are initially situations of partial conflict, there are reasons why it should not admit, as moral, judgements which specially favour their maker, but there are not similar reasons why it should not admit ones which specially disfavour him. That may be overkill, but it will not frustrate the object of the exercise.

Stage 2, particularly 2a, is related to a well known standard method of moral reasoning; one criticizes an action by making the agent consider a relevantly similar situation in which he is in the other person's place. But even 2a goes far beyond this standard form of argument, carrying it to an ideal limit in requiring that the judgement should be endorsed for all generically identical but numerically different possible worlds, and, as I have said, the demand for such sweeping endorsement can be made realistic only subject to the requirement that the moral judge must endorse *some* relevant principle in this universal way. The standard argument does not incorporate so strong a requirement, so it is not plausible to say that this degree of universalizability is actually required by the logic of moral concepts, and the same applies, *a fortiori*, to 2b. The most we can say is that this logical requirement is a development of a tendency implicit in the standard form of argument. By imposing it, we tidy up moral thinking and make it more systematic along lines that are only suggested by its actual features.

However, this tidying up or systematization would be required as a consequence of the sort of objectivity that is commonly ascribed to moral principles. If the wrongness of my doing X is an objective fact—if the judgement 'I must not do X' does not merely express a feeling or attitude or sentiment which I or others have— then it seems that this wrongness must result from some general features of the situation. Objective moral principles, it seems, could not be respecters of persons in any way at all. So the wrongness would have to hold not only for all of some class of relevantly similarly placed persons, but also for all the similarly placed persons in all the possible worlds covered in 2a. So if someone endorses a proposed rule only for the actual world, he is implicitly abandoning the claim that its validity is an objective truth. Similar considerations will support 2b; though a certain moral rule may hold only for worlds that are just like this one in certain general ways, this must be because it is a derived rule, resulting from the conjunction of some non-moral facts about how things are in the actual world with some more basic moral principle which holds for all possible worlds. If something is objectively valid morally only in the actual world, there must be some reason why it is so, and this will rest on the facts about how things are, in relation to a basic moral principle which would hold however things were.

Thus if the claim to objectivity is part of the meaning of moral terms, or is firmly incorporated into our moral concepts, then universalizability up to degree 2b will be part of their logic; but not otherwise. This gives rise to a dilemma for Hare. He denies that moral terms involve such a claim to objectivity. But this denial deprives him of the only strong reason for asserting the logical theses of the first two stages of universalization, leaving him with no more than a preference for a tidier system of thought. Also, Hare has repeatedly protested against the use of fantastic examples to criticize utilitarian moral principles. But if universalizability is defended in the suggested way, as a consequence of the claim to objectivity, then *fundamental* principles, such as the utilitarian ones are supposed to be, must be endorsable, as stage 2b requires, for all possible worlds, however unlike our own.

The third stage of universalization, however, is not supported by such a claim to objectivity. Quite the reverse. For the most natural (though not the only) way of interpreting this claim to objectivity is to take it as the view that certain specific values are objective, and this view automatically resists third stage universalization as we have described it. Though such objective values might, indeed, be perceived from every point of view, or from no point of view at all, this would not impose on the moral judge the complete neutrality which is needed to generate a utilitarian conclusion. One who holds that there are such specific values cannot be *nothing but* impartially benevolent. Nor can stage 3 be plausibly said to be implied by our ordinary moral concepts. In *Freedom and Reason* Hare seems to classify as fanatics all those who adhere to specific values; but if we adopt this way of speaking we shall have to admit that there are a great many fanatics around. There is not only the Nazi who is fanatical about the elimination of Semitic features of character and culture, but also John Stuart Mill, who is fanatical about the higher pleasures. Kant is a fanatic about retribution, and Herbert Hart is, I suspect, a fanatic about gratitude. Elizabeth Anscombe is a fanatic about contraception, apostasy, and the judicial murder of the innocent, in that she holds that these are all wrong in all circumstances, even where someone who was nothing but impartially benevolent would support them. Bernard Williams's theoretical thinking is riddled with fanaticisms (though not his practical thinking, as reflected in the recent Report on Obscenity and Pornography). Ronald Dworkin is a fanatic, in that he holds that all people have a right to equal concern and respect, and to various specific rights which can be derived from this in concrete historical circumstances, and that it is the essential nature of a right that it shows at least some resistance to utilitarian calculation. Sometimes, indeed, he recommends a kind of utilitarianism, but it is selective, like Mill's, though on other grounds. Dworkin would exclude from the calculus what he calls external preferences, but this exclusion could not be sustained from the utterly neutral standpoint of the third stage. And so on.

Hare has, it is true, a way of dealing with all such apparent counter-examples. Anyone who finds any variety of 'fanaticism' morally appealing is failing to distinguish the intuitive from the critical level of moral thinking. Many, though presumably not all, varieties of 'fanaticism' are acceptable at the intuitive level; but they cannot be carried over to the critical level, where third stage universalization and its utilitarian consequences are in force. It is involved in our developed moral concepts that they are defensible at this critical level; anyone whose thought is fixated at the intuitive level has not fully mastered these concepts, indeed he has not quite grown up.

I am not sure, however, what kind of proof can be given to show that the concepts of some existing conceptual scheme involve thought-procedures which are resisted by many of those who seem, *prima facie*, to be fully in command of those concepts. Even if we agree that moral concepts involve the notion that they are defensible at *some* critical level, it is not clear how it could be *shown*— not merely asserted—that the appropriate critical level is the thinking of one who is nothing but impartially benevolent. Since the third stage is logically distinct from the first and the second, the acceptance of both these sorts of universalization as conceptually necessary would not commit us to the third stage. Equally, it would not follow even if we accepted the claim to objectivity which seems to be involved in our moral concepts. That would indeed require us to base our judgements on principles which could be endorsed from any point of view or from none; but that would still leave room for the objective validity of specific principles, it would not commit us to the neutrality of the spectator who is nothing but impartially benevolent.

But perhaps the argument will run as follows. Anyone who resists this third stage is adhering to some distinctive, idiosyncratic, point of view; he is therefore letting the fact that this is *his* point of view (while he knows that others have other points of view)

determine his judgement; to do this is to retain a residual preference
for himself analogous to those which were excluded by the first and
second stages of universalization—a preference for himself not,
indeed, as a beneficiary but still as a determiner of what is to count
as good.

This argument can easily be rebutted by someone who holds that
the specific values in question are objective. He can say that he is
merely recognizing what is there already. He is not judging from
any idiosyncratic point of view. He is not, therefore, giving any
preference to himself, any more than a scientist who publishes a
truth that he alone has discovered is thereby giving any preference
to himself, if it is indeed a truth, and not just an unsubstantiated
pet theory. This rebuttal is enough to show that third stage universalization is not required by our moral concepts, since they at
least do not exclude the possible objective validity of specific values.

However, Hare has still a possible reply. He holds that the belief
in the objectivity of prescriptive values is incoherent. From this it
would follow that the rebuttal just offered could not be coherently
maintained; hence the previous argument for third state universalization would hold the field. (But that argument requires the
assumption that moral concepts demand the abandonment of *every*
sort of preference for oneself.)

We have thus reached an ironic position. The only strong argument for the logical theses of first and second stage universalization
rests on the view that moral concepts incorporate a claim to objectivity, while the only strong argument for the logical thesis of third
stage universalization rests on the view that any such claim is incoherent. *There is no single view about what moral concepts coherently involve which will provide a good argument for the logical
theses of all three stages of universalization.* This is not to say, of
course, that someone who adopts the *practical* theses of all three
stages is guilty of any sort of inconsistency. Again, someone could,
as a matter of choice, incorporate the logical theses of all three
stages into his own private meanings for all moral terms. But he
cannot show that these theses are supported by the existing public
meanings of those terms. He cannot claim that his practical position is supported in any way by conceptual analysis, or that it is a
necessary answer to the moral questions which we began by asking.

It is of interest to ask whether there is also a coherent position
available for someone who denies the objectivity of values, but who

wishes to adopt first and second stage universalization but to reject the third stage which generates utilitarianism. Could such a person say, for example, with Mill that the higher pleasures are better than the porcine ones, or with Dworkin that some kind of equality or fairness matters *basically*, and not merely as contingently derivative from pure impartial benevolence? There is surely no difficulty here. Such a person just does value intelligence as contrasted with stupidity or fairness as contrasted with unfairness. He is thereby expressing a preference, indeed, which he knows that not everyone shares. But he has no need to say anything of the form 'X is specially valuable because I prefer it'. Since he is, by hypothesis, a stage 2 universalizer, he is valuing X even with regard to possible worlds in which he does not have these preferences. But there is not even a psychological paradox in this, and the logical distinctness of the various stages of universalization guarantees that there can be no incoherence. Even if, contrary to what I have argued elsewhere, the belief in objectively prescriptive values were incoherent, there would be no reason why someone who chose to adopt the practical theses of the first and second stage should on that account feel committed to that of the third stage as well, or, therefore, to its utilitarian implications.

In conclusion, then, I would repeat what I said at the beginning. Conceptual analysis has no practical force: even if the analysis of moral concepts did show that they entailed all three degrees of universalizability and, thereby, utilitarian conclusions, this would not rationally constrain us to make utilitarian choices of action. But in any case conceptual analysis does not support the logical theses for all three stages of universalization: rather it shows that the very consideration which tends to support those for the first two stages undermines the case for that of the third stage. And, finally, the three stages are coherently separable, in particular in such a way that one could reasonably make the practical decision to adopt the first and second stages of universalization without the third.

XIV

RIGHTS, UTILITY, AND UNIVERSALIZATION

MANY different forms of utilitarianism have been put forward and discussed in some detail, and several very different right-based moral and political theories have been at least outlined.[1] But I shall be concerned mainly with the contrast between one form of utilitarianism, that advocated by R.M. Hare, and one right-based view, my own. Hare's theory has been fully stated, especially in his recent book *Moral Thinking*;[2] mine has not yet been adequately presented, but I shall indicate its main outlines, using comparisons with utilitarianism for this purpose.

The fundamental point of contrast, and conflict, between utilitarian and right-based views is that the former, at least in their basic theory, aggregate the interests or preferences of all the persons or parties who are being taken into account, whereas the latter insist, to the end, on the separateness of persons.[3] For the utilitarian, the ultimate determination and the ultimate justification of every moral requirement lies in its relation—perhaps a complex and indirect relation—to something that represents the pooling of all individual purposes. The rights theorist takes it to be morally important to respect and protect—at all levels, not at some only—the separate interests of each individual in a way that goes beyond the mere counting of them, however fairly, as elements in the pool.

Of course this does not mean that a utilitarian must literally deny that persons are separate, or that any utilitarian has ever done so. What it means is that this separateness does no work in the

Reprinted from *Utility and Rights*, edited by R.G. Frey (University of Minnesota Press and Basil Blackwell, 1984).

[1] Right-based theories include those of Robert Nozick and Ronald Dworkin, and, if Dworkin is right, that of John Rawls. Another is sketched in my 'Can There Be a Right-Based Moral Theory?', in *Midwest Studies in Philosophy*, Vol. III (1978). [See Chapter VIII above.—Edd.]

[2] R.M. Hare, *Moral Thinking* (Oxford, 1982).

[3] Cf. J. Rawls, *A Theory of Justice* (Oxford, 1972), pp. 23–7, 187.

utilitarian method of determining what is good or just, that in the utilitarian calculus the desires, or the satisfactions, of different individuals are all weighed together in the way in which a single thoroughly rational egoist would weigh together all his own desires or satisfactions: on a utilitarian view, transferring a satisfaction from one person to another, while preserving its magnitude, makes no morally significant difference.

A right-based moral theory attempts to develop and clarify the popular notion that everyone should have a fair go. This is something more than the utilitarian principle, enunciated by Bentham and echoed by Mill, that everybody is to count for one and nobody for more than one. It is also more than Hare, as we shall see, provides by saying that the moral point of view is that in which an agent imaginatively occupies in turn the positions of all those who would be affected by his action, and gives equal weight to all the preferences which he thus, in thought, acquires. One whose interests have been thus fairly taken into account may still, in the end, have much less than a fair go: the maximizing of utility may turn out to require that his well-being should be sacrificed, without limit, in order to promote that of others. It is this that a right-based theory is meant to bar.

The formal structure of such a theory will be something like this. Having started with the assignment to all persons alike of the rather vague right to a fair go, we first make this somewhat more explicit, in the light of ordinary human needs and purposes, by an assignment of some basic abstract *prima facie* rights. These, I suggest, will include the traditional rights to life, health, liberty, and the pursuit of happiness. We also need basic rights with regard to possessions. Here I suggest a right to the products of one's own labour, in so far as these can be distinguished; but also a right to share equally in or have equal access to all natural resources. I suggest also a similar right with respect to such products of the labour of previous generations as have reverted to the status of natural resources. This applies both where special claims are untraceable and where, though traceable, they are no longer in force. Such claims gradually fade out because the recipient of a bequest has a weaker right than the original producer, and this effect is cumulative. I suggest also a right to the fulfilment of reasonable expectations based on a fairly stable system of laws, institutions, and practices; and, finally, a right—which, unlike the others, can be not *prima facie* but absolute—to equal respect in the procedures that determine the compromises and adjustments between the other, *prima facie*, rights. Any specific moral or political theory or system can then be defended or criticized (or both) by considering to what extent its provisions and workings—including, no doubt, assignments of concrete, institutional, rights, but also including rules, concepts of duty, the recognition and encouragement of certain dispositions as virtues, and the discouragement of others as vices—can be seen as applying, implementing, and realizing those basic abstract rights in view of the actual purposes, choices, negotiations, actions, and interactions of persons over the course of time.

Since the ultimate rationale of such a theory is the respecting and protecting of separate interests, it seems likely that any practical system which it would endorse and defend to any significant extent would centre, as do most actual working moralities, on norms of reciprocation and conditional co-operation. Among other things, it will direct us to show gratitude, to help those who help us, to join in mutually beneficial enterprises and play our part in them, and to display the various sorts of honesty, fidelity, loyalty, and agreement-keeping that are in general likely to facilitate such conditional co-operation.

As this sketch shows, a right-based theory can and naturally will incorporate the distinction on which Hare insists between two levels of moral thinking. What I have called a specific moral or political theory or system belongs to what he calls the intuitive level, whereas the basic assignment of rights belongs to what he calls the critical level. The fact that most of the suggested rights are only *prima facie* ones, capable of being overridden in particular cases, does not mean that they are, like the rights that would be recognized in many utilitarian systems, merely derived principles whose rationale lies in their tendency to promote something else, say the general happiness. The suggested rights are basic, though defeasible. They must be defeasible, since they can in particular circumstances conflict with one another. But the conflicts are to be resolved by balancing these *prima facie* rights themselves against one another, not by weighing their merits in terms of some different ultimate standard of value, such as utility.

This notion of balancing may seem obscure, and may be thought to compel recourse to utilitarian methods at some point. This obscurity can be removed, and both the character of the proposed right-based theory and the contrast between it and utilitarianism can be made plainer, if we compare it also with the Marxist slogan, 'From each according to his ability, to each according to his needs'. My proposal incorporates Locke's two principles of property, that all natural resources belong, fundamentally, to all persons equally and in common, but that each individual has a private property in his own body, energy, talents, and labour, and therefore also in the traceable products of his labour. The Marxist slogan presupposes rather that not only natural resources but also each individual's labour, talents, energy, and perhaps his body too, belong to everyone in common: the needs of other persons constitute valid claims on whatever I can contribute. However, the second part of this slogan is ambiguous: just how are goods and services to be distributed in relation to needs? This might be read as proposing a utilitarianism of needs: utility might be equated with need-satisfaction (it being assumed that we can distinguish needs from mere wants or preferences), and the total of this utility or need-satisfaction maximized. But an alternative and more natural reading would give each person an equal *prima facie* right to have his needs satisfied, so that an ideally just arrangement would be one in which everyone's needs were satisfied to the same degree: the practical principle of redistribution would be 'Your need is greater than mine'. These two interpretations are not even extensionally equivalent. Equalizing marginal need may well not minimize total unsatisfied need or maximize the satisfaction of need: when A's and B's levels of need are equal, we may be able, by transferring resources from A to B, to increase B's need-satisfaction by an amount greater than that by which A's is reduced: B may be a more efficient converter of resources into need-satisfaction than A, even where their levels of need-satisfaction are initially equal. If we were choosing simply between these two readings of the Marxist slogan, the second would be not only the more natural but also the more attractive. There is a similar choice to be made between methods of adjusting conflicts between our more Lockean rights. The two principles of property quoted above are not absolute, either in my proposal or in Locke's own theory: initial property rights have to be weighed together with the rights to life, health, liberty, and the pursuit of happiness. Locke himself says 'so ... when his own Preservation comes not in competition, ought he, as much as he

can, *to preserve the rest of Mankind* ...'[4] Conflicts between these
prima facie rights might be handled by a utilitarianism of rights, so
that what would count as the ideally just arrangement would be
that in which total right-fulfilment was maximized, or total right-
infringement minimized. Alternatively, they might be handled by
assuming that, ideally, one person's rights should not be infringed
more than another's. Again the two methods are not even extensionally equivalent, and again I suggest that the second is the more
attractive. Such equality of sacrifice in compromises between our
Lockean rights is, of course, not equivalent to the equal need-
satisfaction in our second reading of the Marxist slogan, precisely
because our rights include each individual's private property in his
own body, energy, talents, and labour, and because each has a
prima facie right to be free and to pursue happiness in whatever
way he chooses, doubtless with very varying degrees of success.
Does this mean that what I am advocating is equality of opportunity rather than final equality? Not if this means that justice would
be secured if only each young adult started with equal resources
and chances, no matter what happened thereafter. Rather we
should include what we might call the prodigal son principle, that
even someone who has squandered his initial opportunities has,
later, some claim to be helped to make a fresh start. We want a
continuing or at least a recurrent equality of opportunity, not
merely an initial equality of opportunity, once and for all.

These contrasts have been drawn in terms of various ideal principles of justice. In practice each of the rival ideals could be realized
only approximately and indirectly through some concrete system
of institutions. Nevertheless, the ideal formulations are useful, both
as guiding lights for the criticism or defence of institutions and to
bring out the contrasts between the different possible views. Our
Lockean proposal is, not surprisingly, more individualist and less
collectivist than the Marxist one. Yet even the latter, with the
second, egalitarian, reading, is, paradoxically, *less* collectivist than
any utilitarian principle. For a utilitarian principle also—as
William Godwin in particular made clear—presupposes that everyone's labour, talents, energy, and body are in principle common
property, to be used in whatever way maximizes overall utility. The
utilitarian, no less than the Marxist, is committed to the clause,
'From each according to his ability'. And whereas 'to each accord-

---

[4] J. Locke, *Second Treatise of Government*, Section 7.

ing to his needs' can be read as prescribing *equal* need-satisfaction between individuals, a utilitarian is committed rather to *maximum* overall satisfaction—whether of needs or of preferences—which may well be at the cost of every sort of equality except equality of consideration, the right to be taken equally into account.

Hare's theory is based on features which, he believes, conceptual analysis shows to be characteristic of moral thinking: moral judgements are prescriptive, universalizable, and overriding. The kind of universalizability on which he relies is made very clear in his recent book: to endorse something as a moral judgement is seriously to prescribe it for a whole set of possible worlds each of which is exactly like the actual world in all its general features, but in which individuals change places in all possible ways. Essentially, this means that for me morally to choose some action is for me to prefer that action to any alternative with respect to an imaginary situation in which I not only occupy in turn the positions of all the persons affected in any way by this choice, but also take on all their preferences, detaching myself completely from my own actual preferences and values and ideals, except as those of one affected person among others. What is morally right, therefore, is what would be chosen from a point of view which thus combines or amalgamates all points of view. Hare infers that this will be equivalent to the output of a preference utilitarianism, in which the 'utility' that is to be maximized is the balance of satisfactions over frustrations of all the preferences of all the persons concerned.[5] (The range covered by this phrase 'the persons concerned' is indeterminate: it presumably includes all actual human beings, present and future, but it is not clear whether it includes merely possible people, non-human animals, and perhaps all sentient beings whatever. But a right-based theory suffers initially from the same indeterminacy. This is a problem common to the two approaches, and therefore irrelevant to the choice between them; so I shall leave it aside.)

The practical effect of this theory is very significantly affected by Hare's stress on the distinction between two levels of moral thinking. At the lower, practical, working, level—the intuitive level, as Hare calls it—various rules, principles, and dispositions are in place; but thought at the higher, critical, level has the task of deciding *what* rules, principles, and dispositions are to be adopted

[5] Hare, *op. cit.*, Chapter 7.

or cultivated for use at the lower level. This distinction provides two quick answers to anyone who complains—as so many recent writers have complained—that utilitarianism, including the proposed preference utilitarianism, has counter-intuitive consequences. One answer is that the true consequences, for a practical working morality, of this preference utilitarianism do not conflict but rather coincide with our ordinary intuitions. A prescriptively universalizing (and therefore utilitarian) critical thinker would encourage the adoption and development of firm principles and dispositions of the ordinary moral sort, rather than the direct use of utilitarian calculation as a practical working morality. There are at least six reasons why this is so. Shortage of time and energy will in general preclude such calculations. Even if time and energy are available, the relevant information commonly is not. An agent's judgement on particular issues is liable to be distorted by his own interests and special affections. Even if he were intellectually able to determine the right choice, weakness of will would be likely to impair his putting of it into effect. Even decisions that are right in themselves and actions based on them are liable to be misused as precedents, so that they will encourage and seem to legitimate wrong actions that are superficially similar to them. And, human nature being what it is, a practical working morality must not be too demanding: it is worse than useless to set standards so high that there is no real chance that actions will even approximate to them. Considerations of these sorts entail that a reasonable utilitarian critical thinker would recommend the adoption of fairly strict principles and the development of fairly firm dispositions in favour of honesty, veracity, agreement-keeping, justice, fairness, respect for various rights of individuals, gratitude to benefactors, special concern for some individuals connected in certain ways with the agent, and so on, as being more likely in general to produce behaviour approximating to that which would be required by the utilitarian ideal than any other humanly viable working morality. Since utilitarianism itself would thus generate an apparently non-utilitarian intuitive morality, it is idle to appeal against it to just such intuitions. Hare's second answer to the common complaint grants that there may be some very unusual situations, or some fantastic imagined situations, in which this reconciliation fails, in which utilitarianism, even after all the above-mentioned considerations have been allowed for, recommends choices that are at variance with our ordinary moral intuitions. But, it says, this shows only that these are situations with which our intuitions are not competent to cope. These intuitions have been developed in the real, normal, world, and they are appropriate only for it: in fantastic situations they have no authority against the implications of universalizing critical thinking, if those implications are themselves clear.[6]

These answers are powerful enough to dispose of the majority of the stock objections to utilitarianism or to the kind of overridingly prescriptive universalization that, in Hare's opinion, generates it; it would, therefore, be both misguided and tedious to reiterate them. Instead, I shall raise three other objections.

One of these is internal to Hare's theory. Let us accept, provisionally, the thesis that first emerges from his kind of universalization, that what is morally right is, ultimately, what would be chosen from a point of view that combines or amalgamates all points of view. Is there, then, a uniquely correct way of amalgamating those points of view? Does it follow that what is right is what maximizes utility defined as the balance of the aggregate of the satisfactions of preferences over the aggregate of frustrations of preferences? Or might the appropriate amalgamation still be one that took serious notice of the separateness of persons, perhaps in a way that would be expressed by the assigning of some basic abstract rights to each individual? If I am, for the purpose of ultimate moral decision, to be everyone, must I be everyone in such a way that all are blurred together into a mere aggregate of preferences, or can I be everyone with the boundaries between all these persons still visible and important? Can I not still want *each* of my multiple incarnations to have a fair go?[7] And, if I do, will I not assign to each of them *prima facie* rights which, when conflicts arise between one incarnation's rights and another's, are to be adjusted in the way indicated above, so that the ideally acceptable compromise will not infringe the rights of one more than those of another? In contrast with this, it is not enough that in the utilitarian method, or in Hare's utilitarian way of combining points of view, each individual is fully considered and his preferences counted, all preferences being given equal weight. The boundaries between persons are here being ignored, in that one person's satisfaction can

---

[6] Hare, *op. cit.*, Chapter 6.
[7] This point was made in discussion by Ronald Dworkin.

simply replace another's, and outweigh that other's miseries or frustrations.

An analogy between the different personae that one would assume through universalization and the different temporal phases of the life of an ordinary individual will throw some light on this issue. Suppose that as a young adult one could look forward to a fairly long life, and had some rough idea of the various satisfactions and frustrations likely to be experienced as a result of each of several alternative choices of a plan of life. Suppose that one could also allow for probable changes in one's preferences and ideals as one grew older, and was able to detach oneself from one's present youthful purposes and values and to look fairly at the alternative plans of life from the points of view of all one's future selves as well as the present one. Is it obvious that if a reasonable person were able to do all these things, he would opt for whatever plan of life promised the greatest aggregate utility? Or might he try to ensure that no substantial phase of his life was too miserable, even if very great satisfactions at other times were to compensate for this? I am not merely saying, as Hare might concede, that in general one would be most likely to maximize the aggregate of utility by providing for one's well-being at each successive phase. I am suggesting that looking after each substantial phase might be the sensible thing to opt for in its own right, not merely as a means to maximizing the aggregate. Yet the separateness of phases, in this case, just because they are only phases of the same person, would matter much less than the separateness of persons within the whole that is created and embraced by the adoption of the universalizing procedure. I might the more readily tolerate *my* misery over one five year period if it was compensated by *my* great happiness over another five years simply because it is the same I that will be, or has been, happy. But if I adopt a way of thinking which commits me to being, as it were, both Smith and Jones, but separately, it is not so clear that I can tolerate unmitigated misery *as Smith* merely because that will enable me, *as Jones*, to be extravagantly happy. So if there is any force at all in the suggestion that the young adult might be reasonably concerned for the well-being of *each* of his temporal phases, it follows *a fortiori* that Harean universalization might generate a persisting concern for each separate individual.

I need not insist that what Hare's universalization leads to *is* a rights theory rather than an aggregative utilitarianism even at the

critical level: it is enough to point out that it does not give unequivocal support to the latter. There is no uniquely correct or rational
way of amalgamating the indefinitely many points of view which
are brought together by universalization, so there is no support to
be derived from Hare's basic principles for utilitarianism as contrasted with a right-based theory.

My second objection is external to Hare's theory, in that it challenges even his basic approach through prescriptive universalizability. In earlier writings, Hare has placed great weight on conceptual analysis, maintaining that a correct understanding of
ordinary moral concepts and moral language shows that overridingly prescriptive universalizability is built into them, and hence
that to follow any other method would be tantamount to refusing
to answer the moral questions we began by asking: while one can,
without incoherence, simply opt out of the moral game altogether,
this is the only consistent alternative. But this approach can be
questioned on three grounds. First, even if analysis of established
moral concepts shows that they involve some sort of universalizability, it is far from clear that they involve the precise sort which
Hare is now using. His present method embraces all three of the
stages of universalization that I have distinguished, but our ordinary concepts may well involve only the first, or perhaps the first
and second, without the third.[8] Secondly, since there are these
complications, opting out of the moral game and ceasing to ask
recognizably moral questions is not the only alternative to using
Hare's method. Thirdly, even if we accepted his conceptual
analysis, we might well ask why that should matter, what power
the analysis of existing concepts has to constrain our thinking, if
there are other coherently possible ways of thinking about choices
and patterns of behaviour.

These points are important, since between them they destroy
whatever force there might be in Hare's reliance on conceptual
analysis and linguistic intuitions. Since there are coherent ways of
thinking morally other than the one he describes, and moral language does not determinately involve his specific method of universalization, we have not only the choice whether or not to speak
and think morally, but also, if we choose to do so, the further
choice whether to speak and think morally in Hare's style or in

[8] Cf. J.L. Mackie, *Ethics, Inventing Right and Wrong* (Harmondsworth, 1977),
Chapter 4.

⌞some other. Since he vehemently advocates one specific kind of moral thinking, he is under pressure to find further ways of recommending it.

However, I need not labour these points here.[9] Hare himself now seems willing (at a pinch) to concede them. He says:

> If anybody either does not believe that I have given a true account of the moral concepts as we have them, or thinks that investigations of the logic of words in ordinary language are unhelpful, it is open to him to proceed in a different way. He could set out the logic of an artificial language, identical in its properties with the logic which I claim our ordinary words have; then he could show that anybody reasoning in such a language would have to think in the way in which *I* say our existing concepts constrain us to think; and then he could, using the same arguments as I shall use, show that there would be an advantage in our adopting such a language. Though I should not like such a method as much as my own ... I do not think that the difference between the results of the two methods would be very substantial.[10]

In short, he is now prepared to join with others in sawing off the branch on which he has been sitting all these years. But though the branch is sawn off, Hare does not fall with it: he has provided himself with alternative means of support, in the claim that 'there would be an advantage in our adopting such a language'. But what can this mean?

It might mean that adopting this as an artificial language (or retaining it if it is, after all, our ordinary moral language), and thinking in terms of it to determine a practical working morality, would do more than any alternative system of action-guiding thought to fulfil together all the preferences of all human (or perhaps all sentient) beings. Now, provided that it really is possible to think properly in terms of this language, this must be true, since what the use of the Harean moral language aims at is precisely the fulfilment of all these preferences—subject, of course, to the query in our first objection about whether there is a unique way of amalgamating them. Hare assigns his critical thinking to a class of 'archangels' presumed to be thoroughly rational and fully informed, and of course a system of thoroughly rational and fully informed thinking aimed at achieving X must be a better way of achieving X than any other sort of thinking. But precisely because

---

[9] Some of them are developed in the chapter referred to in note 8.

[10] Hare, *op. cit.*, Chapter 1, p. 20.

this is so obvious, it is no real defence of, or support for, this kind of thinking.

Alternatively, this claim might mean that the adopting (or retaining) of such a language and way of thinking by *each* person is advantageous to *him*; in other words, that Hare is prepared to mount a prudential defence of moral thinking. And this is indeed what he does. He admits that to do what we ought to do is not always in our prudential interest, and remarks that it is hard to see how anybody could have thought that it was always so in default of divine rewards and punishments. But he says that we can still 'achieve something more modest, which nevertheless is adequate for the defence of morality'. His argument is that if one were bringing up a child, and had *only* the child's interests at heart, one would not inculcate in him a purely egoistic principle; rather, one would try to develop in him not only such virtues as courage but also 'moral *prima facie* principles of just the same sort as the act-utilitarian archangel would select'. The reason is that it is not easy to be a successful immoral egoist. 'Mankind has found it possible to make life a great deal more tolerable by bringing it about that on the whole morality pays.' Since 'by far the easiest way of seeming to be upright is to be upright ... perhaps the most effective way of bringing up our child to obey the principles would be to inculcate moral feelings ...' And if this holds for the supposed case of educating a child in his own interests, it must hold also with regard to each agent on his own: it would be prudent for him, so far as he is able, to adopt or retain the moral way of thinking.[11]

What I have given here is a précis of quite a long discussion. Clearly it makes important empirical claims; but are they true? I agree that if one were bringing up this child with a view simply to its own interests one would not try to make it into a directly-calculating egoist. One would try to provide it with such self-strengthening virtues as courage, perseverance, some sort of temperance, and so on. Also, one would try to provide it with the specifically moral dispositions of some sort of morality. But not, I think, exactly the same moral dispositions as would be selected by Hare's act-utilitarian archangels, even allowing for all the above-listed considerations that would make a reasonable Harean critical thinker settle for an apparently non-utilitarian practical working morality. Rather, one would develop in the child dispositions that

[11] Hare, *op. cit.*, Chapter 11.

would enable it to accept and take advantage of unequal social structures to a greater extent than would the product of an education directed by Harean critical thought. For example, if the child happened to be born into a slave-owning aristocracy, one would educate him so as to be a well-behaved member of that class, and no doubt so as to be disposed to treat his slaves reasonably well. But Hare's critical thinking might well say that we should develop even in so fortunately endowed a child principles that might lead him to support some tendency to reform this unequal social structure, rather than merely to accept it and flourish within it, if there were any real possibility of successful reform.

In short, Hare slides far too easily from the admitted point that to have some sort of morality is very likely to be to the advantage of any individual to the conclusion that his specific sort of morality is so, and is maximally so. This thesis is, on the face of it, highly implausible; if Hare wants to make use of it, the onus is on him to defend it far more thoroughly than he has done. It is not enough simply to reiterate his belief that it holds.

However, let us suppose, merely in order to investigate a further step in the argument, that he is right in this empirical claim. Suppose, that is, that the practical morality that would be chosen with a view simply to the agent's interests coincides perfectly with that which would be chosen by a Harean critical thinker. Even so, this would not yield a prudential vindication of Hare's style of critical thinking or of its basic utilitarianism. The prudential support would go straight to the working morality, not by way of the utilitarian critical thinking. It would be at most a lucky accident that the two lines of thought led to the same practical results. Even if they did, what the prudential argument would vindicate would be something like our ordinary morality with its norms of reciprocation and co-operation, special duties of honesty and agreement-keeping, special obligations of loyalty to family and friends, gratitude to benefactors, the legitimacy of the pursuit, within limits, of one's own interests, and of resentment of injuries, and so on. It *may* be that, contrary to initial appearances, the universalizing critical thinking, interpreted in the aggregative utilitarian way, would recommend acceptance of just this same practical moral system. But this would not mean that we had thereby a prudential vindication of that sort of critical thinking; at most we would have an absence of any prudential case against such critical thinking, as a general programme. In particular—and this is crucial—we should have no reason for regarding utilitarian calculation as the method on which we should fall back in really hard cases: these, like the basic method itself, would lie beyond the scope of the prudential vindication.

By 'hard cases' I mean ones where appeal to the established principles of a practical working morality fails, either because those principles conflict with one another or because the situation is abnormal. Here, by Hare's own account, we shall have to suspend the normal operation of even the best 'intuitions', and since the assumed defence of the ordinary reliance on those 'intuitions' has been a prudential one, there is no case for saying that what we should fall back on here, to replace those 'intuitions' and principles, is the utilitarian style of critical thinking, merely because the output of this normally coincides with that of prudential critical thinking.

There is, then, no sound, non-trivial, interpretation of the thesis that 'there would be an advantage' in adopting (or retaining) the moral language and the basic method of moral thinking that Hare favours. His alternative means of support gives way, and he does, after all, fall with the sawn-off branch of conceptual analysis.

But what else, he may ask, can we offer as a method of critical moral thinking? We surely need something on this level. We cannot be content simply to accept whatever morality is conventionally in force, or to respect all the threadbare 'intuitions' to which popular moralists appeal—particularly when we see how they conflict with one another, and how some of them stem from religious traditions to which we have no good reason to ascribe any authority. We need some way of revising a community's working morality, and of making adjustments when discrepant working moralities come into contact with one another. Certainly; but there are at least two possible rivals to utilitarianism as a guide to thinking at the critical level.

One of these, which Hare himself might on reflection find acceptable, results from my first objection, which is, as I said, internal to his theory. His thoroughgoing prescriptive universalization might amalgamate the points of view of all the individuals concerned in a way that took serious account of the separateness of persons, by assigning such basic abstract rights as I have suggested to each person. That is, we could have a right-based method of critical thinking, and it could be supported, with at least as much plausibility as the aggregative utilitarian one, by the approach through universalization.

But I would not myself support it in this way, because, as I have indicated, I do not find the argument from conceptual analysis for prescriptive universalization compelling as a method for choosing ultimate constraints on action. Rather, I would fall back on the thesis for which I have argued elsewhere, that right and wrong have to be invented, that morality is not to be discovered but to be made.[12] We have to start somewhere, simply adopting some basic practical principles, though no doubt not in an arbitrary or casual spirit, but with reflection on the range of alternative sets of principles, and on the entailments and likely consequences of each such set. I suggest that on reflection we might find an assignment of basic abstract rights to persons a more acceptable starting point for critical moral thinking than any other.

A second suggestion is harder to state succinctly. Let me approach it by way of a digression through a speculative account of the origins of morality. Hare has spoken as if our existing 'intuitive' moralities were the product of his style of critical thinking:

It is no accident that the world and society are such that crime does not in general pay ... It is better for nearly all of us if social rewards and penalties are attached to socially beneficial and harmful acts; *and so it has come about that on the whole they are* [my italics].[13]

Similarly Hume, in the *Enquiry concerning Morals*, thinks that it is a sufficient explanation of moral rules and practices that they have utility:

The rules of equity and justice owe their origin and existence to that utility, which results to the public from their strict and regular observance ... Common interest and utility beget infallibly a standard of right and wrong among the parties concerned.[14]

But this is emphatically not an adequate method of explanation. There is no sound general principle either of biological evolution or of socio-historical development that tendencies or dispositions or practices will be fostered and encouraged simply because they are beneficial to a community as a whole in a utilitarian sense. The

---

[12] Cf. Chapter 1 of the book referred to in note 8.
[13] Hare, *op. cit.*, Chapter 11.
[14] D. Hume, *Enquiries*, edited by L.A.Selby-Bigge, 2nd ed. (Oxford, 1902; repr. 1946, 1955), pp. 188, 211; see also pp. 202, 208, etc.

true explanation, of which this is a distortion, runs rather as follows.

Sociobiologists have outlined processes of natural selection by which genetically determined tendencies are developed in favour of 'kin altruism'—that is, helping offspring and other close relatives—and reciprocal altruism—that is, helping those who help you. Tendencies to co-operate in small groups, where each agent's participation is conditional on that of most of the other members, can be fostered in similar ways, as can the resentment of injuries and hostile retribution. All these are what we might call spontaneous pre-moral tendencies: they can be found, and understood, in many non-human species as well as in humans. They are typically spontaneous, being genetically fostered, and give only an appearance of calculation: here, as elsewhere, natural selection mimics purposiveness. Further, social evolution is superimposed on biological evolution. Here the most important element is the development of conventions. These can be understood as arising out of, and helping to resolve, problems of several sorts: co-ordination problems and especially problems of partial conflict of interests, either of much the same form as the prisoners' dilemma or of non-symmetrical variants of this form. Then the internalization of rules of behaviour will turn conventions into norms. In this social evolution, as in biological evolution, mechanisms of interaction can generate spontaneous tendencies that mimic purpose and calculation, and the solutions of problems can be produced and maintained by the very forces which initially create the problems. Hume, in Book III of the *Treatise*, at least hints at this explanation of morality in terms of conventions, though in the *Enquiry* he substituted for this the simpler but less correct attempt to explain morality directly by its utility.[15]

If it is by such processes as these that first pre-moral and then specifically moral tendencies have actually developed, it is not surprising that actual moral systems have the features we usually find in them: norms of co-operation (including co-operation on terms that are differentially advantageous to parties of different sorts); norms of reciprocation; principles that secure various rights. In general, we find moralities that look like the product of many contractual or quasi-contractual relationships, although actual his-

---

[15] For a fuller explanation of these matters, see J.L. Mackie, *Hume's Moral Theory* (London, 1980), Chapters 6 and 9.

torical contracts have not as a rule contributed significantly to their development.

My second suggestion, which this digression has been designed to introduce, is that moral thinking at the critical level might resemble the processes by which practical working moralities really have developed, rather than the control by utility to which Hare, and Hume in the *Enquiry*, mistakenly ascribe their origin. That is, critical thinking might itself be a process of interaction, negotiation, and debate between diverse groups with different starting points, different traditions of thought. Rather than proceeding *de haut en bas*, being pursued by one or more detached thinkers who try to stand above the whole conflict of interests and ideals, it would work up from below, from those conflicting views and claims themselves. The details of this process would be contingent upon the input to it, and are therefore not open to any precise description *a priori*, but it is reasonable to expect that any such process of interaction, negotiation, and debate would be roughly equivalent to some distribution of entitlements which are not merged into a pure collectivity—in other words, that this too would be, in effect, a right-based approach.

In criticizing an earlier draft of this essay, Hare has demanded that more should be said about the ground rules for such negotiation. This may, indeed, be a fruitful line of enquiry, but I cannot say much about it here. An attractive principle would be the above-mentioned one of equality of sacrifices in compromises between our Lockean rights, but realistic ground rules for negotiation would need to take some account of the strength of the bargaining positions of the parties. I would stress, however, that Hare's thoroughgoing universalization, which means that each party abandons his special interests, values, and point of view in taking on those of all parties alike, is not a ground rule for negotiation, but a move that would make negotiation unnecessary. Equally, Rawls's notion of a hypothetical contract made behind a veil of ignorance destroys what is characteristic of a contractual or negotiating method. In speaking of negotiation I mean real negotiation, conducted in the full light of day, while the parties retain their self-conscious individuality and divergent aims.[16]

<hr/>

[16] A proposal for basing a liberal theory of justice on 'constrained dialogue' has been put forward by Bruce A. Ackerman in *Social Justice in the Liberal State* (New Haven, Conn., 1980). I have criticized Ackerman's proposals in a review article,

This second suggestion is plainly different from the first, but it could be supported in the same sort of way, simply as a possibly acceptable starting point for critical moral thinking. There is, however, something else that might be said for it; and this brings me to my third main objection to Hare's theory, which, like the second, challenges his basic approach.

Hare's critically thinking archangels are supposed to be performing a task which Bishop Butler assigned more appropriately to God. (Hare has himself noted this in an earlier essay.[17]) Butler's God is presumed to have perfect knowledge and complete benevolence towards all his creatures; he therefore is in a position to choose the best practical working morality for human beings, with their limitations as he knows them, and to write it into their consciences in the form of moral intuitions. But this viewpoint which Butler plausibly ascribes to God is simply not accessible, either intellectually or emotionally, to anyone else.

It is obvious that it is not intellectually accessible. Critical thinking, it is to be remembered, is concerned primarily with the choice of sets of moral principles and dispositions, and this choice will affect indefinitely many present and future persons. No human thinker or small group of thinkers can possibly know what it is really like to be each of these people. Hare takes trouble to argue that one can really put oneself imaginatively in the place of *some* other people. This might be sufficient for universalization used as a test of the rightness of some particular choice of action; but it cannot be sufficient for the main task of critical thinking.

I would have supposed that the required viewpoint is also emotionally inaccessible, that no-one can really *take on* the feelings of all persons, present and future, even if he could surmount the intellectual barriers to his discovery of them. However, Peter Singer, in a recent book, has tried to meet this challenge. His title, *The Expanding Circle*,[18] refers to the well known thesis of Westermarck and others that the history of human moral thought has been, in part, the history of a progressive enlargement of the circle of persons

---

'Competitors in Conversation', in *The Times Literary Supplement*, 17 April 1981, p. 443.

[17] R.M. Hare, 'Principles', in *Proceedings of the Aristotelian Society*, LXXIII (1972-3), pp. 1-18.

[18] P. Singer, *The Expanding Circle: Ethics and Sociobiology* (New York and Oxford, 1980).

towards whom altruism is morally prescribed and towards whom, to some extent, altruistic feelings and actions are really directed. Singer describes and accepts very much that same sociobiological account of the origins of morality in kin altruism, reciprocal altruism, and co-operation in small groups as has been sketched above. But he then argues that the expansion of the range of altruism is not due merely to wider practical opportunities for useful co-operation or to widening sympathies, but is rather to be ascribed to *reason* in something like a Kantian sense. This is not what Hume would have called reason: there is no strict deductive requirement to go on from altruism (or universalization) with respect to a small community to altruism (or universalization) with respect to a large community or the human race or all sentient beings. But it is reason in a looser sense: it is the avoidance of an arbitrary cut-off. Singer appropriately compares this moral expansion with the gradual progress of arithmetic from the recognition of the integers from, say, 1 to 10, *via* the extension to an infinite sequence of integers, the introduction of negative numbers, fractions, irrationals, and so on, to the full modern development of mathematics. He connects both of these with biological theory. The growth of the ability to develop the higher mathematics could not be explained *in itself* as a product of natural selection: this ability could never itself have given its possessors a genetic advantage. But this ability may well be so closely linked with practically useful and genetically advantageous forms of intelligence that natural selection could not help introducing them together. We could not have the useful abilities to count sheep and to think conditionally without having also the useless ability and motivation that have led the mathematicians into Cantor's paradise. Similarly, Singer suggests, the kinds of moral thinking that are genetically advantageous, that would be, and have been, produced by the above-mentioned sociobiological mechanisms, together with the practically useful ability to generalize, tend automatically to produce the unrestricted prescriptive universalization of Hare's archangelic critical thinkers. And the latter, *unlike* the higher mathematics, may really be useful after all, although it could not have been selected genetically—or, I would add, culturally—for its usefulness.

If Singer were right, then, the archangelic viewpoint would in principle be emotionally accessible even to humans, not only to Butler's God, in so far as there would be a tendency in thinking, closely linked with reasoning powers that we already have, which would carry us from the already existing kind of morality (directly produced by biological and cultural evolution) to a Harean universalization.

However, this suggestion slides too easily over the contrast between norms of reciprocation and conditional co-operation on the one hand and that of pure rational benevolence on the other. To go from the first to the second of these would be a qualitative change in moral thinking, different from a mere expansion of the circle within which altruism *of the same kind* operates. The 'reason' that avoids arbitrary cut-offs will not carry us over this gap. Also, the supposed evidence that there already is a significant amount of pure rational benevolence is weak. Singer makes much of the altruism of blood-donors, but after all this is a comparatively inexpensive form of altruism. More spectacular forms of self-sacrifice typically come under the heading of the taking of risks within what is normally a co-operative enterprise, and are governed by norms of reciprocation. Despite Singer's argument, therefore, I still deny that the archangelic viewpoint is emotionally accessible to humans in any real sense, and I repeat that in any case it is not intellectually accessible.

There is, then, a good reason why critical moral thinking should take the form sketched in my second suggestion above, that of a process of interaction, negotiation, and debate rather than something closely analogous to the thinking of Butler's God, namely that the former is humanly possible, while the latter is not.

This criticism may seem to tell not only against Hare's theory but also against my own first suggestion. But I think it is less damaging to the latter. We should need less close an approximation to divine omniscience and universal benevolence in order seriously to assign some basic abstract rights to all persons alike, and to criticize practical working moralities by reference to that assignment, than in order seriously to adopt an unqualified aggregative utilitarianism, even if we confined this to the critical level. There are two reasons why this is so. First, the right-based approach, since it keeps everyone covered to some extent, keeps *us* covered among others. And, secondly, since its aim is to keep everyone covered, it can proceed in a more piecemeal way. We can say roughly whether some local arrangement, over a finite geographical area and a modest time span, does or does not constitute a decent approximation to an application and realization of the basic rights of those directly involved, without necessitating sacrifices of the corresponding rights of persons outside this spatio-temporal region. We can say this more confidently than we can say that any scheme, however local its immediate bearing may be, is likely on the whole to come close to maximizing the aggregate satisfaction of preferences of the whole body of human (let alone sentient) beings, present and future. In effect, this means that while my first and second suggestions about possible methods of critical thinking—the first, universalization in the form of an assignment of basic abstract rights to all persons, the second, a process of interaction, negotiation, and debate—are in principle different from one another, they are still not very far apart: the second could be seen as a way of approximately realizing the first.

Let me sum up, then, the ways in which we might want to stress the role of rights in moral theory. First, it is clear that we shall want rights to be recognized and taken seriously as elements in our practical working morality. But this is not a point at issue between Hare's view and mine: he would be emphatic about the importance of rights at this level, as was another utilitarian, J.S. Mill, when he wrote:

Justice is a name for certain classes of moral rules, which concern the essentials of human well-being more nearly, and are therefore of more absolute obligation, than any other rules for the guidance of life; and the notion which we have found to be the essence of the idea of justice, that of a right residing in an individual, implies and testifies to this more binding obligation.[19]

The real dispute, then, concerns the choice between 'utility' and 'rights' as the central concepts in higher level, critical, moral thinking.

Secondly—and this is now a point at issue—I have questioned whether the analysis of moral concepts yields the precise kind of universalization which amounts to the identification of morally defensible choices with ones made from a point of view which amalgamates the points of view of all persons. But even if the analysis of existing moral concepts did have this as its output, why should this be seen as an important constraint on the kind of critical thinking whose function is to choose a practical working morality, that is, a body of rules, principles, and dispositions that

---

[19] J. S. Mill, *Utilitarianism*, Chapter 5.

would directly guide and control what people do? The authority of moral concepts is no more sacred than that of particular 'intuitions', and I have argued that Hare is not able to substitute for this authority a prudential vindication. The way, therefore, is at least open for a theory based on rights and the separateness of persons rather than on aggregative utility.

Thirdly, Hare's style of universalization assigns to his archangelic critical thinkers a point of view which belongs rather to Butler's God, and is not accessible to human beings either intellectually or, despite Singer's ingenious argument, emotionally. Lacking this point of view, we could not really carry out the utilitarian critical thinking: rather, if we aimed at this, we should achieve only guess-work purporting to be an application of preference utilitarianism. But two other methods are humanly possible. One of these accepts, as the moral point of view, one which amalgamates the points of view of all persons, but interprets this amalgamation in a way that still allows for the separateness of persons, and so issues initially in an assignment of basic abstract rights, in terms of which concrete moral and political systems and proposals can be defended or criticized. The other abandons the attempt to work down from any supreme principle or over-arching point of view, and instead works up from below by a procedure of interaction, negotiation, and debate. Though different in principle, these two methods are not far removed from one another in practice. I suggest, therefore, that rights not only should be prominent in a practical working morality, but can also replace utility at the critical level.

XV

MORALITY AND THE
RETRIBUTIVE EMOTIONS

THE Finnish philosopher Edward Westermarck, in the first two chapters of *Ethical Relativity*, argues against the supposed objectivity of moral judgements, claiming that the concepts which are used as predicates in these judgements are ultimately based on emotions. In the next two chapters he tries to substantiate this claim by identifying the special class of moral emotions on which these concepts are based, moral approval and moral disapproval or indignation. He says that these are a subclass of what he calls retributive emotions, resentment and retributive kindly emotion (which also includes anger, revenge, and gratitude), and are marked off from their non-moral counterparts by disinterestedness and at least apparent impartiality. He explains these differentiating features by the fact that 'society is the birth-place of the moral consciousness', that 'tribal custom was the earliest rule of duty'.[1] Westermarck also argues that disapproval is more important than approval, and that the resentment of which it is a subspecies is likewise more important, and occurs more widely in the animal kingdom, than retributive kindly emotion. He maintains that the retributive element in punishment is uneliminable, and cannot be wholly replaced by such principles as deterrence and reformation, though he also says that there is 'some connection between these ends and the retributive aim of moral resentment'.[2]

These theses are all, I believe, substantially correct, but the arguments Westermarck gives for them are inconclusive. He does not really show that moral concepts are derived from what he identifies as the moral emotions, nor that these emotions are derived from their non-moral counterparts, nor how disinterestedness and

Reprinted from *Edward Westermarck: Essays on His Life and Works*, edited by Timothy Stroup (*Acta Philosophica Fennica*, 1982).

[1] Edward Westermarck, *Ethical Relativity* (London, 1932), p. 109. Subsequent references to this book will be to '*ER*', with page numbers.

[2] *ER*, p. 80.

apparent impartiality result from society and its customs. The causal claims implicit in his account are not strongly supported by the merely descriptive facts that there are resemblances between, for example, the various feelings that he classes under the heading of resentment, and while he says that 'rightly understood, resentment is preventive in its nature',[3] he does not explain this except by showing that resentment tends to be modified by the offender's repentance and that an act of moral resentment is 'apt to resemble a punishment inflicted with a view to deterring from crime'.[4]

But a more conclusive case can be made out for his theses. This turns upon what I shall call the paradox of retribution. This paradox, I shall argue, cannot be resolved except with the help of a hypothetical account in which all of Westermarck's main assertions take their place. The paradox is that, on the one hand, a retributive principle of punishment cannot be explained or developed within a reasonable system of moral thought, while, on the other hand, such a principle cannot be eliminated from our moral thinking. As Westermarck says, 'It is one of the most interesting facts relating to the moral consciousness of the most humane type, that it in vain condemns the gratification of the very desire from which it sprang.'[5]

To explain this paradox, I must first identify the crucial retributive principle and then show how all attempts fail to make moral sense of it. Within what can be broadly called a retributive theory of punishment, we should distinguish negative retributivism, the principle that one who is not guilty must not be punished, from positive retributivism, the principle that one who is guilty ought to be punished. We can, indeed, add a third principle of permissive retributivism, that one who is guilty may be punished. In these principles, 'must not', 'ought', and 'may' are meant to express moral judgements. For completeness, we should think also of quantitative variants of each principle, that even one who is guilty must not be punished to a degree that is out of proportion to his guilt, that one who is guilty ought to be punished in proportion to his guilt, or may be punished in proportion to his guilt. Also, while it might be possible to defend such judgements, perhaps all three (or all six) of them, as derived rules within, say, a utilitarian moral

[3] *ER*, p. 83.
[4] *ER*, p. 81.
[5] *ER*, p. 86.

system, that would not constitute a retributive theory of punishment. To yield anything worth counting as a retributive theory, such principles must be thought of as having some immediate, underived moral appeal or moral authority. Now I suggest that in moral thinking they are very widely, perhaps universally, felt to have such an immediate appeal and underived authority. This is undoubtedly true of negative retributivism, including its quantitative variant. Permissive retributivism, too, is immediately plausible. When the three principles are distinguished, many people are inclined to reject that of positive retributivism, to say that only some possible future benefit, such as deterrence or reformation, can justify punishment; yet I suspect that when we consider actual or possible cases of crimes or wrong-doing of kinds that we really regard as unmitigated and inexcusable, then we do after all tend to see them as in themselves calling for the infliction of some adequate penalty. Indeed, if we did not feel that there was such a positive retributivist reason for imposing a penalty, we should not feel that even sound arguments in terms of deterrence or reformation or any similar future benefit would make it morally right to inflict suffering or deprivation on the criminal. Certainly this is Westermarck's opinion, though his discussion of the point is obscured by his failure to distinguish positive retributivism, which is the really controversial issue, from the negative and permissive views.

If these retributivist principles have such immediate appeal and apparent authority, how are we to make sense of them, to relate them to some system of moral ideas? One suggestion which we must mention, though only in order to dismiss it, is that the connection between crime or wrong-doing and punishment is analytic. An old and often-criticized move of this sort is to say that negative retributivism is not needed as a moral principle, because it is logically impossible to punish the innocent. It is very doubtful whether this is true, but even if it were true it would be trivial, it would not cover quantitative negative retributivism, and there would still be room for, and a strong call for, the moral principle that one who is not guilty must not be made to suffer in any of the ways that would ordinarily count as punishment, call them what you will. A less familiar move of the same sort is to say that we simply have not fully grasped the concept of punishment unless we integrate it with the three retributive principles: in particular it is part of that concept that punishment is called for by wrong-doing. But again, even if this is true, it merely shifts the crucial problem to another place: how are we to make moral sense of a concept which includes this requirement, which envisages suffering or deprivation as being called for by a previous wrong action? Let us run through some possible answers to this question.[6]

It would be idle in this context to refer to the satisfaction that may be felt by the surviving victims of a crime when the criminal suffers, or to the likelihood that they will have recourse to more damaging kinds of retaliation if there is no legal penalty. This would be an attempt to justify punishment by its consequences, and does not help us to make sense of an essentially retributive principle. True, it presupposes that those victims themselves have retributive sentiments, but that does nothing to explain the retributivist moral principle. Similarly the suggestion that the punishment will satisfy the outraged feelings of the public at large, or will placate a god who has been offended by the crime, is equally forward-looking or consequentialist, equally useless for making sense of the backward-looking principles of retribution. Indeed, it presupposes that a morally respectable public or a morally respectable god already accepts such principles, and therefore must assume that there is some *other* morally coherent defence and explanation of them. The notion that punishment may impress upon the public the wrongness of the crime, and so have a useful educative effect, is also consequentialist, and it too seems to presuppose independent retributivist views: the public will take a penalty as a dramatic assertion of the wrongness of the act for which it is imposed only if it already has the concept of punishment as being called for by wrong-doing.

It is often suggested that by being punished a criminal pays a debt to society. But how can this be, unless what he suffers does some good to society? Reparation might be justified in this way, but reparations are clearly different from punishments; only the

---

[6] J.G. Cottingham, in 'Varieties of Retribution', *The Philosophical Quarterly*, Vol. 29, No. 116 (July 1979), lists the following nine different approaches, each of which has been called retributivist: Repayment Theory; Desert Theory; Penalty Theory; Minimalism; Satisfaction Theory; Fair Play Theory; Placation Theory; Annulment Theory; and Denunciation Theory. Of these, Minimalism is negative retributivism; Penalty Theory is the above-mentioned reference to logical necessity; and Desert Theory seems to be the bald, unexplained assertion that crime simply does deserve punishment; all the others on this list, as well as two further suggestions, are examined below.

already rejected principle of satisfaction would turn punishment into a sort of reparation.

A more serious attempt to explain the retributivist principle as the retrospective principle that it is, without turning it into something that is primarily forward-looking, is the suggestion made explicitly by Hegel, but perhaps anticipated by Kant, that an appropriate penalty annuls or cancels the crime. If left unpunished, the crime would still be alive and flourishing, but punishment tramples on it and wipes it out. But this really is incoherent. The punishment may trample on the criminal, but it does not do away with the crime. It may, perhaps, by way of deterrence, reformation, and the like help to prevent future similar crimes, and it may put a temporary or a permanent stop to this particular offender's criminal career; but again all of these are only possible consequentialist justifications, yet it seems that it is merely by confusion with them that it could be thought that the punishment annuls the crime. It should be clear beyond all question that the past wrong act, just because it is past, cannot be annulled. Might a crime be like a marriage or a contract or a conviction which can be annulled in the sense of being made to be without legal effect or validity? Though the act has occurred, can it be made to be no longer a crime? Perhaps this is the notion of expiation, that the suffering of the penalty absorbs and wipes out the guilt. This would make sense if the guilt were itself seen as consisting essentially in the wrong action's calling for an appropriate penalty: that call would die out when it was satisfied. But again this line of thought presupposes and therefore cannot explain positive retributivism.

A related suggestion uses the notion of fair play. All the members of a society are seen as being engaged in some kind of competition in accordance with rules; the criminal has gained an unfair advantage by breaking the rules; fairness is restored by the imposition of a penalty that takes this advantage away from him. Now what is annulled or cancelled is not the past crime, but the present advantage that has accrued from it. This suggestion at last offers us something that is both coherent and genuinely retributive. This explanation is retrospective, non-consequentialist, in that the justification for the penalty is complete as soon as the penalty has itself been carried out; the balance is thereby restored, irrespective of any future results. This principle has well-known and obviously reasonable exemplifications in what are literally rule-governed competitive games, such as association football. If a player commits a foul in the 'penalty area', that is, wrongly obstructs an opponent or his shot in the neighbourhood of his own goal, then the other side is awarded a penalty kick which gives it a good chance of scoring a goal. But the notion is that fairness has been (roughly) restored whether a goal results or not. However, this principle has little application to the punishment of most wrong-doing or crime. Above all, it would make penalties proportional not to the degree of wrongness or guilt, but to the advantages gained thereby; unsuccessful criminal attempts would not be punished at all. This is clearly so in the games where this principle is at home: a foul not near the offender's goal is penalized less, and there is an 'advantage rule': the referee will not stop play to penalize an infringement if the innocent side has the advantage anyway. All this is very far from the central notion of positive retributivism, which sees punishment as having its point in somehow counterbalancing the wrongness of the previous act, not in correcting the present advantage that the wrong-doer has gained by it.

It is often argued that the retributive approach to punishment respects the dignity of the people concerned in a way that the rival utilitarian approach does not. Each person is seen as a responsible agent. He has the right not to be made to suffer as long as he commits no wrong. If he does something wrong he loses his immunity in proportion to the degree of his guilt; but only by his own choice. If he has unfairly invaded the rights of others, he cannot reasonably complain at what would otherwise be a corresponding invasion of his own rights. This line of thought does seem to make sense of negative and permissive retributivism; but it still leaves positive retributivism unexplained. It is sometimes said that this is covered by an extension of the same line of thought. The criminal has freely chosen his own punishment is so far as he, as a citizen, has shared in the making of the law in accordance with which he is punished; he endorsed this law in general and in application to others, so he cannot fairly protest against its application to himself. This is plausible, and it would yield a partly retributive justification of punishment in that if such a law had really been endorsed, explicitly or implicitly, by the criminal among others, and if such endorsement could itself be seen as reasonable, then the only further justification required for the imposition of the penalty in a particular case would be the retrospective one that an offence of the sort condemned by the law had indeed been committed. But now all the weight falls on the conditional clauses. This justification would apply only in a society whose laws were themselves fair in their incidence upon various classes of citizens and had been made by something like Rousseau's general will; those who support retributivism may be happy to accept this restriction.[7] But, further, the law imposing this penalty must be one which the free and equal citizens of such a society could reasonably make. What reason could they have for doing so? Since no other explanation of positive retributivism has stood up to criticism, this condition requires that there should be some other, forward-looking, consequentialist, reason for having such a law. The general practice of punishing requires, for this approach to be coherent, a consequentialist justification, though, given this practice, reasonably endorsed by the general will, the imposing of individual penalties needs only retrospective grounds to justify it.

This survey shows that all these attempts to make sense of the principle of positive retributivism, as an independent principle with immediate moral authority, have signally failed. And we have, I believe, covered all the main lines of thought that have been used to try to make retributivism coherent. Yet this survey has also indicated how deeply ingrained retributivist—even positive retributivist—ideas are, if only by bringing to light the circularity of many of the explanations that have been widely thought to be satisfactory, that is, the tendency of proposed accounts to build upon the supposed existence of already valid positive retributive principles. People find the proposed accounts plausible because they are so firmly wedded to retributivist ways of thinking that they find it difficult to confront the task of justifying retributivism from cold, without implicitly assuming what they are setting out to explain. We do have a concept of punishment which involves positive as well as negative and permissive retributivism, and, as Westermarck says, attempts to reconstruct that concept so as to free it from that involvement are radically

---

[7] For example, Jeffrie G. Murphy, in 'Marxism and Retribution', *Philosophy and Public Affairs*, Vol. 2, No. 3 (Spring 1973), says that 'there may be some truth in Marx's claim that the retributive theory, though formally correct, is materially inadequate' in that the 'presupposition that all men, including criminals, are voluntary participants in a reciprocal system of benefits' is empirically false about actual societies.

unsatisfying. We are indeed faced, therefore, with the paradox of retribution.

For all that has been said so far, it might be thought that this is just a special problem about one particular concept, that of punishment. But if we analyse the concept of a morally wrong action it will be seen to have much wider significance. In the central cases, the wrongness of an action is thought of as being made up of three elements, its being harmful, its being forbidden, and its calling for a hostile response. No one of these elements, if the others are somehow denied, is sufficient to make an action wrong in the full sense. Even if we try to think of 'an action's having any two of these features, but not the third, we hesitate to say that it would then be wrong. In particular, if we think of an action's being both harmful and forbidden, but nevertheless try to withhold the judgement that it calls for any sort of hostile response, I suggest that we cannot then judge whole-heartedly that it is morally wrong. Moreover, all three elements involve what Westermarck calls objectivization. The wrong action is not harmful just to this or that person, it is harmful *simpliciter*, or, as Sidgwick put it, from the point of view of the universe. It is not forbidden just by this or that authority, it is somehow forbidden intrinsically, absolutely; it simply should not be done. Its moral quality includes both a generalized harmfulness and an intrinsic not-to-be-done-ness. And similarly it is not just from this or that particular person that it calls for a hostile response; rather, it is such that a hostile response *from somewhere* is needed, the situation is somehow generally unsatisfactory if the wrong action gets by without any proportional reaction.

To complete the analysis of this concept, we have to note that the three elements we have identified are not merely conjoined. It is not that we have moral wrongness whenever all three just happen to occur together: they are rather seen as being necessarily connected with one another. A wrong action is intrinsically forbidden because it is harmful from the point of view of the universe, and it calls for a hostile response because it is both harmful generally and intrinsically forbidden.

It might be thought that this analysis makes redundant the vain search in which we have been engaged for some way of making moral sense of positive retributivism. What need is there for any further explanation of the principle that one who has done wrong

ought to be punished, if it is involved in the very concept of wrongness that a wrong action calls for a hostile response? But this is a
mistake. Buried inside the complex concept of wrongness, lying
behind the analytic judgement that what is wrong calls for a hostile
response, is the synthetic judgement that what is harmful generally
and intrinsically forbidden calls on that account for a hostile response. It is for an elucidation and justification of this synthetic
judgement that we have so far sought in vain; what would come to
the same thing would be a 'deduction' in Kant's sense of the complex concept of moral wrongness itself.

On other occasions I have stressed the difficulties in the second
of these three elements, the notion of intrinsic not-to-be-done-ness,
or the supposed objective prescriptivity of moral features of which
this is an instance. I have argued that our central moral concepts
are prescriptive but also include a claim to objectivity for that
prescriptiveness itself. I have argued, as Westermarck does, against
the actual objectivity of moral qualities or moral facts, while insisting that this subjectivist conclusion cannot be established by the
mere analysis of moral concepts and judgements, since, as I say,
such analysis reveals this claim to objectivity. My main argument
has been based on the 'queerness' of this notion of objective prescriptivity, on the metaphysical and epistemological difficulties it
involves; these are such that the best explanatory hypothesis to
account for the phenomena of moral thinking does not include the
postulate that there are any such objectively prescriptive truths;
instead, it will use Westermarck's view that the belief in such truths
results from moral emotions, whose distinctive features are developed by social interactions and then, through objectivization,
yield the misleading appearance of objective reality.[8]

Now, however, we can reinforce this argument in another way.
The central moral concept of the wrongness of an action includes,
as we have seen, the synthetic judgement that what is harmful
generally and intrinsically forbidden calls for a hostile response:
this concept contains a very general form of the positive retributivist principle. In this general form, it applies not just to the special
topic of punishment, but pervasively, wherever the central concept
of moral wrongness is in force. But the apparent impossibility of
making moral sense of this retributive principle must then add to

---

[8] These arguments can be found in Chapter 1 of my *Ethics, Inventing Right and
Wrong* (Harmondsworth, 1977).

the implausibility of the moral concepts' claim to objectivity. Although many, perhaps most, or even all moral thinkers have an apparent intuition in favour of this principle—a moral intuition, not merely a linguistic or conceptual one—it cannot be defended as an immediately valid and authoritative principle with the status of an objective truth. This is over and above the general metaphysical and epistemological difficulties that beset the notion of *any* objectively prescriptive truth; but, because it affects the very central concept of moral wrongness, it casts its shadow over moral thought as a whole.

I have concentrated on hostile rather than on kindly retribution, on punishment rather than on gratitude and reward, on the wrong rather than on the good and the right, because gratitude and reward do not generate so acute a paradox as their hostile counterparts. Reasons for doing good are not so hard to integrate into a moral system as reasons for doing harm. Yet there is some element of paradox even here, as extreme utilitarians have seen. Why should previous good actions be in themselves a reason for doing good to these agents in particular, rather than simply seeking to maximize overall utility? But hostile retributivism is more of a problem, and, as Westermarck says, kindly retributive tendencies are less pervasive and less central in morality than hostile ones. The more forceful moral notions, of what is obligatory or of what justice requires or of rights that must not be infringed, all involve the concept of its being wrong to do something, or wrong not to do something, and the concept of wrongness, as we have seen, itself includes the principle of positive retributivism.

How, then, are we to resolve the paradox of retribution? It ceases to be puzzling when, like Westermarck, we make the Humean move of saying that moral distinctions are founded on sentiment, not on reason, and so ask not, 'Why do wrong actions deserve penalities and good actions deserve rewards?' but rather, 'Why do we have an ingrained tendency to see wrong actions as calling for penalties and good actions as calling for rewards?' I suggest that we can find a biological explanation for the tendency to feel non-moral resentment of injuries and gratitude for benefits, and a sociological explanation for the development, out of these, of their moral counterparts.

Suppose that an animal, human or non-human, is injured by another, either of the same species or of some other, where the first is able to do some harm to the second which the second can associate with its aggression and perhaps recognize as a reaction to it. Then such retaliation will tend to benefit the retaliator, since the aggressor will be discouraged from repeating the attack. This mechanism can operate either at the psychological level, by negative reinforcement in an individual aggressor, or at a genetic level, where there will be some selective pressure against a kind of aggression that commonly proves harmful to the aggressor. For both reasons there will then be some selective pressure in favour of the tendency to retaliate. This need not be, and originally will certainly not be, the result of calculation and deliberate choice by the retaliator; it is rather that the mechanism of natural selection mimics calculated, purposive, action. Spontaneous retaliation will thus develop because it is often beneficial, either immediately or in a longer term, but it will be spontaneous, not chosen by the retaliator for the sake of the benefit. Of course, we need not assume that retaliation is always beneficial, as it clearly is not, and we can well admit that what is thus biologically developed is likely to be a 'mixed strategy', a combination of retaliatory tendencies with tendencies, say, to flight or, at least among members of the same species, to conciliation. All that we need is that there should be a retaliatory component in whatever mixed strategy is developed, and it is easy to see why this should be so. And the spontaneous repaying of benefit with benefit may be developed in a corresponding way.

Initially what is thus explained is retributive behaviour, but in creatures that have the capacity for emotion this will naturally be accompanied by the development of retributive emotions directed towards the sources of injury or help. However, these are still only the non-moral retributive emotions. In order to account for their moral counterparts we must, as Westermarck says, turn to society as the birthplace of the moral consciousness. Among animals that live in social groups, it is easy to explain co-operation in the resentment of injuries. The helping, in this as in other ways, of individuals closely related to an agent will be of direct genetic advantage, of a sort that results in selection in its favour, in so far as close relatives will tend to share the agent's genes. There can also be selective pressures in favour of reciprocal altruism, the tendency to help those who help the agent in return.[9] But what may be most

[9] For an account of these genetic mechanisms, see R. Dawkins, *The Selfish Gene* (Oxford, 1976). In my 'The Law of the Jungle: Moral Alternatives and Principles of

important, especially among human beings, is that co-operative social practices or conventions can grow up by social interaction. A simple model will illustrate this possibility. If two agents will do better in some way if they co-operate, they may begin to do so gradually and tentatively, each making his further co-operative moves conditional upon a favourable response from the other. Such a tentative development of a co-operative practice is easy to describe in terms of a series of conscious choices; but it could equally well grow up more automatically, through agents coming habitually to adopt ways of behaving in relation to one another that tend to help each in whatever pursuits are already established as part of his behaviour. Reciprocal sanctioning, the fact that each will be less co-operative if the other is less co-operative, can generate and maintain co-operative conventions even without any series of conscious choices.[10] Since co-operation in general is thus explicable, co-operation in resentment can be understood in social animals and particularly in human beings once resentment itself has been explained. And co-operation in resentment is more likely to be useful to those who develop it than co-operation in gratitude: the repelling of injuries will often require greater concentrations of force than are needed in order to make a worthwhile return for a benefit.

From co-operation in resentment to moral disapproval or indignation is a further step, but not an enormous one. It requires that certain *kinds* of behaviour should be co-operatively resented and opposed and seen as generally harmful. For this will yield the 'disinterestedness' and 'apparent impartiality' that are characteristic of the moral sentiments. The fact that it is kinds of behaviour that are resented is linked with what I call the first stage of universalization and with disinterestedness, while the notion that they are harmful generally, not just to this or that person or group, is linked with the second stage of universalization and with apparent

Evolution', *Philosophy*, Vol. 53, No. 206 (October 1978), I have shown that although, in general, tendencies will not be favoured by selection simply because they will benefit a group in whose members they occur, such 'group selection' can take place in special circumstances, and the example used was one of reciprocal altruism. [See Chapter IX above.—Edd.]

[10] Hume, in the *Treatise of Human Nature*, Book III, Part II, finds the origin of the 'artificial virtues' in such 'conventions' established and maintained by the indirect operation of self-love. I interpret and develop his account in my *Hume's Moral Theory* (London, 1980).

impartiality.[11] But both these moves result from the need for a morality to be accepted by a society as a whole, to be strengthened by each person's influencing of others in its favour and to be passed on by collective teaching to later generations. All of this is only a further development of such conventions as those mentioned above and is supported in the same way by social interaction where there is a partial conflict of interests. Such a development presupposes fairly advanced intellectual powers associated with the retributive emotions and the socially maintained retributive behaviour. Nevertheless, the essential drives, the directing forces which sustain the resulting patterns of action, still come from the emotions and the conventions, and are only further canalized by the recognition of kinds of behaviour. And the judgement that a certain kind of behaviour is harmful, even when it is true, may often follow rather than precede the co-operative resentment and opposition to it. For, as we have seen, there are both genetic and social mechanisms which can pick out what is harmful and develop hostile reactions to it, reactions that will themselves be beneficial, without the agents themselves having consciously realized that these reactions are beneficial or that what they are reacting against is harmful. The apparent purposiveness is explained throughout by procedures of natural selection and the growth of conventions.

Of course, this is only a sketch. Further explanations are needed for all the details of human moral attitudes and their objectivization into moral beliefs, and much of Westermarck's work was meant as a contribution to such explanation. But what was crucially required, and was not, I think, given by him with sufficient clarity, was an outline of the basic mechanisms and main steps by which recognizably moral thinking could arise in the first place.

We can, then, describe a possible course of evolution by which retributive behaviour and emotions, co-operative resentment, and the disinterested moral sentiments could have developed in turn. It is an essential feature of this hypothetical account that at every stage it involves spontaneous, non-calculating, retributive tendencies, mainly hostile, though there is room for some kindly retribution too. In this lies the solution of our paradox of retribution. For what we have sketched is the development of a system of sentiments (which, through objectivization, yield beliefs) which from the

[11] I distinguish the various stages of universalization, and discuss their place in moral thinking, in Chapter 4 of *Ethics, Inventing Right and Wrong*.

point of view of those who have them are both originally and persistently retrospective. They are essentially retributive, essentially connected with previous harmful—or, occasionally, beneficial—actions. When we seek to rationalize our moral thinking, to turn it into a system of objective requirements, we cannot make sense of this retrospectivity. We either, with the utilitarians, attempt to deny it and eliminate it or to subordinate it to forward-looking purposes, or, with their retributivist opponents, try various desperate and incoherent devices, none of which, as we have seen, will really accommodate the principle of desert within any otherwise intelligible order of ideas. But if we recognize them simply as sentiments—though socially developed sentiments—we have no difficulty in understanding their obstinately retrospective character. Moreover, we can now elucidate Westermarck's otherwise obscure reference to 'some connection between these ends [such as deterrence and reformation] and the retributive aim of moral resentment'.[12] These utilitarian 'ends' are the results for which moral resentment, and its non-moral forerunners, have been selected and encouraged by genetic and social evolutionary mechanisms. They are functions in terms of which we—as scientists, not as moralists—can explain the development of moral resentment: they are the apparent ends in evolution's imitation of purposiveness.

Since an objectivist moral view can neither avoid nor resolve the paradox of retribution, which pervades moral thinking in so far as the positive retributivist principle is involved in the central concept of a wrong action, whereas a sentimentalist or subjectivist view can resolve it, this whole problem constitutes a powerful support for the latter sort of view, and therefore for Westermarck's thesis that the moral concepts are ultimately based on emotions. Our resolution of the paradox also included a hypothetical account of how the moral emotions could have developed from their non-moral counterparts by the addition of disinterestedness and apparent impartiality; and though this was only a hypothesis, it is confirmed by its success in helping to explain what otherwise resists explanation. Thus we have been able to supplement and round out Westermarck's theory, fitting his various theses into a more tightly argued and causally coherent account.

[12] *ER*, p. 80.

XVI

RIGHTS, UTILITY,
AND EXTERNAL COSTS

THIS paper takes its departure from a view stated by H.L.A. Hart in his article 'Between Utility and Rights'.[1] 'We are currently witnessing', Hart says, 'the progress of a transition from a once widely accepted old faith that some form of utilitarianism, if only we could discover the right form, must capture the essence of political morality. The new faith is that the truth must lie not with a doctrine that takes the maximisation of aggregate or average general welfare for its goal, but with a doctrine of basic human rights, protecting specific basic liberties and interests of individuals, if only we could find some sufficiently firm foundation for such rights ...' In other words, we are moving towards a right-based political morality, but we have not yet discovered a defensible one. Hart develops this thesis by criticizing two very different right-based theories, those of Robert Nozick and Ronald Dworkin, and argues that we shall not reach a satisfactory right-based theory as long as our approach is determined mainly by a reaction—indeed an over-reaction—against utilitarianism.

I shall not retrace, though I largely agree with, Hart's criticisms of Nozick and Dworkin. Rather, I shall take up Hart's challenge to formulate a more defensible right-based theory, and then try to show that it is not a trivial restatement of a utilitarian view, and is neither empty nor too vague to serve as a practical guide, by applying it to a specific sort of problem about how to allocate the external costs of an enterprise.

We need not, however, take too seriously the difficulty that Hart mentions for a right-based theory, '... if only we could find some sufficiently firm foundation for such rights'. I am confident that no normative theory, whatever its basis, whether it centres on utility

---

Previously unpublished: written late in 1979, read as a paper in the U.S.A. early in 1980.
   [1] *Columbia Law Review*, Vol. 79 (1979), pp. 828-46.

or on duties or on rights, can in the end be held to be objectively valid. Normative systems, of whatever sort, are made by men, individually or collectively, by explicit invention or by unconscious development.[2] There is plenty of scope for reasoning, and for the use of causal and other information about human nature or social relations, in the detailed development of such systems, but their fundamental principles are not a matter of truth or falsehood, but of choice and endorsement. So we are not to look for any set of self-evident truths about what basic rights people have, nor to think our theory any the weaker because we cannot discover such truths. Rather, we have to look for some system of basic rights which we are ourselves prepared seriously to ascribe to people in general, and which there is some hope that people in general may come to recognize one another as having. In this search, we may reasonably be guided by the considerations that have led many thinkers to turn from utility to rights.

As Hart says, here agreeing with Nozick, what we want a right-based theory to do is to take serious account of the separateness of persons: rights are to 'form a protective bastion enabling an individual to achieve his own ends in a life he shapes himself'. But, as he also says, now in criticism of Nozick, 'for a meaningful life not only the protection of freedom from deliberate restriction but opportunities and resources for its exercise are needed. Except for a few privileged and lucky persons, the ability to shape life for oneself and lead a meaningful life is something to be constructed by positive marshalling of social and economic resources. It is not something automatically guaranteed by a structure of negative rights.' Let us then consider what sort of system of rights really could achieve this aim.

We need to distinguish the detailed and complicated network of rights which it is the business of the legal institutions in a particular country to enforce from some basic and perhaps fairly simple set of rights in which, on the present approach, we shall locate the ultimate justification of those institutional rights, in so far as they are justified, and also criteria for their adjustment and correction and reform—these basic rights are what Dworkin calls abstract rights. The derivation of institutional rights from abstract rights may itself be complicated. Some institutional rights can, perhaps,

---

[2] I defend this view in *Ethics, Inventing Right and Wrong* (Harmondsworth, 1977) and in *Hume's Moral Theory* (London, 1980).

be seen as applications to concrete circumstances of certain abstract rights. Others will have been constituted or created by various things that people have done, either recently or more remotely, in the course of history, in exercise of certain of their basic rights; in particular, they may have arisen through the interaction between the activities in which people have used their abstract rights. Some, again, will arise from the need to compensate for previous violations of rights. Yet others, paradoxically, may have arisen from actions which have in greater or lesser degree violated certain abstract rights, but even so may be at least partly, temporarily, and provisionally validated by certain other abstract rights: there will be room in our system for such principles as those of adverse possession and a statute of limitations. What basic or abstract rights, then, should we postulate?—remembering that their purpose is not that we should, in general, appeal directly to them for practical decisions, but rather that they should serve as principles by which we can either justify or criticize the institutional rights on which practical decisions will be more immediately based.

I suggest that these abstract rights can be seen as falling under three headings. Those in the first group are concerned with protected opportunities for choice and activity; those in the second with the control and distribution of property or, more generally, of resources; those in the third with the ways in which institutional rights are developed, maintained, or changed. Under the first heading I put such traditional rights as those to life, health, liberty, and the pursuit of happiness, the rights stressed by Jefferson and before him by Locke. More explicitly, we could formulate rights not to be deprived of life or health (since these are preconditions of almost any worthwhile activity) and to be protected against both human and natural agencies that might deprive one of life or health; also rights to be able to make one's own choices and decisions about the matters that concern oneself most closely, and to be able to work towards the bringing about of results that one strongly desires and to continue to enjoy such results in so far as they are achieved. Under the second heading I suggest three principles. One is that each person has a *prima facie* right to use and dispose of such goods as he creates or to the part of the value of any goods that is traceable to his efforts and skill; this can also be extended from individuals to groups. The second is that, by contrast, all persons have equal *prima facie* rights to share in natural resources or in the use of such resources, and hence to share that part of the value of any goods that is traceable to natural resources. The third is that elements of value that are in fact derived from the labour and skill of previous generations, but where no clear derivation can be traced, revert to the status of natural resources, so that all persons have equal *prima facie* rights also to these, and that even where such a derivation can be traced we should recognize only an evanescent right of inheritance, so that these goods too revert gradually to the status of natural resources.

All these rights, under both headings, are put forward only as *prima facie*, not absolute or conclusive, rights—necessarily so, since in practice they are liable to come into conflict with one another, though in some respects also to support one another. The extent to which someone's life or health can be protected will of course depend on what resources are available and what legitimate competing claims there are for their use. But the fairly egalitarian principles suggested with regard to property should harmonize well with the notion that everyone has a right to the pursuit of happiness.

Since these are all only *prima facie* rights, and also only abstract rights, there is a very great problem of adjusting their interactions and deriving institutional rights from them. This leads to my third heading. Here I would suggest two principles. One is that on which Dworkin has laid so much stress, that people have a right to equal concern and respect, or, as Rawls puts it, that people have a right to equal respect and consideration in determining the principles by which a society's basic arrangements are to be regulated. This could be seen as a principle that underlies the democratic idea that citizens have the right to participate in the political process and to have some chance of influencing the laws and governmental decisions that are made. But it also goes beyond the idea of simple majority rule in requiring that minorities, especially permanent minorities, should not be ignored or brushed aside. Where there really is something that approximates to Rousseau's legislation by the general will, where all members of a community agree to be bound by laws that will apply to all, then clearly no one's rights are infringed. But where this sort of unanimity is unattainable, then some sort of compromise is in order, governed by the rule that the more vital interests of some are not to be sacrificed to the less vital interests of others. The other principle under this heading is that

all persons have a *prima facie* right to the fulfilment of reasonable
expectations based on a fairly stable system of laws, institutions,
and practices. This is a moderately conservative principle: it obviously implies that some sort of brake should be put upon changes
in institutions even where other *prima facie* rights would tell in
favour of such changes, and could support such principles as those
of adverse possession and a statute of limitations, which I mentioned above.

This whole scheme may be contrasted with an argument of Nozick's which sums up his whole theory. 'The major objection', he
says, 'to speaking of everyone's having a right *to* various things
such as equality of opportunity, life, and so on, and enforcing this
right, is that these "rights" require a substructure of things and
materials and actions; and *other* people may have rights and entitlements over these ....'. The particular rights over things fill the
space of rights, leaving no room for general rights to be in a certain
material condition' (*Anarchy, State, and Utopia*, p. 238). It is true
that if Nozick's particular rights were absolute they would fill the
space of rights. I want deliberately to start from the other end,
laying down *prima facie* but non-negligible rights to things like life
and health, and therefore to conclude that while there can be rights
to property, founded in various ways, these too can be only *prima
facie* rights.

Now it may be objected to this outline that while the proposed
rights have some plausibility, and indeed different ones among
them may appeal to different tastes, the scheme as a whole is too
vague and indeterminate to be of any use except as a rhetorical
smokescreen to cover decisions that are really made on other
grounds, particularly since it combines reforming and conservative
principles, and everything practical will depend on the relative
weights assigned to these. But this will not be so if serious attention
is given to the principle of equal concern and respect and the notion
of letting more vital interests outweigh less vital ones. At the same
time, it is fair to remember, if this scheme is in competition with
utilitarianism, that that theory also was never more than a rough
guide: there neither was nor could be a *calculus* of utility. However,
the best reply to this objection may be to try to discuss a type of
real issue in the light of this approach, and to see whether it does
indeed suggest any practical guidance.

Let us then apply these principles to the familiar problem of external costs. Many activities, productive or non-productive, have, in addition to the internal costs of the labour, materials, energy, and capital which they use and pay for, external costs for which they do not pay, which they unload onto other people and other enterprises. A factory in a city pours out smoke and fumes which damage the health of people living around and the paintwork and stonework of their buildings. It drops smuts on any clothes that are hung outside to dry, so that people have to use electric driers instead. An airport brings the noise of planes taking off and landing which disturbs people's peace, spoils their appreciation of music, interrupts lessons in schools and conversation in homes, or else forces people to install double glazing, keep their windows closed even in summer, and use air-conditioners. Another factory discharges waste chemicals into a river, which kill the fish and ruin the sport of those who used to catch them. And so on. But the factories and the airport do not pay for all this incidental damage which they cause. In recent years everyone has become more aware of these problems, more ready to protest against them. But there are at least three distinct kinds of possible hostile reaction. One is the nostalgic or Luddite reaction: 'How much better it was when we didn't have factories or airports, when goods were made by hand and people didn't rush aimlessly all over the world, but either stayed at home or, if they had to travel, went on foot or on horseback or by sailing ship. What we wrongly regard as progress ruins the environment: let us try to get back to a simpler way of life, an alternative technology.' Attractive though this reaction is, I shall simply leave it aside. A second reaction is to say that it is unfair that enterprises should be able to unload part of their costs onto other people; a factory doesn't expect its workers to work without wages, it doesn't expect to get its energy supplies free; why should it not equally pay for the damage which it does, which is just as real a part of its total costs? A third reaction supports this second one with an economic argument. In a reasonably competitive economy, an enterprise will be engaged in only if it is in a fairly obvious sense socially worth while, if the social value of its products, measured by what people are prepared to pay for them, is at least as great as the social cost of its inputs, measured by what it will have to pay for them, competing with other enterprises for capital, labour, materials, and energy. But this pricing mechanism will fail if some of the real costs of the enterprise are not charged to it. An enterprise may be engaged in because it is profitable even when its total social cost is greater than the value of what it produces. The classical recommendation of welfare economics, therefore, which goes back at least to Pigou, is that enterprises should somehow be made to pay for their external as well as their internal costs.

However, there is a counter-argument, originally put forward in a well known article by R.H. Coase ('The Problem of Social Cost', in the *Journal of Law and Economics*, 1960). The core of Coase's argument runs as follows. Suppose that an enterprise's income from the sale of its products is \$a, its internal costs \$b, and its external costs, initially borne in various ways by other people, are \$c, and a > b but a < b + c. Then the enterprise ought to be stopped or modified, since its real costs are greater than the real benefits it produces, and Pigou's thesis is that this will be achieved if, by some administrative, governmental, or legal action the enterprise is compelled to pay out \$c, to compensate all those who are injured by its side effects. But, Coase argues, the same desired result can be achieved without administrative action, by the mere operation of *laissez-faire* economic mechanisms. If other people are really being damaged to the extent of \$c by this enterprise's activities, it will pay them to get together and offer those who run the enterprise anything up to \$c to close down or go somewhere else; and if a < b + c, simple algebra shows that c > a − b, that is, what they can afford to offer is greater than its present margin of income over costs, so the enterprise *will* be closed down or moved elsewhere.

In fact Coase makes a stronger claim than this. Suppose we take the old-fashioned example of a railway which runs coal-burning locomotives through farmland, and sparks from the locomotives set fire to the farmers' crops; up to a point, the higher the speed the more profitable it will be for the railway, but, also, the higher the speed the wider the strip of farmland on which the crops are likely to be destroyed. Now if the railway were compelled, in accordance with Pigou's principle, to pay the farmers the full value of whatever crops it destroyed, and if it could still afford to run at a certain speed, because the relative advantage of running at that speed would outweigh the value of those crops, then it would pay the farmers to plant crops right up to the track, knowing that even if the crops were burnt they would still be paid for them. And this would be, socially speaking, a sheer waste of resources. Whereas if the farmers had to bargain with the railway, having found the speed below which it was not worth their while to bribe the railway to run, they would not waste their labour and materials in planting crops in the zone where they were pretty certain to be burnt.

However, this argument rests on a misinterpretation of the Pigou principle. That would rather require the farmers to be compensated only for losses that the railway's running *imposes* on them, not for any further losses which they deliberately incur by planting crops where they will be destroyed. That is, the farmers will be paid for the loss of the use of a certain strip of land, they will receive the difference between the profit they would have made if they could have used all their land and that which they make if they simply do not use the strip that would be burnt by sparks from the railway. Thus reasonably interpreted, Pigou's principle can be shown to give exactly the same adjustment between activities—the same speed for the locomotives, the same unused strip of farmland—that would be reached by Coase's method of free bargaining.

However, although we get the same adjustment between activities, and hence the same maximizing of social utility, in either way, it may still be held that it is *unfair* to let the external costs rest initially where they fall, to force those on whom they fall to buy off the polluter to whatever extent it is most economical for them to do so. The farmers have a right to the use of the contested strip of land, the railway does not.

To evaluate this objection, let us consider a more modern problem. Suppose that a city needs a new airport, and there is a choice between three sites, A, B, and C, where B is further from the city centre than A, and C is further away still. Site A will be expensive, but it will benefit the city more than either B or C, in that it will cost travellers less in time and money to go between the airport and the city centre, so that the choice of A will do more to attract both business and tourists. On the other hand, site A is near a residential area, and the people there protest about the noise, the added ground traffic, and the consequent loss of value of their homes. The same is true of site B, but to a lesser extent. Site C is so far from any residential area that the external costs of using it would be negligible, but it is in a swamp where it would be costly to build an airport, and it is so far from the city centre that it would be much less beneficial. Suppose that the benefits and the internal and external costs of the three sites, over some period of time, are estimated as follows, say in millions of dollars:

	A	B	C
Benefits	200	150	100
Internal costs	80	60	80
External costs	100	50	—
Balance of benefits over total costs	20	40	20

We are inclined to say that if these estimates are correct site B should be chosen, since it is the one which yields the greatest balance of benefits over total costs. Also, this is the site that will be chosen if the city is legally compelled to compensate the residents for whatever damage they suffer. But, equally, in accordance with Coase's argument, site B will be chosen if the issue is left to private enterprise and fair bargaining. The city authorities will no doubt initially prefer site A. The residents in that area will be up in arms, holding meetings, writing to the newspapers and to their representatives, complaining of all the injury and inconvenience they will suffer. But the authorities can say to them: 'If it will really damage you as much as you say, what are you prepared to pay to have the proposed airport moved to, say, site B?'—to pay not surreptitiously to senators or representatives or city councillors, but openly to the city treasury itself. And clearly the residents of area A will be willing to offer, say, $30m to make it as satisfactory for the city to transfer to site B, where its total profit, including the $30m, will still be $120m, as at site A. Perhaps they will have to offer a shade over this, to tip the balance. The residents of area B will, no doubt, now be similarly up in arms. But the city can call their bluff, asking them whether they are prepared to offer the $70m needed to make site C equally attractive to the city; and of course they are not. So again site B, the one we automatically recognize as the right one, will be chosen. And this bargaining procedure has the merit that its results depend on what the parties who are or may be affected are really willing to pay, which will correspond to their real costs, whereas if the Pigou principle were legally enforced there would be every temptation for the residents of area B to exaggerate the damages they would suffer, so as either to get greater compensation or to induce the city authorities to go on to site C, which, as we can see, would not be the socially correct decision.

Thus—and this, of course, is Coase's contention—the socially desirable result will be reached more certainly by letting the damages rest initially where they happen to fall and leaving the further outcome to be determined by direct bargaining, rather than by attempting to impose legal principles of compensation that will make enterprises bear their own external costs.

But, everyone will protest, this is not fair. Why should the residents of area B in particular suffer $50m worth of damage so that the city as a whole can have a better airport? And why should the residents of area A have to pay out $30m in order to keep such damage away? Even if the Coase principle is at least equally efficient, is not the Pigou principle more just? Is this not a classic illustration of the need to supplement, at least, considerations of aggregate utility with distributive considerations about rights? The rights of the residents of areas A and B are being infringed if they are put into a position where they must either suffer damage or pay to keep it away.

Suppose, then, that we adopt the Pigou principle, leave area A alone (since it would cost the city too much to compensate the residents there), put the airport on site B, and pay the residents of area B $50m. The city's airport enterprise is then much less profitable than it might have been: it brings in on balance only $40m when it might have brought in $120m. Can we not argue, then, that this relative loss to the city is an external cost of the activities of the residents of areas A and B? Those pampered dwellers in area A, listening to music on their front lawns on summer afternoons, breathing fresh air through their schoolroom windows, sleeping peacefully at night, are costing their fellow-citizens millions of dollars, and so are those only slightly less pampered dwellers in area B, who are taking in compensation and getting free double-glazing and air-conditioning. Why should we not apply the Pigou principle now the other way round, and require them to compensate the city for these external costs of their enterprises?

An obvious answer would be that the residents of these areas were there first. Their enterprises are already established, and perhaps have been established for a long time; the present residents bought their houses at higher prices than they would have had to pay if it had been known that an airport would be planked down among them. Their reasonable expectations are the foundation of continuing rights. The proposed airport is an intrusion into an existing network of social and economic relations.

But this is only a fairly good answer. If this were all that could be said, it might be countered by asking why so much weight should be given to mere temporal priority, why past uses should be able to outweigh possible future ones. And even if we did give some weight to temporal priority, would this not lead only to a short-term preference for the residents' uses, so that they would be compensated more fully for the damages they suffered in the first year than in the second, and so on?

A more radical challenge to the 'other way round' application of the Pigou principle would be to deny that the lowered profitability of the city's airport enterprise is an external cost of the residents' way of life, to ask in what sense of 'cost' this can be so. But this challenge is easily met. The meaning is simply that if the residents' activities were not there, demanding protection or compensation, the airport would be so much less expensive and more profitable. The ideal procedure for the city would be to put the airport on site A and not compensate anyone, and so make a profit of $120m. The difference between the profit that it would make from this ideal procedure and that which it actually makes if it goes to site B and pays $50m to the residents of that area is $120m minus $40m, that is $80m. In fact we can compute costs in either of two ways, according to which baseline we take. If we take the *status quo*, before the airport project is suggested, as the baseline, then the $30m paid by the residents of area A to keep the thing away and the $50m damages then suffered by the residents of area B are indeed external costs of the airport. But if we take what is the ideal procedure from the city's point of view as the baseline, then if it has to go to site B and also pay $50m in compensation to the people in that area the total of $80m by which the city is then worse off than it might have been is an external cost of the activities of the residents of areas A and B. We can bring this out dramatically by imagining a situation in which these areas are initially vacant, the city decides on site A, and then people pour into areas A and B, forcibly prevent any construction work, and compel the city both to alter its plans and to pay compensation. Can anyone doubt that in these circumstances the residents' activities would be imposing external costs on the city? So is not all that makes the difference between this and the actual case the fact that the residents were there first? And, as was said above, is this temporal consideration sufficient to carry all the weight so as to justify using the Pigou principle only the one way round? If not, then some compromise solution might seem reasonable. If what is evidently the best practical choice, that of site B, is made, then all the parties together are *somehow* going to be $80m worse off than if, *per impossible*, every party had got what was best for it at once. Perhaps, then, the city should bear $40m of the cost of this compromise and the residents $40m between them—for instance, the residents of area A might pay $20m to those of area B, and the city $10m to the residents of area B, who would then be only $20m down. Or we might regard this equal division as the final arrangement, to which we should move only gradually, starting with one more favourable to the residents, in view of the temporary, but only temporary, weight of their plea that they were there first.

Let us relate this issue to the set of abstract basic rights outlined above. One crucial question will be whether the existing situation, before the problem of the new airport arose, was itself a just one, whether the institutional rights, in particular the property rights, that the various interested parties then had could be seen as having arisen from our set of abstract rights by way of various decisions and actions over time, or could be defended with the help of the principle about protecting reasonable expectations. Suppose that this is so. Then of the two alternative baselines the *status quo* has a clear advantage over the one that represents the ideal procedure for the city, for there can be no presumption that it is equally fair, since it completely disregards any *prima facie* rights of the residents of areas A and B. Whatever needs the city as a whole has, the rights of these residents cannot simply disappear. This is enough to show that an equal compromise, as suggested above, will not be the just solution—given the assumption that the original situation was itself just.

On the other hand it does not follow, even with this assumption, that the just solution in altered conditions will fully respect the pre-existing property rights. They may be weakened by the competition of new claims that arise, ultimately validated by the same abstract basic rights. Suppose, for example, that someone has originally a just title to some land which then increases sharply in value because minerals are found in it or because it is very much needed, say as residential land for a growing city or as including the only possible route for a new highway; our basic principles clearly give no presumption that the owner is entitled to the whole of such 'windfall' profits. Even if the owner does not seek to collect such profits, but merely to continue to enjoy his present use of the land, it does not follow that he is entitled to do so. Through whatever relevant changes have occurred, this land has become the object of more intense general demand or need than it was before, and the ownership which was part of a fair allocation in the previous need-situation may no longer be so.

It may be argued that if, in our airport case, the pre-existing situation was fair, the fair solution after the airport problem arises cannot be one which makes anyone worse off. If the airport is worth building at all, it must be, on aggregate, advantageous to all those concerned; if so, it must be possible to distribute its costs and benefits so that no one is worse off than he was, while some at least are better off. This argument is not watertight, for two reasons. First, the airport may be needed not to make the city as a whole better off but to prevent it from becoming worse off; a city without an efficient airport is in danger of becoming a derelict area, so perhaps all its citizens will have to bear some losses to prevent greater ones. Secondly, it is not in general necessary that the move from a just solution before a worthwhile technological change to a just solution after that change will be a Pareto improvement. For example, suppose that two twins, J and K, share very limited resources, but initially J suffers from an incurable disease which will kill him at the age of twenty, leaving K to enjoy all the resources for the rest of his three-score and ten years. Then a discovery is made which enables J also to live for seventy years. The just sharing of resources after this discovery is introduced may well make K worse off than he would have been. Admittedly, it would be *possible* to make a Pareto improvement here: for example, J might be made K's slave for those fifty years, for then J is better off as a slave than if he were dead, and K is better off with a slave, even though he has to use some of the scarce resources to keep J alive. But though this would be a Pareto improvement, it would not be just, according to our principles.

Nevertheless, it seems clear that the just solution will be at least close to that which would follow from the Pigou principle. The residents of area B cannot, in the face of the need of the city as a whole for a new use of this area, justifiably claim an absolute right to the undisturbed enjoyment of what, *ex hypothesi*, they previously justly enjoyed. Yet if the original situation was just it is likely that the just solution in the changed situation will spread the costs as well as the benefits of the new airport in some proportional way over all the citizens, and this implies that the residents of area B should not be worse off, on balance, in comparison with similarly situated residents in some other, unaffected, area, say D, merely because they happen to live in the area for which a new use is now appropriate. The same basic principles which tell against windfall profits tell also against what we might call jetstream losses.

Of course, this is only one problem among many. I put forward the present discussion mainly as an illustration, in an attempt to show that the proposed system of basic abstract rights is not toothless, that it does have some bite on practical issues, and in particular that such a right-based approach leads towards solutions which are more acceptable than would be those supported by a simple appeal to social utility, such as Coase's proposal, or even the view that we should be neutral between Coase and Pigou, since their methods lead to solutions which are indistinguishable with respect to social utility. But, in conclusion, I must admit that this argument may be unfair to utilitarianism. It may be that more subtle and indirect appeals to considerations of utility would also lead us away from Coase's solution and perhaps in the direction of the solution I have favoured. Even if this is so, I would argue that the right-based approach is superior in that it leads towards this solution more directly and for more obvious reasons.

XVII

NORMS AND DILEMMAS

PARFIT has raised a question about what sorts of norms are needed to solve multi-person prisoners' dilemmas involving public goods and public harms—cases where if each of a large number of people rationally pursues his private interest the result will be that everyone is worse off than he would have been if each had acted in some alternative, more co-operative, way. This practical problem can be and often is solved by the development of norms which check or modify people's pursuit of their private interest; but what norms will serve this purpose? One would be trustworthiness, the principle that one should honour agreements, promises, and contracts. Another would be the principle that one should not be a free rider, but should play one's part, where others are playing theirs, in a pattern of activity that promotes some public good or prevents some public harm. A third is the Kantian principle that one should act only on a maxim which one can will to be a universal law of nature, that is, only on a rule of conduct which, if everyone followed it, would have satisfactory results. And a fourth is the principle of altruism, that one should aim directly at the well-being of others and should choose, rationally and clearsightedly, whatever actions are most likely to promote this.

This fourth suggestion raises a point of terminology. 'Altruism' means, strictly, the pursuit of the good of *others*: the agent's own good is not included in its object. This is a nineteenth-century word, introduced by Comte and his followers. A related principle or motive is *benevolence*, the pursuit of the good of all, in which the agent's own good is included, equally with that of each other person. Eighteenth century writers often spoke of benevolence, since the term 'altruism' had not yet been coined. But which of the

Like 'Parfit's Population Paradox' (Chapter XVIII this volume), 'Norms and Dilemmas' was read to a discussion group in June 1980, in response to a paper by Derek Parfit. It has not previously been published and the typescript (dated 16 June 1980) has not been revised in any way. A later version of the material on which 'Norms and Dilemmas' comments is to be found in Derek Parfit, *Reasons and Persons* (Oxford, 1984), Chapters 2-3.

two do we want to speak of? If we are concerned with the direct pursuit of the public good, we should speak of benevolence rather than altruism. No doubt altruism would in practice usually give rise to the same choices as benevolence, either because the difference made by leaving one's own good out of the total would be negligible, or because what is practically in question is a public good which automatically includes some element of one's own good, so that an altruistic motive could produce only benevolent actions. But in special circumstances altruism, strictly so called, can be self-defeating, in fact it can produce multi-person prisoners' dilemmas—the *nolo episcopari* or 'After you, Claude' syndrome— so it would be better to concentrate on benevolence, which, I think, modern writers often have in mind when they speak about altruism.

With this change of terminology, Parfit has in effect argued that the norm of rational benevolence will solve certain dilemmas which it has been thought unable to solve. One of these concerns voting. Suppose that you are an American citizen and you believe that it will be better for the United States as a whole if the Democratic candidate becomes president than if the Republican does. However, you think it is most unlikely that your vote will make the difference: no presidential election has ever been decided by a single vote. And if it does not make the difference it has no significant effect at all. Voting is a nuisance, and if your vote is not going to affect the result of the election you would do more for the general good by not voting—if your own good is included, merely by sitting in comfort at home instead of going to the polling booth, but, even if it is not included, by some minor altruistic effort, like helping your son with his homework or by making your garden a bit less of an eyesore for your neighbours. Thus it seems that the principle of either benevolence or altruism will actually prevent you from voting. Benevolence, therefore, or altruism would reinforce rather than resolve the prisoners' dilemma about voting that is initially created by selfishness. If everyone were benevolent or altruistic, no less than if everyone were selfish, no one would vote and democracy would collapse, which is presumably an even worse outcome than the election of a Republican president. In practice this will not happen, but only because most people are neither purely selfish nor purely benevolent or altruistic, nor any mixture of these alone; their actions are influenced by various other motives—partly, no doubt, by sheer muddled thinking, but partly also by the anti-free-rider and Kantian norms.

However, Parfit argues that, after all, rational benevolence would do the trick. Suppose that you are a registered voter in New York state. New York might go either Democrat or Republican, and which way it goes may well determine the outcome of the whole election. Moreover, there is a small but finite chance that the result in New York will be decided by a single vote. This chance can be estimated as follows. Given the hard core of those who are certain to vote Republican and the hard core of those who are certain to vote Democrat, there is a range of possible results, stretching perhaps from a Republican majority of five million to a Democratic majority of five million; that is, there are only ten million (strictly, ten million and one) possible results. These are not all equally likely, for those in the middle of the range are more likely than those at the extremes; we shall therefore be *underestimating* the chance of a single vote's making a difference if we take it as two in ten million—two, because it might either turn a defeat into a tie or a tie into a victory. The chance that the result in New York will decide the whole election is not less than one in ten. So the total probability that your vote will decide the election is at least two in a hundred million. It is not surprising that this chance has never yet come off; but it is there none the less. Also, the public good of having the Democrat rather than the Republican as president, being the sum of the advantages that this will (in your opinion) bring to all or at any rate to most of the two hundred million Americans, is very great. Suppose the average advantage to each American is a—a significant amount. When you multiply the sum of these advantages by the small probability that your vote will make the difference between their being realized and their not being realized, the expected good-productivity of your vote is $a \times$

$200000000 \times \dfrac{2.}{100000000,}$ which works out at $4a$. This will clearly

outweigh the good you will certainly do by sitting at home or helping your son or tidying up the garden, since a, the advantage to you yourself of having the better president, would outweigh each of these. So rational benevolence would lead you to vote.

This is Parfit's argument, and it is undoubtedly correct. But the norm of rational benevolence does rather less well as a guide to voting decisions in a state like Maine, which is certain to go Republican, or in one like Georgia, which is certain to be won by the Democrats. In either of these, you, as a convinced Democrat, can be certain that your vote will not affect the result, so that rational benevolence will prevent you from voting. But now we have a difficulty. The same reasoning seems to hold for every single voter, whether Democrat or Republican. So if all were governed by rational benevolence, none would vote; but then neither of these would be a safe state for either party, so each voter's rational benevolence would lead him to vote after all. And so on, in an endless circle. Thus universal (and universally known) rational benevolence yields no stable directive for voters of either persuasion in Maine or Georgia, though it gives a single voter who can assume that most others are obeying some different norm the clear directive not to vote.

However, let us leave this problem aside and assume that some considerable number of these dilemmas resemble that of voting in New York, where rational benevolence would yield the desired solution. Nevertheless, we still face the empirical fact that the norm of rational benevolence is not, in general, what actually does the work. In so far as we manage to escape from multi-person prisoners' dilemmas it is usually other attitudes, beliefs, or norms that enable us to do so. Very few New York Democrats, I imagine, are really motivated by the consideration that each of them has one chance in fifty million of personally saving the nation from Reagan. Each thinks either that he is actually doing some good each time he votes, in which case he is not rational, or he thinks that he ought to do his bit, not leave it all to the other guys, or he made a promise to a canvasser and now feels that he cannot let him down, or he wants to be able to put a 'Don't blame me' sticker on his car window, and so on—that is, he is not simply benevolent.

If the norm of rational benevolence actually *does not* do the work, it may be reasonable to speculate that it *cannot* do it, that despite Parfit's proof that it would yield the desired results if it operated, there is some psychological or sociological reason why it will not operate. It may have practical defects which make it less viable than some of the alternative norms. In order to look into this question, let us list some of these rival norms.

1. Make, and keep, mutually beneficial agreements with others.

2. Help (i.e. keep on helping) those who help (i.e. keep on helping) you.
3. Help those who have helped you.
4. Join in enterprises that promote public goods in which you will share and play your role in them.
5. Join others in refraining from activities that would produce public harms from which you, along with others, would suffer.

We can associate with these norms some related principles about mainly retrospective feelings and judgements.

1a. Feel bad about breaking agreements, and about making ones which you do not intend to keep; blame others who do so.
2a. Feel ashamed if you constantly receive benefits without returning them; blame others who do so.
3a. Feel bad about biting the hand that fed you, and blame others who do this.
4a. Take a share of the credit for any good results of enterprises in which you have joined, without trying to calculate the differential effects of your participation; give credit similarly to others.
5a. Bear a share of the blame for any bad results of activities in which you have joined, without trying to calculate the differential effects of your participation; distribute blame similarly to others.

What we are to contrast with these are the corresponding principles of rational benevolence.

6. Act so as to maximize the expected production of the general good.
6a. Commend yourself and others for having made rational choices in accordance with 6, whether or not they differentially caused any good result, and blame yourself and others for having failed to make such choices, whether or not these failures differentially caused any bad result.
6b. Feel pleased when your action has differentially caused a good result, and sorry when it has differentially caused a bad one.

We can see at once a difference between 6, 6a, and 6b on the one hand and 4, 5, 4a, and 5a on the other. The principles of the latter group provide for collective action and for collective credit and responsibility. And this means that they ensure more credit and more responsibility. For example, if our Democrat votes in New York state because he is guided by 4, and his party happens to win both New York and the whole presidential election, he will feel, in accordance with 4a, that he can take a share of the credit, even though, as is almost inevitable, his own vote was superfluous, and even if it was an easy win, and the New York votes in the electoral college were not needed. Thus his choice of action will be psychologically reinforced by success. And even if the worst happens and the Republican wins, no doubt because many potential Democratic voters have changed sides or abstained from voting, he can at least feel free from the blame that he would have incurred in accordance with 5a, if he too had stayed away from the polls. He can still put that sticker on his car window, and he may be able to say 'Well, anyway, we gave Reagan a run for his money'. But what if he had voted in the same way but in deference to 6? Then he can indeed commend himself afterwards in accordance with 6a, but even if his party wins he will be able to feel no pleasure in accordance with 6b, since in the event his vote will have made no difference. In a very bleak sense he must take his virtue as its own reward. On the other hand someone who, while he feels some pressure from 6, flouts it and stays at home, must no doubt apply to himself the abstract blame of 6a, but since even if his party loses his action will have done no harm he will bear, under 6b, no responsibility for the disaster.

Another difference emerges if we contrast 6 with 1, 2, and 3. The latter principles all involve some form of reciprocity: the benefits which they instruct the agent to confer on others are all related to benefits that he receives from them. This is plainest in 1, where the reciprocal benefits are directly and explicitly conditional upon one another. It is only a little less obvious in 2, where the continuation of the benefits that each party confers is still roughly conditional on the continuation of those it receives, and vice versa. This is less true of 3, but where this norm is in force mutually beneficial tendencies will be psychologically reinforced by rewards and expressions of gratitude. Each of these three norms can therefore in an important way be built upon the self-interest of agents. 'There is no passion', Hume says, 'capable of controlling the interested affection, but the very affection itself, by an alteration of its direction' (*Treatise* III ii 2). This is not quite correct. What restrains self-love need not be the indirect operation of self-love through calculation: it may be a norm or convention. But such a norm or convention is more likely to arise and to become powerful if it protects in not too remote a way the prior interests of each of those among whom it develops, so that it is reinforced by tangible rewards. Principles of reciprocity have thus a psychological advantage over others.

This advantage extends also to principles 4 and 5. The collective promotion of a public good, or the collective forbearance from public harm, can be seen as a way of helping others who are helping you, and each agent's participation is at least roughly conditional upon that of a sufficient number of others to give the enterprise a significant chance of success.

It may be objected that 6 too can be brought into this fold. If rational benevolence is established as a norm, then in general each person's observance of it will help all the others. That is true. But the reciprocity thus achieved is far more remote and more chancy. In observing and propagating this norm I do not provide for my own welfare so securely or directly as I do when I follow and support principles 1 to 5. Moreover, each person's observance of the norm of rational benevolence does not automatically involve its observance by other people, whereas the observance of 1, 2, 4, and 5 does.

The cluster of alternative norms 1 to 5 has, therefore, clear psychological and sociological advantages over that of rational benevolence. We can understand why the former flourishes more than the latter, and does far more of the real work of resolving multi-person prisoners' dilemmas. These alternative norms could, no doubt, be represented as derived rules, as consequences of 6 or as indicating ways of implementing it; but that is not the role they play in actual thinking and behaviour. Rather, they are seen or felt as basic norms and are developed directly as conventions in their own right.

Parfit will point out that these alternative norms will sometimes have undesired consequences. They will sometimes lead people to do things that are pointless or even harmful both from the agent's own point of view and from that of the general good. This is true, but this disadvantage is outweighed by their advantages.

The recent discussion has not mentioned the Kantian norm, 'Act only on a maxim which you can will to be a universal law of nature'. Taken strictly, as a negative constraint on choices, it is acceptable and fits in well with norms 1 to 5. Though it does not explicitly involve collectivity or reciprocity, it allows for them and may arise out of practices that involve them, and it does play a real part in our thinking, though its better known variants (e.g., 'Do as you would be done by') are more explicitly reciprocal. But if it is transformed into a positive recommendation to act unilaterally in ways that *would* be beneficial *if* everyone followed them, without regard to the reality or likelihood of such general participation, it could lead to deplorable results; perhaps it is just as well, therefore, that in this positive form it plays only a small role in the thinking of ordinary people, and seriously influences only a minority of visionaries.

XVIII

PARFIT'S POPULATION PARADOX

PARFIT'S statement of the problem refers mainly to possible states of the world and to one of these being better or worse than another, but occasionally to one group rising or gaining or falling or losing, and some of the discussion referred to choices of action or policy. For the sake of clarity, let us initially set aside all practical questions about what anyone ought to do, and even about the merits of changes from one situation to another, and consider only relations of better or worse between abstract conceivable distinct states of the world. 'Better' and 'worse' may here stand either for supposed objective degrees of goodness or for some theorist's considered, reflective, preferences from some impartial point of view. Let us begin with a restatement of the problem.

We assume that there is some level of welfare or of the quality of life such that the existence of a person at this level is, all other things being equal, a marginally better state of affairs than his non-existence. Call this level m (for 'marginal'). Level m need not coincide with the level at which a person himself judges that it is marginally better to be living than never to have been born, but may be significantly higher than this. For the person himself is a biased judge, and what we want is an impartial judgement.

Next, we consider a level of welfare or of the quality of life that is much higher than m, one such that a person at this level can be

---

This paper and 'The Combination of Partially-Ordered Preferences' (Chapter XIX, this volume) were written as discussion notes in June 1980, and have not been previously published. Mackie had intended to incorporate the material from these two notes in a single article for inclusion in his *Selected Papers*. He did not carry out the revision, and the two papers are published here without alteration.

As its text indicates, 'Parfit's Population Paradox' was delivered to a discussion group in response to a paper by Derek Parfit, in which a version of the problem set out in the following paragraphs was raised and discussed. A revised form of the material on which Mackie's paper comments is to be found in Parfit's *Reasons and Persons* (Oxford, 1984), Chapter 19. (See also Parfit's 'Future Generations: Further Problems', *Philosophy and Public Affairs*, Vol. 11, No. 2, Spring 1982.) It should be noted that Parfit's own version of the paradox differs slightly from that given here, in that Parfit does not maintain that A + is better than A, but only that A + is no worse than A.

said to be really flourishing, to be practising and enjoying in a high degree some range of activities that together constitute a good human life. Call this level f (for 'flourishing').

Now consider a state of affairs in which a considerable number of people—say, one hundred million—are all living at level f; call this state A. Also, consider a state Z in which there are a thousand times as many people as in A, but where each of them is at a level of welfare or the quality of life which is above m by only one thousandth of the amount by which f is above m. That is, each person in Z is at a level very little above that at which it is only marginally better that a person should exist rather than that he should not exist. Intuitively, A is a better state than Z.

However, let us compare with A a state of affairs in which as well as a population just like that of A there exists another quite separate population of the same size all of whose members are living at level m; the two populations do not communicate or interact in any way and do not even know of each other's existence. Call this total state, with these two separate populations, $A+$. Then $A+$ is a better state of affairs than A. This seems to follow from the definition of level m.

Next, consider a state of affairs B^* in which there are two populations, each of the same size as each of those in $A+$, but now with equal levels of welfare or quality of life, where this common level is just a shade closer to f than to m. That is, the second population in B^* is better off than the second population in $A+$ by a slightly greater amount than the first population in B^* is worse off than the first population in $A+$. Call this common level c_1 (for 'first common level'). In other words c_1 is slightly above the average of f and m; algebraically, $c_1 = \dfrac{f+m}{2} + \delta = m + \dfrac{f-m}{2} + \delta$, where δ is a small amount.

Then B^* is a better state of affairs than $A+$. The quality of life as a whole is not lower, but slightly higher, and the same is necessarily true of the average quality of life, since the numbers are the same; and there is greater equality, in fact complete equality.

Finally, consider a state of affairs B, in which there is a single population, with communication and interaction among its members, but which is otherwise just like the sum of the two populations in B^*. That is, in B there is a single population twice as large as that of A, and all its members are at level c_1. Then B is not worse than B^*: there being one population rather than two separate ones, each half the size, with the same uniform level of welfare or quality of life, could not constitute a worse state of affairs.

Then since $A+$ is better than A, and B^* is better than $A+$, and B is not worse than B^*, it follows that B is a better state of affairs than A.

This whole argument can be repeated. We can identify a state C which is related to B as B is to A. In C there is a single population, twice as large as that of B, all of whose members are at what we can call the second common level, or c_2, where c_2 is a shade above the average of c_1 and m. That is, $c_2 = \dfrac{c_1 + m}{2} + \delta = m + \dfrac{f - m}{4}$ $+ (1 + \frac{1}{2})\delta$. By the same reasoning, C is a better state of affairs than B, and therefore C is a better state of affairs than A. And so on.

After n iterations, we reach a state R_n in which there is a population 2^n times the size of that in A, at a level of welfare or quality of life c_n, where

$$c_n = m + \frac{f - m}{2^n} + \left(1 + \frac{1}{2} + \frac{1}{4} + \ldots + \frac{1}{2^{n-1}} \right) \delta.$$

In this formula, the last term is always slightly less than 2δ, so we can take c_n as approximately $m + \dfrac{f - m}{2^n} + 2\delta$. For example, after ten iterations we have R_{10} with a population one thousand and twenty-four times that of A, and the level of its members is approximately $m + \dfrac{f - m}{1024} + 2\delta$. That is, the quality of life of each person in R_{10} is above m by only about one thousandth of the amount by which that of each person in A is above m.

From the iterated argument it follows that R_n is always a better state of affairs than A, however large n is, and however small, therefore, may be the superiority of the level of welfare in R_n to m, the level which is just marginally better than non-existence. But intuitively it seems that where n is at all large R_n is markedly worse than A. For example, R_{10} is almost exactly the same as the state we introduced above as Z, and A seemed to be a better state than Z. Here, then, is the paradox. Plausible judgements about the relative goodness of conceivable states of affairs seem to make 'better than' not transitive but cyclical: R_n is better than ... which is better than B which is better than A, but A is better than R_n.

How, then, can we resolve the paradox? In the iterated argument we have used (repeatedly) three principles. What we can call the principle of addition yields the superiority of $A+$ to A, of $B+$ to B, and so on. What we can call the principle of equality yields the superiority of B^* to $A+$, of C^* to $B+$, and so on. And what we can call the principle of consolidation yields the equivalence of B to B^*, of C to C^*, and so on. What the argument shows is that the unrestricted holding of these three principles is incompatible with the judgement that A is a better state of affairs than R_n or, say, Z.

One conclusion that might be drawn from this is that we do not have and cannot find a consistent set of judgements about the relative goodness of states of affairs considered abstractly and on this scale. This would presumably have the corollary that choices of action and policy in this sort of area, if there are any, must be based on something other than the relative goodness of states of affairs. This is by no means an absurd conclusion, but before we resort to it we can reflect further on the three principles and on the view that A is better than Z, to see whether one of these might be rejected or qualified.

We can present the choice between these conflicting elements more starkly by considering two further states, X and Y. In X there are two populations, one exactly like that of A, the other 1023 (that is, $2^{10}-1$) times as large as that of A and living at level m. In Y, there are two populations of the same sizes as those in X, but with all members of both societies at the c_{10} level, that is, $m+\dfrac{f-m}{1024}+2\delta$. In effect, the above-marginal welfare which was concentrated into one population in X is spread evenly over both populations in Y, and raised by the negligibly small term 2δ. The paradox is now condensed into the four pairwise comparisons between A and X, X and Y, Y and Z, and Z and A. The unrestricted principle of addition requires that X is better than A, the unrestricted principle of equality that Y is better than X, that of consolidation that Z is equal to Y; the conjunction of these confronts the intuition that A is better than Z.

Once we have this stark confrontation, we can see how different thinkers will happily choose different ways of resolving it. Anyone who takes a quantitative view of welfare and the quality of life and who regards equality as contributing to the goodness of states of affairs will accept all three principles and reject the 'intuition' that

A is better than Z. After all, there is a shade more of the quality of life above the marginal level in Z than in A; it is just more thinly spread, and for one who adheres firmly to a quantitative view that is no disadvantage. The supposed contrary intuition is due to the tendency to take the small superiority of c_{10} to m as no superiority at all.

On the other hand, one who takes a non-quantitative view of the quality of life will say that the algebraic representation of levels used here is misleading. Somewhere in the transition from f to c_{10} we lose something of quality that is not automatically compensated by the increase in the number of those who share the lower level of welfare. This thinker will therefore reject the unrestricted principle of equality, and say that X is better than Y, and can therefore maintain that although X is better than A, A is better than Y and than Z. He may, of course, allow *some* applications of the principle of equality: all he need say is that in at least one of the iterations of our basic argument equalization without overall loss is not possible. It is not true that the quality of life above m is simply an aggregate quantity which can be either concentrated or spread out thinly without limit: rather there is one or more than one critical level k_1, k_2, etc., such that the flourishing of one person above such a critical level is not balanced by the flourishing of two people (or, perhaps, or any number) below that level.

A third possible approach would be to say that there is a mistake in the formulation of the puzzle, in the assumption that f can be much higher than m. A level that is really marginally better than non-existence must already constitute a high degree of flourishing, and beyond this little further improvement is possible. One who takes this view will again say that Z is better than A, but that this is not counter-intuitive because Z simply adds many more people who are all flourishing thoroughly, at the sacrifice, as compared with A, merely of a superfluity of well-being for a relatively few people, which is inconsiderable from an impartial point of view.

Any one of these three approaches is coherent and not obviously unacceptable, and I imagine that different people will quite happily settle for different ones. All that is then left of the paradox is the fact that some of us are inclined to dither between them. Such dithering may be encouraged by our use throughout of the two terms 'welfare', which tends to have connotations that suggest the quantitative view, and 'quality of life', which suggests the non-quantitative view.

Further confusing factors come in when we reintroduce the practical questions that we set aside at the beginning, about what people ought to do and about the merits of *changes* from one concrete situation to another, as opposed to abstract comparisons between conceivable distinct states of the world. For example, if the two populations of $A+$ are already actually in existence, and we see ourselves as having power and authority over them, so that it is for us to decide whether they *remain* on the widely separated levels f and m or whether those very same people all *move* to level c_1, as in B^* or B, then it may well seem unfair for us to leave them in the $A+$ condition. The second population has as strong a claim on us as the first, so distributive justice requires us to reassign welfare equally, particularly if this can be done without overall loss, if it is in our gift. But note that this is an altogether different consideration from the abstract judgement that B^* is better than $A+$. Though these two considerations may combine to support an equalization policy, the former does not support the latter. The case for equality as a requirement of distributive justice does not show that B^* as a distinct abstract state is better than $A+$, nor, therefore, does it tell against the non-quantitative solution of the abstract form of the paradox. Someone might well deny the unrestricted principle of equality for the determination of what is better or worse among distinct states, and yet give weight to a claim for equalization put forward by one of two groups over whose well-being he has an impartial authority. He might reasonably say: 'Of the two choices open to me, one is fairer but the other leads to a better state of affairs; regrettably, I have to choose between fairness and goodness'.

This reacts also upon the practical counterpart of the abstract comparison between A and $A+$, and those of other applications of the principle of addition. Though in the abstract $A+$ is better than A, it does not follow without qualification that one who had it in his power to do so should always change an A type situation into a corresponding one of the $A+$ type. For to do this would at once expose him to the claim, based on an appeal to distributive justice, that this should then be transformed into the corresponding B^* or B situation; yet this, for non-quantitativist reasons, might well be a worse state of affairs than the given A type situation.

We can look at this in another way. Let us think of a practical variant of the paradox, addressed to some body that had the power and authority to control the existence and size of populations and the distribution of advantages among them which would determine the quality of their lives. 'If you start with A, you should change this to $A+$, because this is better. Then you should change $A+$ to B^*, because it is fairer. And you have no reason to prevent the change (which will tend to come about automatically) from B^* to B, since they are equally good; then you should change B to $B+$, and so on, until you arrive at R_{10}—in effect, at Z. But this is paradoxical, because you should *not* change A to Z, because A is better than Z and no less fair. In fact if you have Z you should change it back to A, at least if you can do so without being unfair to anyone. And so on, in an endless circle.'

Faced with this practical paradox, we can reply first that if the authoritative body is supposed to be guided in its policies simply by the relative goodness of states of affairs, then one of the three solutions suggested above for the abstract paradox will resolve its difficulty—which is the right one depends upon the further judgements indicated. For example, it might take the non-quantitative view and refuse to change $A+$ to B^* (or reject some corresponding move later in the series of iterations), saying that on this supposition fairness and the claims of the actual second population in $A+$ (etc.) do not matter. If, alternatively, the body is supposed to be guided by a plurality of distinct considerations, such as *both* the relative goodness of states of affairs *and* fairness to people over whom the body has impartial authority—the latter being particularly important if this body is itself responsible for these people's being there at all—then it is not surprising if this body is thereby committed to a cyclic series of changes. This would be no paradox, though it might be a nuisance.

XIX

THE COMBINATION OF
PARTIALLY-ORDERED PREFERENCES

A.K. SEN showed (in *Collective Choice and Social Welfare*[1]) that a combination of the Pareto principle with a liberal one could lead to inconsistency. Albert Weale (in 'The Impossibility of Liberal Egalitarianism'[2]) has shown that inconsistency can result also from a combination of the Pareto principle with an egalitarian one; and Iain McLean (in a not yet published paper[3]) has shown that there can be a similar conflict between liberal and egalitarian principles. However, these proofs do not reveal any special mutual hostilities between liberalism, egalitarianism, and the Pareto principle. Rather, they rest upon and bring out a purely formal point which these principles can be used to illustrate. We can, indeed, state the following simple theorem:

> T1: Whenever two logically independent principles of preference P and Q, of which P yields only a partial ordering, are combined to produce resultant preferences by P's being given lexicographical priority to Q, it is possible to generate an inconsistent set of resultant preferences.

To prove T1, let us write '$a >_Q b$' for 'a is preferred to b by principle Q', '$a \sim_P b$' for 'principle P yields no ordering of a and b', and so on. Then we may be able to find three states of affairs a, b, and c, such that $a \sim_P b$, $b \sim_P c$, $c >_P a$, $a >_Q b$, $b >_Q c$, and (consequently, if Q is transitive) $a >_Q c$. Since P has priority over Q, but wherever P fails to rank two states Q determines the resultant preference with regard to them, the resultant preferences are $a > b$, $b > c$, and $c > a$; that is, they are cyclic and hence inconsistent. If P

Previously unpublished: typescript dated June 26 1980. For further details, see the note to 'Parfit's Population Paradox' (Chapter XVIII, this volume p. 242).

[1] San Francisco and Edinburgh, 1970.
[2] *Analysis*, Vol. 40, No. 1 (January 1980).
[3] [Subsequently published as 'Liberty, Equality and the Pareto Principle: A Comment on Weale' in *Analysis*, Vol. 40, No. 4 (October 1980).—Edd.]

and Q are logically independent of one another, it should always be theoretically possible to describe three states so related, though of course such states may or may not arise as practical possibilities, as real objects of choice.

The examples mentioned above illustrate this theorem. The Pareto principle yields only a partial ordering, and the combination rule Sen considers is in effect:

Where one state is Pareto superior to another, prefer it; where neither of two states is Pareto superior to the other, prefer the more liberal.

The combination rule examined by Weale is in effect the same as this with 'equal' substituted for 'liberal'. And the rule examined by McLean is in effect 'Where one state is more liberal than another, prefer it; where neither of two states is more liberal than the other, prefer the more equal'—and 'more liberal than' also yields only a partial ordering.

The moral to be drawn, then, is simply that we cannot, without risk of inconsistency, determine resultant preferences in what seems at first to be a sensible way, namely to give priority to some attractive principle despite the fact that it yields only a partial ordering, but to fall back on some second principle when the first fails to determine an order.

In other words, T1 shows to be unsatisfactory any rule of this form:

R1: If P ranks x above or below y, then this is the resultant ordering; if P ranks x equal with y, then if Q yields any ranking of x in relation to y, the resultant ordering agrees with that of Q, but if Q fails to rank them then x and y are equal in the resultant ordering; if P fails to rank x and y, the resultant ordering (or lack of any) agrees with that of Q.

This sort of difficulty does not, however, beset only those combination rules which give lexicographical priority to a partial ordering principle. A similar problem arises if we try to put two principles, of which at least one gives only a partial ordering, on a level with one another. Suppose that we have two such principles, and consider the following rule for combining them:

R2: If the two principles agree on an ordering of x and y, then this is the resultant ordering; if one principle ranks x in relation to *y* while the other either ranks them as equal or fails to rank them, the resultant ordering agrees with that of the first principle; if one principle ranks *x* above *y* while the other ranks *y* above *x*, or if neither principle ranks *x* in relation to *y*, then there is no resultant ordering between them.

This rule still produces an inconsistency with regard to the three states a, b, and c as given in the example above. For it yields the resultant preferences a>b, b>c, and a~c, whereas we should expect resultant preferences to be transitive. It is even less satisfactory if we have two principles each of which yields only a partial ordering. For then we may have four states of affairs a, b, c, and d related as follows: a~$_P$b, a~$_P$c, d>$_P$a, b>$_P$c, b~$_P$d, c~$_P$d, a>$_Q$b, a~$_Q$c, a~$_Q$d, b~$_Q$c, b~$_Q$d, and c>$_Q$d. Among these states R2 generates the cyclic resultant preferences a>b, b>c, c>d, and d>a.

We can, therefore, state a second theorem:

T2: If two logically independent principles of preference of which at least one yields only a partial ordering are combined in accordance with R2, it is possible to generate an inconsistent set of resultant preferences.

A more complicated relationship is shown by some principles implicit in a discussion by Derek Parfit of the problem of population policy.† Each of the following three principles has some initial moral plausibility.

Addition: If a state of affairs *y* differs from another state of affairs *x* only in that there is, in *y*, as well as a population just like that in *x*, an additional population all of whose members are at a level of welfare such that it is clearly better that someone should live at that level than that he should never have existed, then *y* is better than *x*.

Equalization: If in two states of affairs *x* and *y* the total numbers of persons are the same and the total amount of well-being above a level at which it is clearly better that someone should live than that he should never have existed is somewhat greater in *y* than in *x*, while all the persons in *y* are at the same level of well-being as one another, whereas those in *x* are at widely different levels, then *y* is better than *x*.

† See footnote to 'Parfit's Population Paradox' (Chapter XVIII, this volume, p. 242).—Edd.

Quality of Life: If in two states of affairs x and y a higher quality of life is attained by at least some persons in y than by any persons in x, then y is better than x.

These principles, it may be noted, are not logically independent of one another. Thus if y is better than x in terms of Addition, neither can be better than the other in terms of Quality of Life or in terms of Equalization. That is, Addition cannot directly conflict with either of the other two principles (nor can it positively agree with either). On the other hand if one state is better than another in terms of Equalization, it must be worse than it in terms of Quality of Life, though one state can be better than another in terms of Quality of Life without being worse than it in terms of Equalization.

Given these relations between the principles, it might be tempting to lay down the following priority rules. Addition holds without restriction, while Equalization has lexicographical priority over Quality of Life. That is, Quality of Life determines the resultant preferences between two states only where neither Addition nor Equalization has any application.

However, these tempting rules generate an inconsistency, as the following example shows. In a, there is a population all of whose members are at a uniformly high level of well-being. In b there is a population just like that of a, and also another population of the same size at a much lower level but still at a level at which it is clearly better that someone should live than that he should never have existed. In c there is a single population of twice the size of that in a, at a uniform level of well-being a little above the average of that of the two populations in b. Then, given the suggested priority rules, b is better than a (by Addition), c is better than b (by Equalization, since Addition does not apply), but a is better than c (by Quality of Life, since neither Addition nor Equalization applies here). So we have a cyclic and therefore inconsistent ordering.

By contrast with all of these difficulties, it is possible to determine resultant preference orderings with no risk of inconsistency by combining two principles one of which yields a complete ordering, if that one is given lexicographical priority. For then we have recourse to the second principle only where the first ranks two states as equal; they remain equal in the resultant ordering if the second principle ranks them as equal or fails to rank them, but if it ranks one above the other that is the resultant ordering. The second principle can thus only introduce a finer discrimination between states that appear equal from the point of view of the principle that is given priority, and no inconsistency can arise. If P is a complete ordering principle, we could not have three states a, b, and c like those in our first example but with $a =_p b$, $b =_p c$, and $c >_p a$, since equality in a complete ordering is transitive.

The overall lesson seems to be that principles of partial ordering are awkward things to use except in a subordinate capacity. They cannot be trusted either with lexicographical priority or with equal status, so that it is better to give priority to a principle which by itself yields a complete ordering, leaving only the final fine discriminations to a partial ordering principle. It is interesting to reflect on the political analogue of this conclusion. This would be that it is better to give initial and overriding authority to someone who can always make up his own mind, though someone else may be allowed to decide, if he can, between alternatives which the first person firmly ranks as equal. But of course the merit of either this maxim or the corresponding one for principles of preference is merely the avoidance of inconsistency: it may be open to other objections.

INDEX OF NAMES